TRIAL BY COMBAT

BY

GEORGE NEILSON

THE LAWBOOK EXCHANGE, LTD.
Clark, New Jersey

ISBN 978-1-58477-075-6 Hardcover
ISBN 978-1-58477-985-8 Paperback

Lawbook Exchange edition 2000, 2013

The quality of this reprint is equivalent to the quality of the original work.

THE LAWBOOK EXCHANGE, LTD.
33 Terminal Avenue
Clark, New Jersey 07066-1321

Please see our website for a selection of our other publications and fine facsimile reprints of classic works of legal history:
www.lawbookexchange.com

Library of Congress Cataloging-in-Publication Data

Neilson, George, 1858-1923.
Trial by combat / by George Neilson.
p. cm.
Originally published: Glasgow : William Hodge & Co., 1890.
Includes bibliographical references and index.
ISBN 1-58477-075-9 (cloth: alk. paper)
1. Wager of battle—Great Britain—History. 2. Dueling— Great Britain— History. I. Title.

KD8225.W3 N45 2000
345.41'05'0902—dc21 99-059101

Printed in the United States of America on acid-free paper

TRIAL BY COMBAT

BY

GEORGE NEILSON

GLASGOW

WILLIAM HODGE & CO., 26 BOTHWELL STREET

1890

Inscribed,

IN GRATITUDE AND RESPECT,

TO

ROBERT BERRY, Esquire,

M.A., CANTAB.;

LATE FELLOW OF TRINITY COLLEGE, CAMBRIDGE;

LL.D., EDIN.;

FORMERLY PROFESSOR OF LAW IN GLASGOW UNIVERSITY;

NOW SHERIFF OF LANARKSHIRE.

PREFACE.

THIS account of the judicial duel in England and Scotland has grown out of general antiquarian studies. A few facts casually gleaned furnished the staple of a paper read to the Glasgow Juridical Society in the spring of 1888. Subsequently the quest for material was systematically pursued. The evidence gathered seemed to make decisively for several new and relatively important historical conclusions. In support of these a dangerous ambition is now gratified—to break a lance in the lists of history.

If debts of gratitude were mortgages 'Trial by Combat' would enter the world heavily burdened. My chief purpose in writing a preface is to register the more considerable of my obligations.

To Professor Frederic W. Maitland of Cambridge I owe warm thanks for direct help in dealing with the early English duel of law. That section is a very small part of the wide field of 13th century English law which the editor of 'Bracton's Note Book' has made so peculiarly his own. I cannot forget the friendly and generous spirit of his criticisms.

Dr. Thomas Dickson of the Historical Department of the Register House, Edinburgh, is a never-failing friend of those who strive to penetrate the secret of the past. To me he has throughout my Scottish sections been most helpful with facts and counsel. His genial interest in the labours of an untried student has made my intercourse with him one of my highest pleasures.

Many courtesies have been shewn me in many libraries. Though chiefly indebted in Glasgow to the Faculty of Procurators' Library—the extensive collection of my own profession—I have had much advantage from Stirling's Library and some from the University Library and the Mitchell Library. At Edinburgh in the Advocates' Library and the University Library I had opportunities of dipping into the manuscript sources of Scots law. Besides, the Curators of the Advocates' Library have kindly granted me permission to print my transcript of an unpublished ancient Scottish MS., 'The Maner of Battale.' This has been collated with another version in the British Museum by a record-agent in London, Miss Wright, 16 Belsize Park Gardens, N., who also transcribed the letter regarding a projected border-duel in 1586.

My near neighbour Mr. J. T. T. Brown gave me unlimited license to bore him during the incubation of my thesis—a privilege exercised without mercy. Besides this passive service he actively helped me otherwise, and gave me sundry useful references. Thanks to Mr. Alexander L. Davidson, Ruthwell, and in a minor degree to Mr. J. J. Elliot, Garnethill, some faulty sentences have been modified. My partner in business, Mr. Francis Stoddart, has assisted me in correcting proofs and preparing the index.

In conclusion, let me hope that in spite of numerous defects, avoidable and unavoidable, my book may prove of some service towards a clearer understanding of the place in British history, and especially in Scots history, of the wager of battle.

> I have, God wot, a large feeld to ere,
> And wayke ben the oxen in my plough.

CHAMBERS, 58 WEST REGENT STREET,
GLASGOW, 1*st January*, 1890.

CONTENTS.

PART I.—PRELIMINARY: EUROPE:

Chap. 1. Before the Middle Ages.
2. King Gundobald, A.D. 501.
3. Mode of Battle.
4. Among the Norsemen.
5. The Church.
6. Decadence and Extinction.

PART II.—ORIGIN IN BRITAIN:

Chap. 7. A Question Stated.
8. Norse Evidence.
9. English and Scotch Evidence.
10. The Question Answered.

PART III.—ENGLAND, 1066–1300: LAW:

Chap. 11. Legal Outline.
12. Sketch of Procedure.
13. The Duel in Finance.
14. The Approver.
15. The Champion.
16. Some Churchmen's Champions.
17. Another Champion's Contract.
18. Three Early Duels, A.D. 1096–1163.
19. A Hibernian Hero.
20. Charters and Charter Stories.
21. An Incident, A.D. 1267.
22. Reactionary Signs.
23. Review and Prospect.

PART IV.—SCOTLAND TILL 1300: LAW:

Chap. 24. In Early Scotland.
25. Under David the First.
26. Under William the Lion.
27. Writ of Right.
28. The Battle.
29. An Argument.
30. Exemptions from Duel.
31. Regiam Majestatem.
32. In the Regiam.
33. Crime in the Regiam.
34. Under Alexander II. and after.
35. The Duel Described.
36. March Law.
37. 'The Lawis of Merchis,' A.D. 1249.
38. Recorded Duels from 1155.
39. A Great Trial, A.D. 1242.
40. Merse and Kyle, A.D. 1264–66.
41. Baron Courts of the Bruces, A.D. 1292.
42. By 1300.

PART V.—ENGLAND, 1300–1603: LAW AND CHIVALRY:

Section First—THE DUEL OF LAW.

Chap. 43. Continued Decline after 1300.
44. The Prior of Tynemouth's Champion.
45. Magic, A.D. 1355.
46. The Last Approver's Duel, A.D. 1456.
47. An Elizabethan Scene, A.D. 1571.

Section Second—THE DUEL OF CHIVALRY.

48. A French Edict, A.D. 1306.
49. The Rise of Chivalry.
50. Precedents, A.D. 1350–52.
51. Transmarine Treason, A.D. 1380–84.
52. The Court of Chivalry.
53. In Chaucer.

PART V.—ENGLAND, 1300–1603: LAW AND CHIVALRY:

Section Second—THE DUEL OF CHIVALRY—*continued*:

Chap. 54. A Contrast and Conclusion.
55. Richard II.
56. A Royal Jest, A.D. 1399.
57. Some Treason-Duels.
58. The end of Chivalry.
59. A Summary with an Exception.

PART VI.—SCOTLAND, 1300–1603: CHIVALRY:

Chap. 60. Before Bannockburn.
61. Before Halidon Hill.
62. The Law and Custom in 1354.
63. Three half-told Stories, 1362–95.
64. Border Duels till 1396.
65. 'Vegetius' in Scotland.
66. 'The Maner of Battale.'
67. International Tilting.
68. A New Conclusion.
69. Precedents for the Inch of Perth.
70. Preliminaries—Inch of Perth.
71. The Inch of Perth, A.D. 1396.
72. Facts and Suppositions, 1398–1412.
73. On 'The Order of Combats.'
74. 'The Order of Combats.'
75. The Scottish Court of Chivalry.
76. Stray Duels, A.D. 1426–56.
77. In Parliament and Burgh Court.
78. Note on the Passing of Chivalry.
79. Pitscottie's Dutchman, A.D. 1500.
80. John Major's Homily.
81. Under James V.
82. Rise of Private Duels.
83. An Interlude, A.D. 1549.
84. Two Historic Cartels.

PART VI.—SCOTLAND, 1300–1603: CHIVALRY—*continued:*

Chap. 85. The last Trial by Combat.
86. The Act of Parliament of 1600.
87. A Final Episode.
88. On the Borders.
89. Scottish Summary.

PART VII.—BRITAIN, 1603–1819:

Chap. 90. Last Words on Scotland.
91. England under James I.
92. England under Charles I.
93. Appeal of Murder Act, 1819.
94. The End.

SOME REFERENCES EXPLAINED.

Antiq. Celto-Scand.,	Antiquitates Celto-Scandicæ, by James Johnstone, 1786.
Arng. Jon. Chrym.,	Chrymogæ Rerum Islandicarum, by Arngrim Jonas, pub. with his Epistola, 1618.
Bain's Cal., . .	Calendars of Documents relating to Scotland, by Joseph Bain.
Bann., . . .	Bannatyne Club.
Barrington, . .	Observations on Statutes, ed. 1769.
Black Book, . .	Black Book of Admiralty, Rolls Series, ed. Twiss.
Bower, . . .	Scotichronicon, ed. Goodall, 1747.
Bracton, . .	Rolls Series, ed. Twiss.
Brac. N.B., . .	Bracton's Note Book, ed. F. W. Maitland.
Brakelond, . .	Jocelin of Brakelond, Camden Society.
Britton, . . .	ed. Nicholls.
Cal., . . .	Calendar.
Cal. Rot. Pat., .	Calendarium Rotulorum Patentium (Record Commission).
Calderwood, . .	History, Wodrow Society.
Camden, . .	Britannia, ed. Gibson, 1695.
Chart., . . .	Chartulary.
Cornhill Art., .	See page 9.
Crown Pleas, . .	Select Pleas of Crown, Selden Society, ed. F. W. Maitland.
Du Cange, . .	Glossarium.
Dugd. Orig., . .	Dugdale's Origines Juridiciales, 1671.
Exch. Rolls, . .	Exchequer Rolls, ed. Geo. Burnett.
Extracta, . .	Extracta ex Cronicis, Abbotsford Club.
Fleta, . . .	Seldeni, 1647.
Fordun, . . .	ed. W. F. Skene, 1872.
Froissart, . .	ed. 1812.
Galf. le Baker, .	Galfridus le Baker de Swinbroke, ed. Giles, 1847.
Gibbon, . . .	Decline and Fall, cited by chapter, page, an volume, from Warne's reprint, 1887.

Gibson, . . .	Paper on Ordeals in Archæologia, vol. xxxii., by W. S. Gibson.
Gregory, . .	Collections of a London Citizen, Camden Society.
Hall, . . .	Hall's Chronicle, ed. 1809.
Hemingburgh, .	ed. English Historical Society, 1848.
Kendall, . .	E. A. Kendall. An Argument on Trial by Battle, 3rd ed. 1818.
Knyghton, . .	in Decem Scriptores, 1652.
Madox, . . .	History of the Exchequer, ed. 1711.
Mait., . . .	Maitland Club.
Meyrick, . .	Ancient Armour, 1824.
N. & Q., . .	Notes and Queries.
Pike, . . .	History of Crime in England.
Pipe Rolls, . .	Publications of Pipe Rolls Society.
P.C. Reg., . .	Privy Council Register, Scotland.
Pitcairn, . .	Pitcairn's Criminal Trials, Maitland Club.
R. S., . . .	Rolls Series.
Robertson, . .	View of State of Europe, prefixed to History of Charles V.
Rot., . . .	Rotuli.
Rot. Scot., . .	Rotuli Scotiæ.
Rymer, . . .	Fœdera, 2nd ed. 1727.
Stat. Eccl. Scot., .	Statuta Ecclesiæ Scoticanæ, by Joseph Robertson.
Scalacron., . .	Scalacronica, Maitland Club.
Scots Acts, . .	Acts of Parliaments of Scotland, ed. Thomas Thomson and Cosmo Innes.
Spald., . . .	Spalding Club.
Stow, . . .	Stow's Annals, ed. 1615.
Stubbs' Charters, .	Select Charters, by Bishop Stubbs, 1884.
Thorpe's Cal., .	Calendar of Scottish Documents, 1509-1603.
Walsingham, . .	ed. Rolls Series.
Wyntoun, . .	Cronykil, ed. David Laing, 1872.

ERRATUM.—Page 133, line 16, for *Richard* read Robert.

TRIAL BY COMBAT.

PART I.—PRELIMINARY: EUROPE.

CHAP. 1.—*Before the Middle Ages.*

THIS book attempts a plain straightforward sketch of a British chapter in the biography of a great European institution, with more intent to present facts than to deal with the ethics and philosophy of its origin, progress, and decline. Trial by combat came into existence—no tradition knows when. It had attained a vigorous manhood amongst the tribes of Northern Europe before their written history began. It reached its legal prime in the early feudal ages, and enjoyed a new era of activity under the auspices of later chivalry. Its hardy constitution enabled it to set at naught the attacks of time, religion, and civilization, till it was a hoary-headed anachronism long surviving its usefulness.

Ordeals of various kinds, in their essence a passive appeal to the power of nature as the voice of God, once formed part of the judicial system of almost every nation, whether of the east or west.[1] Trial by combat, on the contrary, in which the litigants were instruments in the appeal as well as subjects of it, had no such universality. Angry men have fought from the beginning, and will fight until the end. But trial by combat—a deliberate staking of a plea upon the issue of a duel—is a different and far higher thing. It was not known to the Oriental races until after contact with the nascent chivalry of the west.[2] It did not exist among the ancient Egyptians. We must reject, as Pope Nicholas the First did in the year 867, the argument that it was divinely instituted when David with his sling slew the mighty man of war of the Philistines.[3] It was not practised by the Greeks. It was a department of jurisprudence which found no place in the codes of Roman emperors or the treatises of Roman jurists. It is true that it comes to the front in history at a time when the mistress of the world began to 'droop and slowly die upon her throne'; but it was not a growth likely to spring from the decaying tissues of a high civilization grown corrupt. Its roots must be sought in lands inhabited

Not universal.

[1] Gibson (on Ordeals). Blackstone, iv. ch. 27.

[2] Kerboga, Emir of Mosul, in 1098, is said to have offered to decide his quarrel with the Crusaders by a combat of five or ten champions. James's History of Chivalry, 147.

[3] Corpus Juris Canonici (1747) i. 389. This argument nevertheless was not extinguished. It shone anew in the Mirror of Justice in the 14th century. Blackstone, iii. ch. 25.

by a people not yet advanced beyond the barbarian stage.

Where the hazel grew.

It appears to have been indigenous to Central Europe—perhaps, as has been suggested, within the limits where the hazel grew[1]—and it flourished amongst those Scando-Gothic tribes before whom Rome fell. The empire all along its frontier had a ring of barbarism in which there are not a few indications that some sort of trial by battle prevailed. That 'monstrous birth of ferocity and superstition,' as Hallam[2] termed it, held there a place which the calm abstractions of Roman law were little likely to fill. Livy records that Corbis and Orsua, disputing about a principality in Spain, spurned the mediation of Scipio, and said that neither god nor man save Mars would be acknowledged as judge between them. Corbis was the devouter votary of the battle-god, and, in the single combat fought in presence of Scipio, his proficiency in arms gave him the victory over his gallant but unskilled opponent.[3] Amongst the Germans also Mars was a popular judge. Thus Paterculus, a Roman soldier

1 Arng. Jon. Chrym. 100.

2 Middle Ages, ch. 2, part 2, Murray's reprint, 156.

3 Livy, book 28, ch. 21. Evidently too there was a tradition of something of this kind in prehistoric Rome itself. The combat of the Horatii, the dauntless three of Rome, with the Curiatii, the three Alban champions, points that way. Horatius, after his two companions had fallen, slew the whole Alban three. Livy says the graves of the two Romans and the three Albans were still to be seen in his day. Book i. ch. 24-25.

and historian who wrote in the first half of the first century, says that when Quintilius Varus thought to soften the barbarity of the Germans 'by the novelty of an unknown discipline, the settlement by law of matters wont to be decided by arms,' his fate very soon proved his folly in believing that men whom swords had not been able to conquer, law would civilize.[1]

CHAP. 2.—*King Gundobald, A.D. 501.*

HOW first in the forest primeval the duel arose who shall say?

> Who can see the green earth any more
> As it was in the sources of time?

All that can be said with certainty is that in the rough boyhood of Europe men fought. There is reason for thinking that more seemly order gained on the duel, and that in consequence of the spreading influence of Christianity it to some extent died out of practice as a mode of litigation, and gave way before a system of oaths[2] which was little better, if not a degree worse. The idea of law was of tolerably early and rapid growth, but justice was excessively slow in finding out a fit method to express herself. In the realm of oaths the church possessed its most

[1] Velleius Paterculus, ii. ch. 117-18. See also Tacitus, Germania, ch. 10.

[2] Esprit des Lois, book 28, ch. 13 and 18. Article, Encyclop. Brit. *voce* Duelling.

solemn sway, and the new system was at once a symbol of clerical authority and a means of power. But the inherent unfitness of such a system for the time ere long produced a powerful reaction which swept it away.

A cure for perjury.

Christianity in abrogating the duel had raised a new evil, and perjury was rife. It is believed that it was this consideration which led Gundobald, King of Burgundy, to revive the ancient barbarism which had been slumbering only, and was far from dead. A means of ensuring the truth in human testimony has been a thing desired in every age. The search hitherto has been as fruitless as the search for the philosopher's stone, and the experiments have been scarcely less numerous. Oaths ever highly reputed have not been an unqualified success, and although some of the oaths of the early middle ages are distinguished by an ingenuity of imprecation entitling them to high rank as works of imagination,[1] yet even they were not satisfactory. That they produced widespread perjury in Gundobald's time is evident, for the declared object

[1] The sweeping curses in the penalty clauses of some Anglo-Saxon charters may serve for proof of this. See one in Ross's Lectures ii. 110, which utters the pious wish, in a certain eventuality, 'sit ipse per colla depressus catenis inter flammivomas tætrorum dæmonum catervas.' Many such are to be found in the Codex Diplomaticus everywhere, but see vol. i. for instances in A.D. 680 and 777, at pp. 24, 158. The oaths, however, against which Gundobald rose in revolt were mainly part of a great partisan system of compurgation.—Esprit des Lois, book 28, ch. 13. For an examination of some evils of that system in England see Pike i. 55.

of his edict in the year 501 was 'to prevent our subjects from attesting by oath what they are not certain of, nay, what they know to be false.' Gundobald[1] evidently thought that his subjects might as well risk their bodies as their souls, and he introduced, or re-introduced, the judicial combat. His edict, an antidote to perjury, was thus a reaction against clericalism, but he was able to turn against the church the arguments of the church itself. Replying to the remonstrances of one of his bishops, he said: 'Is it not true that the event both of national wars and of private combats is directed by the judgment of God? And does not Providence award the victory to the juster cause?'[2]

Very soon after this famous edict the judicial duel was welcomed into almost every European code.

Wide sphere of application.

There is no need to give details in individual states. In some it had probably continued in unbroken traditional practice. Others followed the example of Burgundy. It prevailed amongst all the races from which Britain derived its Teutonic blood. Saxon and Dane, Frisian and Frank,[3] practised it alike. Generally speaking, it was of the most catholic applicability. It was a remedy for nearly every wrong that flesh is heir to.

1 Esprit des Lois, book 28, ch. 17. That it was an antidote to the oaths system is evident from many of the early continental codes. See Du Cange, *voce* Duellum.

2 Gibbon, ch. 38 (ii. 552).

3 Esprit des Lois, book 28, ch. 14, 18. Du Cange, *voce* Duellum.

Nothing was too high for it, nothing too low. It would establish the virtue of a queen,[1] test the veracity of a witness, or redargue the decision of a judge; it would hang a traitor, a murderer, or a thief; it would settle a disputed point of succession, give a widow her dower, or prove a questioned charter.[2] From such high arguments as these, it descended with equal ease to discuss debts of every kind and of whatever amount, and a French monarch earned a title as a reformer when he disallowed it where the principal sum in plea was under five sous.[3]

CHAP. 3.—*Mode of Battle.*

THE modes of fighting employed on the Continent were various. Sometimes the combatants, barefoot and bare-headed, with gloves on their hands, fought with sword and shield. It was thus that the Saxons were armed for the campfight,[4] and when the question was one of life and death, Verstegan says that a bier stood ready to carry away the dead body of him that should be slain.[5] Sometimes the fighting on the Continent was done with clubs or batons. After the tenth century the baton was only used by men of

1 Gibson, p. 288. Corp. Jur. Canon. i. 389. Pope Nicholas I. in 867 declared such a mode a temptation of God.

2 Esprit des Lois, book 28, ch. 26-27. Gibbon, ch. 58 (iv. 230). Robertson, proofs, note 22.

3 Esprit des Lois, book 28, ch. 19.

4 Du Cange, *voce* Duellum, quoting Speculum Saxonicum.

5 Restitution (ed. 1605), 64.

base birth, and knightly antagonists fought on horseback[1] in the panoply of chivalry, with shield and lance and sword and helm.

The progress of chivalry somewhat changed the character of the judicial duel, investing it with a religious ceremonial and tingeing it with a romantic hue which did not belong to its purely legal stages. The influence of the crusades deepened the impression, and tended to an approach to uniformity in practice.[2] Saint George was the saint of chivalry, and it was to 'the good chevalier St. George' that the French knights of the 14th century made their vows when they met for mortal duel in the lists on the appeal of treason.[3]

There were many whimsical variants before the customs became stereotyped. Thus, in mediæval

A breach of promise case.

Germany, when the plea was a delicate question of breach of promise or concerning the marital relations, it was disposed of in a manner certainly odd. The battle was done by both parties in person. The man had his left arm tied to his side, in his right hand he held a short baton, and he stood in a tub sunk waist deep in the ground. His fair adversary was armed with a paving-stone

1 The first recorded duel on horseback took place in 820. This was reckoned a novelty among the Franks, but the reason assigned for the mode was that the combatants were Goths, and the equestrian battle was in accordance with their law. Gibbon, ch. 38 (ii. 552).

2 The Assise of Jerusalem did much to consolidate practice. Gibbon, ch. 58 (iv. 230-2).

3 Philip the Fair's ordinance is duly noted in its place in Part V.

sewn up into the purposely lengthened sleeve of the solitary under-garment which she was allowed to wear. She had full liberty to manœuvre round the tub, and watch for a favourable opportunity to deliver a crushing argument with the paving-stone. As the man's movements were restrained within the limits of his tub, the chances must have been strongly on the virago's side; but an ancient picture of one of these singular encounters represents the woman with her head in the tub and her heels in the air.[1] Female virtue and valour, it is evident, did not always gain the day.

Nor was this a solitary eccentricity in the manner of combat. The Norsemen, who call for a separate chapter, varied occasionally the monotony of the ordinary combat in a mode no less whimsical. Amongst them, according to Arngrim Jonas, the right of appeal after a duel—in other words, the right of revenge—was lost if the victor with a single blow could slay a bull produced for the purpose.[2] A remarkable method of stopping appeals, truly.

CHAP. 4.—*Among the Norsemen.*

AMONG the northern tribes trial by battle ran a course independent of that which it pursued in

[1] For these facts see an able article on trial by battle in *Cornhill Magazine*, 1870, vol. xxii., pp. 715-37. The writer's name is not given. See also Palgrave's Eng. Commonwealth, ii. 201.

[2] Arng. Jon. Chrym. 100. Egill Scallagrimson did this feat.

southern Europe. The real rise of chivalry followed in point of time, and resulted in no small measure from, the junction of north and south in Normandy. The northmen had brought with them from their fiords a fully-developed judicial duel code, which enjoyed amongst them the highest popularity.

When King Frotho the Third, in the misty age of Denmark, sanctioned the settlement of controversies by the sword, he said he deemed it much fitter to contend with weapons than with words.[1] All Scandinavia echoed the sentiment. The Norseman was a fatalist; renown for valour was the jewel of his soul, and battle the breath of his nostrils; his very heaven was a valhalla of warriors spending eternity in feast and fight; with him revenge was a virtue; and supreme in his pantheon was Odin, the God of Battles, whose will alone could give him the victory, whether the cause he fought for was public or private, his nation's or his own. It was no wonder that this rough way of wooing justice commended itself to his free and fearless nature. When, in the ninth century, the overbearing of King Harald of Norway drove into exile the Pilgrim Fathers of Iceland, they carried with them at their 'land-taking' their primitive judicial code. Suspended for a time, for the prudential reason, 'that it became not men to fight with each other whilst there were so few of

[1] Saxo Grammaticus (1744) 86, notes 120.

them in the land,'[1] it was soon reinstated. The sagas, which so nobly combine the law, the history, and the poetry of the north during succeeding centuries, are full of examples. Justice 'with point and edge'[2] had a strong hold on the Norse heart. It underlay the whole Icelandic legal system. The incipient influence of Christianity caused the enactment of the year 1006[3] by which the duel was abolished, but long after that date the old wild remedy held its place as an alternative, and kept alive the fierce tradition of the law as it was in the pagan time.

Of old amongst these northern nations the lists were known as the Hazelstangs, a term derived from the barriers of hazel with which they were once wont to be surrounded. The arena was known as the Hazelsfield or Hesslissvoll, and a challenge appropriately enough became an invitation to go to the Hazels.[4] But in Iceland the prevalent name for the duel was the Holmgang, from the fact that its scene was generally an island

Holmgang.

1 The words of Erik of Gudala, cited in 'Iceland, Greenland, and the Faroe Islands,' 1841, 118.

2 So called in Burnt Njal, ii. 83. For some information about the duel in Iceland, Sir George Dasent's fine introduction to Burnt Njal has been drawn upon.

3 Arng. Jon. Chrym. 101.

4 Saxo Grammaticus (1744) notes, 97-98, Hessliss Steingur, Hesslissvoll, ad hessla. Arng. Jon. Chrym. 100. Heslesteingur, hasla-voll. Steingur is just the plural of the word preserved in Scotch and provincial English—stang, a stick or pole. I believe 'stengesdint' in Stubbs' Charters, 112, 'styngisdynt' and 'stokisdynt' in Scots Acts, i. 336, is a fine for a blow with a stick.

near the hill of laws or the thingvalla, where, under the sky, justice with point and edge was sought and given. A proposal *at gange a Holm*, to go to the island,[1] was a legal phrase of serious import.

CHAP. 5.—*The Church.*

THE influence of the Church, which we have seen directed against the system so early as the days of King Gundobald, seems to have been in the main directed against it during succeeding centuries. But the pious aspirations of churchmen, even when enlightened, united, and consistent, would have been powerless for a time to overturn a deep-rooted popular sentiment. The Church denounced the ordeals of fire and water as a fabric of the devil[2] centuries before these ordeals were banished from the codes of Europe. Even longer was the interval in the case of the judicial combat. Du Cange tells us[3] that from the year 855 'popes and bishops and councils strove to abrogate the impious custom, and damned it by anathemas,' but it did not droop and languish under the Church's frown. Despite the anathemas it continued to flourish, and in some codes

1 Last references. Holm, meaning in early English an island, came also to mean a meadow or piece of land by the strand of a river. Precisely the same has been the case with the Celtic Inis, an inch or island. Inch is often applied to riverside meadows.

2 Blackstone, iv. c. 27. Gibson, 267, has a papal denunciation calling the belief in the ordeal and duel a 'damnabilem opinionem.'

3 Du Cange, *voce* Duellum.

with the added enormity that the clergy, formerly exempt, were brought under its sway.[1] Moreover, ecclesiastical opinion was not always enlightened, and ecclesiastical action was neither united nor consistent.

Clerical precept and practice.

Heedless of the corporate voice of the Church individual churchmen supported and clung to the institution. By the advice of an archbishop a trial of this kind took place in 978.[2] In the eleventh and twelfth centuries Papal denunciations were so far forgotten that the right of jurisdiction in trials by combat was eagerly sought after by the clergy, and many charters conferring it were granted. One of the year 1008, for instance, says—'We give to God and Saint Denis the law of the duel.'[3] Nay, the clergy did not refrain from the duel themselves. In 1165 Pope Alexander III. declared that where a cleric fought a duel he was to be deposed unless he could get the grace of his bishop[4]—a sufficiently elastic exception. And in the same year the same pope ruled, in the case of a priest who had lost a part of his finger in a duel, that as it was only a small piece of his finger which he had lost he was not to be held as maimed and disqualified, but might continue to celebrate the mass.[5] As a rule, however, the clergy did not fight in person

[1] Esprit des Lois, book 28, c. 18.
[2] Robertson, proofs, 22. [3] *Cornhill* article.
[4] Corp. Jur. Canon. (1747) ii. 769.
[5] Corp. Jur. Canon. ii. 127. Mutilation disqualified; this was held not mutilation.

but by proxy, and so general became the practice that religious bodies maintained champions for the express purpose. In 1195 Pope Celestine III. decreed that duels ought not to be undertaken by churchmen, whether they concerned the church or not,[1] and that when a priest's champion killed a man in one of these duels, such a champion was truly a homicide, and the priest ought to cease to minister in holy orders.[2] In 1216 Pope Innocent III. spoke out in still stronger terms, calling any cleric who had to do with duels a man of blood.[3] The church was not a whit in advance of the age.

These citations from papal precept may be followed by some examples of clerical practice. In the eleventh century a great controversy on a matter of ritual arose in Spain, and after a debate of the virulent type usual when the point at issue is in the field of theology, the question which of two liturgies was more acceptable in the eyes of God was actually fought out by knightly champions in the lists.[4] When in the thirteenth century King Louis of France, known later as a saint, prohibited the law of combat within his own demesne, his prohibition was made the subject of grievous complaint by the prior of one of his own monasteries.[5] This did not arise from any special barbarity. It was the old, old obstacle of vested interests. Humanity and religion had to stand

[1] Corp. Jur. Canon. ii. 829.
[2] Corp. Jur. Canon. ii. 769.
[3] Corp. Jur. Canon. ii. 623.
[4] Robertson, *supra.*
[5] Du Cange, *voce* Duellum.

back because reform would have interfered with the fines and perquisites which fell to the possessor of the coveted jurisdiction which St. Louis assailed. At the council of Ravenna in 1312 certain cardinals of the Romish hierarchy brought forward champions to vindicate by arms the memory of a pope.[1]

Thus, although it is admitted that the Church on the whole was on the side of humane reform, it was half-hearted in its anathemas, and its attitude was not one of stern and consistent opposition to this sanguinary and unchristian law. So late as the year 1404 a solemn embassy presented a petition to the Pope himself asking his holiness to ordain a judicial combat to be fought in his own presence at Rome between two European kings. But Innocent VII. dismissed the petition with a smile, and said, 'We do not incline to the shedding of Christian blood.'[2]

CHAP. 6.—*Decadence and Extinction.*

THE shedding of Christian blood, however, was a very small matter to European society from the sixth to the thirteenth century, and much fighting was done in the pure duel of law prevalent all over the continent. One great abstract question of succession was so decided. The doctrine of representation—the right of the sons of a son to be reckoned as children of the family—was determined in the tenth

[1] *Cornhill* article. [2] Adam of Usk, 94 and 224.

century by a combat of champions in preference to a council of judges.[1] But as law grew the duel fell more and more into disrepute in the ordinary courts. Meanwhile a contrary influence was at work, for chivalry had become a great European power. Under its influence the duel had its days prolonged—more, however, as a duel of chivalry—a duel of law still, it is true, but more chivalric than legal in its type.[2]

End approaching.

When the fourteenth century began, the duel had ceased to be in any real sense a living proper part of law. Its day was past. Feeling the hand of time it had fallen behind. Although its name was still on the muster-roll it was no longer an effective combatant in the ranks of the great army of law which wages perpetual warfare for the rights of man, and carries with it in its endless march the ever-increasing spoils of countless victories. Reluctantly it left the field in which, no one who has faith in the innate reasonableness of men can doubt, it served a useful purpose once. When the fifteenth century was at hand there was still a rude faith in its justice—a faith which had not been without its triumphs and had withstood many a shock,[3] and which for a while longer kept it in life.

1 Robertson, proofs, 22.

2 This sufficiently appears from Philip the Fair's ordinance in 1306. His previous attempt to abolish it altogether is satisfactory proof of the next statement in the text.

3 The dog of Montargis which convicted the murderer of its master by defeating him in a trial by battle before the French King (Kendall

Long moribund, it took an unconscionable time to die. Chivalry was long lived; by chivalry it was kept alive, and with chivalry it passed away. In Spain a judicial duel was fought so late as 1522.[1] The French language gained a new phrase in 1547—the *coup de Jarnac*—from the underhand blow which decided the last licensed duel in France.[2] On the Continent and in the British isles it was alive a thousand years and more after the enactment of Gundobald. The anathemas of Rome against it had failed, suggesting to Gibbon his satiric dictum that 'the ineffectual censures of saints, of popes, and of synods, may seem to prove that the influence of superstition is weakened by its unnatural alliance with reason and humanity.[3]

The thunder of the Council of Trent in 1545,[4] threatening wrath and judgment on principalities and powers which sanctioned the duel, was little more than an echo of the conscience of Europe. Trial by battle faded away before the light of civi-

160, Barrington 203) was very famous. The duel of Carouge and Le Gris, arising from a wrong done to the wife of the former, and in which Le Gris was defeated, has had the fortune to be appealed to as an example both of the infallibility and the fallibility of such trials. Compare Froissart ii. ch. 60, Moreri *voce* Carouge, Coûtumes de Bretagne i. 7, with Encyclop. Brit. *voce* Duelling. If an occasional miscarriage ruined a system of law, what about trial by jury?

1 Robertson, proofs, note 22.

2 This duel is named by Robertson, as last cited. It was between M. Jarnac and another Frenchman. Jarnac gained the day by a stroke deemed unfair.—Encyc. Brit. *voce* Duelling; Haydn's Dict. of Dates *voce* Jarnac.

3 Gibbon, ch. 38 (ii. 553).

4 The deliverance of the Council is quoted in Selden's Duello, ch. 5.

lisation; it was not frightened out of existence by a papal bull.

The private duel.

Even when the end came, so venerable an offspring of a deep-seated human instinct of strife could not wholly die. It left behind to carry on the old barbaric line a bastard scion, the private duel, which first asserted its pernicious presence when the eye of its parent had grown dim, and its hand waxed feeble in the extremity of age.[1]

[1] The relations between judicial combat and private duel are touched on later. The private duel began in the 16th and became terribly common in the 17th century

PART II.—ORIGIN IN BRITAIN.

CHAP. 7.—*A Question Stated.*

'I THINK it not easy,' said John Selden, in his Duello,[1] 'to prove this custom in England before the Norman Conquest.' That trial by battle was not indigenous in Britain might be supposed from the fact that it is not mentioned in the Roman authors. It is without memorial in such poor fragments of Celtic law in Scotland as survived the wars of Pict and Scot and the coalition of Saxon and Gael. The earliest British authors, Gildas, Nennius, and Bede, name it not, and neither does the Anglo-Saxon Chronicle. If the thing is to be found anywhere, one would expect to find it in the ancient laws of the legislating kings from Ethelbert to Edward the Confessor; but we search these laws in vain. Such facts raise strong presumptions. Yet, on the other hand, Teutonic Britain was of Saxon and Scandinavian birth. It has been seen that amongst both Saxons and Norsemen, 'like enough to be fathers of such a child,'[2] the custom was well known

Selden's opinion to be examined.

[1] Opera Omnia, 1726, vol. iii., the Duello, ch. 6.
[2] A phrase of Selden's in Duello, ch. 5.

and in high favour. And when we consider in how many respects England was the heir of the Continental ages, when we remember how much of her law came to her through her Germanic ancestry, it will surely be surprising if campfight and holmgang are found never to have crossed the North Sea in Frisian keels or Northern galleys. Moreover, on the Celtic side, the old Welsh laws, designated 'anomalous,' give it countenance, although under the suspicious, borrowed English name of 'Ornest' or 'Gornest,' in cases of theft, homicide, and treason.[1] In Ireland the combat, known as 'Comhrac,' was a familiar institution in the fifth century,[2] and St. Patrick himself had to forbid his clerics to indulge in it.[3] Nothing, therefore, in the antecedents of either Celt or Saxon need predispose against an opinion different from that of Selden.

Before the view of that 'most learned wise arch-antiquary'[4] is either endorsed or rejected, let Scotland be made a party to the inquiry and let the proof be led anew. First in the witness-box let us put some garrulous old Icelandic scalds whose testimony Selden did not hear.

1 Welsh Laws, ii. 211, 315, 516, 623, 625.
2 Ancient Laws, Ireland, R.S. i. 251, 253; iv. 33.
3 Ware's Hist. and Antiq. Ireland, ed. 1764, ii. 153.
4 Selden is justly so styled by Herrick in Hesperides.

CHAP. 8.—*Norse Evidence.*

The Scot abroad.

WHILST some of the Norse sagas display the judicial combat in its finished state with due ceremonials and code,[1] others shew most significantly its primitive rudeness. In its earlier stage a man's whole belongings were staked on the issue of the fight, for the winner took all the property of the vanquished as the spoil of victory.[2] A sure road to wealth, therefore, lay open to a skilful champion. The ubiquitous Scot embraced the golden opportunity and fared over the sea in quest of fortune.[3] In the tenth century we read of Liot the Pale, a gigantic champion,[4] by nation a Scotsman, going to and fro in Norway, and 'by the rite and rigour of single combat' rapidly getting rich. But his career was cut short by the renowned Norse warrior, champion-killer, and poet, Egill Scallagrimson, who overcame him in a duel about an heiress, and so 'vindicated all his goods to himself according to law.'[5]

1 It is said that Cormak's saga, ch. x., contains the regulations.

2 Arng. Jon. Chrym. (a work drawn from saga sources) 100.

3 Quæ regio in terris nostri non plena laboris?

4 Giants and champions in the north are represented as being often of extreme respectability. Olaus Magnus treats at some length of their 'sobriety.' Some there were who went so far as to be teetotallers—qui nunquam ebriosa potione indulsisse dicuntur.—Gentium Septentrionalium Historiæ Breviarium, 1652, book v. chs. 1 to 4, pp. 164-174.

5 Arng. Jon. Chrym. 134. This Egill had a great career both in fight and song. He is reckoned a poet of exceptional merit. (Note by editors of Corpus Poeticum Boreale.) He fought under Athelstan at the battle

Scotland, according to the same authority, had champions at home also; and a like law of escheat prevailed there to give the victor his reward. Thorgisel Orabein, another Norse notable, was sent on a mission from Norway to the Hebrides to recover arrears of tribute. On the voyage his ship was wrecked 'at the promontory of Scotland, Katanes,' but he and his companions were saved. At this time there was infesting Caithness a terrible pirate, Surter, surnamed Jarnhaus or Ironhead, who threatened fire and sword to the whole province if its prince would not give him Gudrun, his sister, to wife. Thorgisel, with a heart for beauty in distress, challenged Surter to a duel. The pirate did not fight fair. He had the gift of magic, by which he used to blunt the edge of an opponent's sword. Forewarned of this, Thorgisel doubly armed himself by taking with him to the field two swords. One of these he hid in the ground—the other he used

The Scot at home.

of Brunanburh in 937, and his extant saga describes the victory his sword helped to gain. See an extract in Antiq. Celt. Scand. He conquered in a duel Atlas, who was surnamed the Short for the *lucus à non lucendo* reason that he was very tall. Atlas was a magician on whom no iron brand could bite. Egill was in the fight before he found this out, but as soon as he did so he tossed his sword aside, grappled with Atlas, and threw him; then, gripping his windpipe between his teeth, held him so 'till at last he breathed out his conjuring soul'—a mode of fighting which Arngrim Jonas justifies by Roman models from Valerius Maximus. Egill attained the age of 90. Long after his death his remains were dug up, and posterity wondered at his skull, 'undulated on every side like waves.' Posterity's wonder at the skull must have been little tempered with respect, for we are told 'a bystander could not break it with an axe.'—Arng. Jon. Chrym. 135.

at the opening of the fight; and when the eye of the magician turned its edge he drew forth the hidden weapon, smote starkly ere the enchanter could tamper with the second blade, and gained the day.[1] To the victor fell not only the fair *casus belli*, the virgin princess, but also the whole ships and warlike gear of the vanquished Surter. Nor was the ironheaded pirate the sole victim of Thorgisel's sword. Snecoll and Snabernon and Gyrder-with-the-Foot-cut-off he overcame in single combat. Besides, he had a very wonderful encounter with 'Randid, a dire champion of Scotland.' The other duels above described were fought with the accustomed arms—helmet, shield, sword, and spear—but that with Randid was exceptional. It was of that peculiar class fought 'in a very capacious vessel closed at the top,' where a wooden baton a cubit long was the weapon of offence. Sword and baton in open field or in closed vat were alike deadly in the hands of the ever-victorious Thorgisel, and the Scottish champion was slain.[2]

In the whole range of the early historical literature of the north no name has such authority as that

[1] Starchater, another terrible Norse champion, vanquished a magician after the same fashion. His plan to outwit his adversary was to cover his sword with thin hide, which the eye of the magician could not pierce. Saxo Grammaticus (1644) 105.

[2] Arng. Jon. Chrym. 101, 150. These Norse champions were a long-lived race. Thorgisel, after he was 70, having been affronted by a Norwegian merchant who said that age was telling on him, fought a duel with the scoffer to prove his unwithered vigour, which he did by killing his man. He lived to tell the tale for other 15 years.—Arng. Jon. Chrym. 150.

of Snorro, the Icelandic scald and statesman. One of his sagas tells how in England, in the tenth century, Alfuin, a great captain and holm-gang-fighter, aspired to the hand of Gyda, widow of an English jarl. But Gyda would have none of him, and pledged her hand to Olaf, a Norseman. Therefore Alfuin challenged Olaf to a duel, with twelve men on each side. Olaf armed himself with a great battle-axe, ordered his men to do the same, and bade them follow his example in the fight. At the very outset, with a blow of his battle-axe he struck the sword of Alfuin from his grasp. A second blow, and Alfuin lay at his mercy. Olaf's men adopted their leader's tactics with like success. So Alfuin was banished, never to return, and Olaf vindicated to himself his whole possessions. In this saga Snorro very expressly says—'Now at this time it was the received custom in England to decide litigations by the holmgang.'[1]

What Snorro says.

Such, then, is the testimony of the Norse witnesses, whose patriotic preferences are decidedly marked. They took care not to let the English and Scotch dogs have the best of the argument.

[1] Antiq. Celt. Scand. 74. 'Enn þat var sidr á Englandi ef ii. keptoz um ein lut, at þar skylldi koma til hólm-gánga,' is the original Norse of the passage quoted. I translate from the Latin version.

CHAP. 9.—*English and Scotch Evidence.*

NEXT shall be heard some English historians who lived in the eleventh and twelfth centuries, and a Scotch one of the fifteenth.

When that dim personage, King Arthur, was besieging Paris, Flollo, the Roman tribune of Gaul, shut up in the beleaguered city, challenged him to single combat. Whoever gained the day was to be king of the other's realm. The battle took place on an island near Paris. In goodly armour, mounted on horses of wondrous speed, as the combatants fixed their lances, set spurs to their steeds and charged, it was not easy—according to the chronicle[1]—to foretell which would triumph. Arthur hurled his spear against the chest of Flollo, and Flollo was unhorsed. Quickly rising he stabbed Arthur's charger, and horse and man fell together. But in a moment Arthur arose unhurt to renew the fight on foot. Not, however, till he was wounded on the forehead and saw his own blood[2] stream over his corselet and shield did he nerve himself to decisive action; then one stalwart stroke drove his good sword Caliburn right through the helm of Flollo and cut his head in two. 'By which wound,' says our veracious

King Arthur.

1 Geoffrey of Monmouth, ix., ch. 11.

2 Compare—'When Maitland saw his ain blood fa'
An angry man was he.'
—Ballad of 'Auld Maitland' in Border Minstrelsy.

authority, Geoffrey of Monmouth, 'Flollo fell, striking the ground with his heels, and gave up the ghost'—as well he might.

The Anglo-Saxon Chronicle, in its account of the peace of 1016 between the Danish king Cnut and the English king Edmund, merely states that they came together at Olney, by Deerhurst.[1] Symeon of Durham says the same, but calls Olney an island.[2] It has therefore been understood to be the Isle of Alney, near Gloucester.[3] William of Malmesbury hints at a prelude to this treaty. He says that Edmund challenged Cnut to a duel, but that Cnut declined.[4] Gaimar has it that the challenge was accepted, and that they met in a ship moored in mid-Severn, while their respective armies lined the opposite banks. The kings were arrayed for battle with hauberk and helm, shield and axe, dagger, sword, and mace, but a compromise was effected and the arms were never used.[5] In Henry of Huntingdon this progressive story advances one stage further. His version sonorously describes the fearful clang and gleaming flash of arms with which the duel opened, the stoppage when Edmund began to thunder on his rival,[6] and the final kiss of peace. The full-developed product appears in a work of Walter

Cnut and Edmund Ironside.

1 Anglo-Saxon Chron. under year cited.

2 Symeon of Durham, R.S. ii. 153.

3 Camden, 234, 246.

4 Gesta Regum, R.S. i. 217.

5 Gaimar, R.S. lines 4267, *et seq.*

6 Henry of Hunt. History, under year 1016, R.S. 185.

Map,[1] a Welsh marchman, who may have gleaned some parts of the tradition in the neighbourhood of the Isle of Alney itself. He tells us that champions originally proposed were discarded. At the commencement of the combat Cnut pressed hard on Edmund, who, we are told with some preciseness, was 'stout and broad, that is to say, rather fat.' This was no common fight—a realm was at stake—and an eager ring of Danes and Englishmen stood round. During a pause Cnut, in the hearing of the bystanders, made a remark to Edmund, who, being 'rather fat,' was out of breath. The remark presents the great Dane in a light somewhat different from that suggested by his wave-compelling attitude on the wild sea shore. 'Edmund,' he said, 'you are panting far too much.'[2] Edmund blushed fiery red; he said never a word, but when the battle-royal was resumed he struck Cnut such a blow on the helmet that it sent him sprawling on hands and knees. Chivalrously holding back, Edmund did not urge his advantage over his fallen foe; he contented himself with an *ad hominem* retort to Cnut's taunt—'I don't pant too much for one who lays so mighty a king at his feet.' When the Danes saw this issue of the duel they were glad to make

[1] De Nugis Curialium (Camden Society) 204-5.

[2] It scarcely comports with legal and historical dignity to say that Cnut 'chaffed' Edmund, but no other verb conveys the idea so well. Boece's version of this duel is in book 12, ch. 2. It is very racy.

peace, and the kings partitioned England between them.[1]

Cnut, in the person of one of his children, is associated with another duel of renown[2]—this time on the continent. Gunhild, his daughter, had married Henry III., Emperor of the Germans. Accused of unfaithfulness by Rodingar, a gigantic German, her defence was undertaken by a mere boy—Mimekin, an underling at the court of her brother, King Hardecnut of England. In the duel the English champion hamstrung and slew his adversary. Thus unexpectedly vindicated, Gunhild retired to a nunnery.

Macbeth and the thieves.

The solitary Scotch witness to be adduced is Hector Boece, who records a stratagem of Macbeth so picturesque that one wonders it did not find its way, through the medium of Holinshed, into Shakespeare's great tragedy. Macbeth—so Bellenden's quaint and free translation of Boece tells us—'devisit ane subtell slicht, to bring all misdoaris and brokin men to his justice and solistit sindry his liegis, with large money, to appele the thevis quhilkis opprest thame maist, in barras, aganis ane prefixit day. And quhen thir thevis war enterit in barras quhare thay suld have fouchtin aganis thair nichtbouris, thay wer all takin be armit men, and hangit on jebatis, according,

[1] It is worth noting that the Knytlinga saga, which tells of this treaty, has not a word about the duel.—Antiq. Celt. Scand. 139.

[2] R. de Diceto, R.S. i. 174, William of Malmesbury, Gesta Regum. R.S. i. 230. This duel is assigned to the year 1041.

justly, to thair demeritis.'[1] Were this story half as true as it is dramatic, it might itself prove that, before 1058, Scotland was well acquainted with the legal duel, the procedure in appeals of felony, and the 'barras' or lists in which they were decided.

The concluding item of evidence is the statement of William of Malmesbury that William the Conqueror, when he laid claim to the English throne, offered single combat to Harold as one of the possible modes of settlement. He suggested 'that they might ventilate the matter by the sword'[2] whilst the armies looked on.

CHAP. 10.—*The Question Answered.*

THE proof,[3] if proof it can be called, is closed, for there is no cross-examining of these dead witnesses. Yet there is little difficulty in dealing with them. Much of their testimony is mere myth-mongering. At the best, had the circumstances been ten times more favourable, Norsemen could not be accepted as authorities on English law. Geoffrey of Monmouth is a historian indeed, but a historian whom

1 Bellenden's Boece, book 12, ch. 4. The original passage, which Bellenden rather amplifies, is on folio 258 of Boece, ed. 1526.

2 Selden's Duello, ch. 2, citing William of Malmesbury, 'ut scilicet spectante exercitu gladio rem ventilarent.'

3 Mr. Kendall was quite satisfied with a passage from Verstegan about the Saxons, the tale of Cnut, and an etymology of 'craven,' as proof of his second proposition, 'That battle did not originate in this kingdom with the Normans.'—Kendall, 141-3, 175-8.

a professor of literature[1] has called the father of English fiction. The tradition of the Isle of Alney, respectable though it be, would, if true, prove little. Nor would William the Conqueror's challenge do more. Gunhild's frail virtue was tested by a German, not an English, duel. Macbeth's trick upon the thieves rests on the single testimony of as arrant a liar as ever turned imagination loose on history. Without

Not proven.

cross-examination at all the proof breaks down, and Selden's Scotch verdict of Not Proven still meets the case. 'All this,' said he, 'persuadeth not such antiquity of the English duel.'[2]

The fact is not easy to account for, but the holmgang or campfight was either not practised in England and Scotland before the Norman Conquest, or if so practised it strangely left no trace.[3] Still the circumstance that some of the earliest British duels on record were fought on islands[4] is not fully explained by the mere fitness of islands for that purpose. The holmgang must have lived in tradition.

1 Henry Morley in First Sketch. 2 Duello, ch. 6.

3 Bishop Stubbs, in Const. Hist. i. 276, remarks that the absence of battle from the Anglo-Saxon courts is far more curious than its introduction from abroad. 4 See index under 'island.'

PART III.—ENGLAND, 1066-1300: LAW.

CHAP. 11.—*Legal Outline.*

IN 1066 wager of battle entered England in the train of William the Conqueror. By the laws bearing his name,[1] an Englishman accused by a Norman of perjury, murder, homicide, or open robbery[2] could defend himself as he preferred—by the ordeal of carrying the hot iron, or by the duel. In the Anglo-Saxon version of William's statutory charter the combat appears for the first time in English law[3] under the name of 'Orneste.' A Norman had the same options as the Englishman, and in addition might clear himself by the oaths of witnesses after the custom of Normandy. The Conqueror seems to have had no desire to thrust upon his new subjects a foreign mode of trial. The Englishman, accuser or accused, can avoid the duel, but still some favour is shown

Under William the Conqueror.

1 Stubbs' Charters, 84. Ancient Laws, England i. 493, 488-9.

2 Called 'ran.'

3 Ancient Laws, England, i. 489. See note in glossary annexed to the laws, *voce* Ordeal. 'Ornest' or 'Eornest' has the same meaning as 'wager': see ch. 12. The word still survives as 'earnest.' Palgrave's Eng. Commonwealth, i. 223-33.

to the Norman. An accused Englishman who will not fight must go to the ordeal; a Norman, accused by an Englishman who will not fight, may clear himself by oath. The duel is thus treated as a Norman institution, and the ordinance affords an additional argument for the belief that the duel was not practised in England before the Conquest. However, in a very short time this distinction between Norman and Englishman disappeared; we never hear of a litigant refusing battle because he was an Englishman. The English had little liking for the judicial combat, but they probably liked still less to be treated as an inferior and unwarlike race. Several passages in Domesday Book[1] shew that the duel had become an integral part of English practice before 1086. There is some doubt about the precise sphere of its operation in civil matters for which the extant laws of the Norman period make no provision, but it certainly was not limited to crimes. Domesday Book proves that at the time of the survey pleas of land were tried by battle or by ordeal, for in cases of disputed ownership an alternative proof is offered, 'vel bello vel judicio,'[2] by battle or the ordeal. From

[1] Domesday Book, popular account by Birch, 314. Its technical name was 'bellum.' The subject is illustrated, I understand, in Bigelow, Placita Anglo-Normannica, 41, 43, 61, 305. See cases cited below from Domesday Book itself.

[2] Domesday Book, ii. 213. 'Hanc terram calumpniat esse liberam ulchetel homo hermeri quocunque modo judicetur vel bello vel juditio.' Also ii. 146*b*. At ii. 176 is the entry, 'Hanc terram calumpniatur

the so-called *Leges Henrici Primi*, a compilation which has been attributed to the reign of Henry I., to that of Stephen, and even to that of Henry II., we learn that there could be no battle in civil (*i.e.* non-criminal) cases unless the property in dispute was worth at least ten shillings.[1] The origin of this restriction is unknown. Henry I., in one of his writs, mentions duel as the method of settling disputes regarding the boundaries of lands.[2] He it was, too, who granted to the citizens of London their much-prized exemption—*et nullus eorum faciat bellum*[3]—a great reform, full of hope for the future. The English people are thought to have disliked the duel as a badge and instrument of tyranny.[4]

Under Henry II.

A great change took place under Henry II., whose administration, it has been said, initiated the reign of law. By several different ordinances or 'assizes' he confined trial by battle within a definite and ever-narrowing sphere. In the first place, he introduced by the side of the 'appeal'—that is, the accusation of felony preferred

godricus dapifer per hominem suum juditio vel bello'—an offer to deraign by champion. For ordeal alone offered, see ii. 193. An instance of battle offered in a plea of land, probably before Domesday, appears in Birch's popular account above cited, 303.

1 Laws of Henry I., ch. 69, § 15-16, in Ancient Laws, England.

2 Stubbs' Charters, 104. 'De divisione terrarum' seems to refer to actions about disputed boundaries.

3 Stubbs' Charters, 108. Liber Albus, R.S. 128. The exemption was confirmed by Henry II. and Richard I. Liber Albus, 130, 131.

4 An inference of Bishop Stubbs'. Constit. History, i. 616. Palgrave had said the same.

by the person who had been wronged or by the heir of the dead man—the process which came to be known as the 'indictment,' an accusation of crime preferred by a sworn body of neighbours (the ancestors of the modern 'grand jurors') who were sworn to present the crimes of their neighbourhood. The person thus indicted went to the ordeal; but soon a practice crept in of allowing him 'to put himself upon his country for good and ill,' that is, to submit his fate to the verdict of another jury of neighbours, the ancestors of the modern 'petty jurors.'[1] When, in 1219, the ordeal was abolished, trial by jury remained the one mode of trying an indicted person, and if he would not submit to this, then he could be starved into submission,[2] for in theory none could be tried by jury who had not accepted that method of trial. Trial by battle was thus excluded from what was to be the ordinary and normal mode of procedure in criminal cases. The old appeal was not abolished. It still remained, but into its procedure trial by jury intruded itself—first, it would seem, as a means of determining collateral issues, such as whether the 'appellor' was too old to fight, or the like; afterwards as a means of determining the main issue whether the 'appellee' was guilty or no. In the course of the thirteenth century it became established that the appellee might always decline the

Trial by jury.

[1] Stubbs' Charters, 142-3. Assize of Clarendon, 1166.

[2] See 3 Edward i. ch. 12. Fleta i. ch. 34, § 33. At first the refractory were more summarily treated. Crown Pleas, Nos. 153, 157.

duel, and put himself upon his neighbours for good and ill.

Secondly, as regards civil actions, the verdict of an assize or jury was introduced in divers forms. Questions about the possession as contrasted with the ownership of lands—about 'seisin' as contrasted with 'right'—were to be thus decided, while, even when the question was as to ownership, when the action began with the solemn and conclusive 'writ of right,' the defender (or, as he was called, the tenant) was enabled to refuse the duel, and submit instead to the verdict of a 'grand assize.' Ranulf de Glanvill, soldier, judge, and crusader, is believed to have been the framer of this reform when he was chief justice of England. In his Tractatus de Legibus Angliæ, written probably in or soon after 1187, the earliest text-book on English law, Glanvill points out the equity, the promptness, and the general advantage of the verdict of a jury of twelve as compared with the delays, the dangers, and the ambiguous result of a duel.[1] It was a far-reaching reform, for in it lay what was to be the essential and central feature of English law. The assize was introduced as an alternative to the duel, just as the duel had been brought in as an alternative to the ordeal. Gradually the verdict of a jury, in one form and another (for we may here neglect the technical distinctions between 'a grand assize,' 'a petty assize,' and 'a jury' strictly so-called), became the

[1] Glanvill ii. ch. 7.

usual means of deciding all disputed questions of fact in civil actions. The duel was reserved for the writ of right, the final remedy for a claimant of land or other real property who could not rely upon recent possession, while even in this case, as just said, it was competent for the tenant, the party attacked, to reject the duel and adopt the grand assize.

Restriction of battle.

There was a steady process of restriction of the sphere of battle to the writ of right and the appeal of felony. When Glanvill wrote the process was not complete; battle was still competent in one or two civil actions besides.[1] But it was complete before Bracton's day, and thenceforth the judicial combat had place only in appeals of treason and felony, and on the writ of right, and even there only if the defender preferred the decision of battle to the verdict of his neighbours.[2] It made no more conquests. The law of England was sweeping into the younger day.

CHAP. 12.—*Sketch of Procedure.*

IN the ordinary thirteenth century criminal prosecution by way of 'appeal' the accuser 'appealed' the accused of the crime charged, stated the facts of the

[1] For duel in Glanvill see ii. ch. 3, iv. 6, v. 5, vi. 11, viii. 9, x. 5, 12, xiii. 11, xiv. 1-7.

[2] I am happy to acknowledge a very special indebtedness to Professor Maitland for some notes embodied in this chapter, of which they form the valuable part.

offence, and offered to prove it by his body or as the Court should ordain. The defender pleading not guilty denied the whole accusation word by word. If he did not wish to fight he might elect to be tried by the country—a local jury. But if he willed to fight he might elect battle and offer to prove his innocence by his body. It was then for the judge to consider whether the duel was competent and proper in the case. If he 'adjudged battle' it is inferred from subsequent practice that the gloves[1] of the parties were exchanged as a symbol of plighted faith and of the challenge and acceptance. They then found 'wads' or pledges—that is, neighbours of theirs became bail for their due appearance on the battle day. This stage of the case from the giving of 'wads' was described in the phrase 'vadiare bellum,' to wage battle; whence the name 'wager of battel,' by which the judicial combat was known to English law. Its earlier name, 'Ornest,' came from the same source. Yet it must be remembered that the 'wager' was not the battle, it was only the pledge to fight. When battle had been waged the judge decreed 'Let them come armed,' and named the day. The regulations and procedure in the actual combat appear as incident to future chapters.

'Wager' in appeal of felony.

1 Matthew Paris refers to the challenge by gloves as a French custom. 'More Francorum chirothecam suam ei porrexit . . . Quam chirothecam quasi duelli vadium ostensam Comes recepit.' This in year 1243. Hist. Maj. (1684) 533, R.S. iv. 252.

Somewhat similar was the process on the writ of right, with the difference that a civil claim took the place of a criminal charge. In that case, once the battle was waged, battle there must be, unless by consent of the judge, to whom in such an event a heavy fine called a 'concord' was payable. Another heavy fine called the fine of 'recreancy'[1] was due when either champion failed to appear. This fine was also payable when the duel was fought out, for one or other of the champions was of necessity beaten and forced to yield, thereby incurring the imputation that he was a 'craven'—not only losing the case in which he fought, but incurring a serious deprivation of civil rights. The event of the duel was held to have proved him perjured, so 'he lost his law.'[2] As an infamous person he could never be heard as a witness again.

Wager in writ of right.

In criminal cases of life and limb, say in a charge of homicide or serious theft, the accused, if defeated, suffered the penalty of his offence and the escheat of his goods. If, on the other hand, he was victorious, the accuser was imprisoned or fined for making a false charge. These and other perquisites[3] formed a species

[1] Glanvill ii. ch. 3, makes the fine 60s., a sum often recurring in the notes to the next chapter of this work. Under the laws of William the Conqueror an accused convicted by battle paid 40s. to the king. In another version the sum is 60s. Ancient Laws, England, i. 488-9, 493. The fine of 'recreancy' seems to have been exactable in the early 13th century in criminal as well as civil case duels. So it may be inferred from the Pipe Rolls, and Brac. N.B. 592, 1460.

[2] Glanvill ii. ch. 3.

[3] In a charter of Henry I. to a church of St. Peter the jurisdiction of

of dues of court which made the jurisdiction of duel a profitable affair, and explain the eagerness with which the power of pit and gallows was sought after by the nobility. Thus it will be seen in the following chapters regarding the finance of the Crown that the duel, while it was the occasion of some expenditure, was still more a source of revenue.

CHAP. 13.—*The Duel in Finance.*

Income.

IN Madox's great history of the Exchequer, and in the pipe-rolls from which it was drawn, there are endless notices of the duel. In the reign of Stephen, for example, the escheat of a vanquished man is credited,[1] and a person is represented as owing 100 measures of wine for the concord of his brother's duel.[2] Under Henry II. large sums are paid to the officers of the Crown for the duel,[3] for the fine of a duel,[4] for recreancy,[5] for refusal to fight, or absence from a duel.[6] There are amercements for

duel is conferred, and it is provided that after the battle the victor was to give thanks to God and St. Peter for his victory, and to offer the arms of the vanquished to the church. Du Cange, *voce* Duellum.

1 Madox, 237, 5 Stephen. 2 Madox, 325, 5 Stephen.

3 Pro duello. The sum varies greatly. Pipe Rolls, 5 H2 (Henry II.) p. 21, 100 marks; 7 H2 p. 16, 1 mark; 9 H2 p. 46, 100s.

4 Pro fine duelli. Amounts again vary. Pipe Rolls, 7 H2 p. 30, 5 marks; 9 H2 p. 1, 3 marks; 12 H2 pp. 21, 31 and 41, 10 marks, 5 marks, and £16 13s. 4d.

5 De recreantisa. Madox, 382; Pipe Rolls, 11 H2 p. 11, 60s. 1d.; 12 H2 p. 69, 60s.

6 Madox, 382. Garcio qui refutavit bellum—j marcam, 4 H2. Same

making a man fight two duels in one day[1]; for being present and allowing it to be done[2]; for not keeping the duel properly.[3] Fines are paid in money and in horses for concords of duels[4] and licence to concord.[4] Another is exacted for trying the theft of a cow in a court which had not the necessary jurisdiction.[5] There are fines for the record of a duel;[6] for fighting a duel in the hundred court which ought to have been before the sheriff;[7] for having a duel in the king's court.[8] Last on the varied list here cited is that paid by a lady to hinder a duel between her and her brother.[9] In the short reign of Richard I. the same thing continues. In his fifth year, notably, a fine was paid by a man who, after confessing to the king that he had no right to certain lands, had the effrontery to wage battle for them.[10] It is needless to trace details further, suffice it to say that analogous entries continue throughout the reigns of John and Henry III., with

5 H2. Pipe Rolls, 12 H2 p. 7, 1 mark; 'quia absentavit se de duello. Madox, 382, 60s.; 'quia retraxit se de duello suo die quo debuit pugnare,' 31 H2.

1 Pipe Rolls, 12 H2 p. 46, 100s.; 'quia fecit fieri una die duo duella ab uno homine.'

2 Pipe Rolls, 12 H2 p. 47.

3 Madox, 378, 100s.; 'pro duello male custodito,' 14 H2.

4 Madox, 355, 71, 325; 14, 28, and 31 H2. In last case fine was a 'ferrand horse.'

5 Madox, 379, 16 H2; 348, 17 H2.

6 Madox, 71, 22 H2.

7 Madox, 379, 24 H2.

8 Madox, 66, 30 H2.

9 Madox, 311, 31 H2.

10 Madox, 349 5 R1. Other fines in this reign appear in Madox 72, 298, in 3 and 5 R1.

strong indications of a falling off under the last-named king.[1]

That these fines were paid occasionally for the gratification of private enmity quite as much as to facilitate the administration of law is very well shown in a suit between William Marshal, Earl of Pembroke, and Fawkes de Breawte in the year 1220. There was a conflict of charters to lands in Bedfordshire. In ordinary course, if decided by duel, the fight would have been by champions; indeed, according to Glanvill, supported by many cases, it was inept for the pursuer to fight in person. But the earl's quarrel with Breawte dated back to King John's time. It had been accentuated by some recent annoyances. So keen was he for revenge that he offered no less a sum than 1000 marks for the privilege of personally fighting his enemy.[2] A similar explanation possibly applies to a number of other cases in which, under cover of an appeal of felony, an attempt was made to try the right to lands.[3]

Expenditure.

Financially the duel was to the Crown a cause of outlay as well as income. During the whole period traversed above, the costs of duels are continually appearing on the

1 Madox, 346, 7 John; p. 351, 9 J.; p. 325, 10 J.; p. 382, 5 H3; p. 307, 6 H3; p. 82, 25 H3.

2 Bracton's Note Book, No. 102. For a subsidiary cause of annoyance in 1219, see Bain's Cal. i., Nos. 725, 736.

3 Crown Pleas, Nos. 35, 88, 90.

debit side of the royal ledger. Leaving for separate treatment payments made to and for approvers, numerous items show that in the courts of the crown, duels, as a part of the judicial system, were fought at the crown's expense. In the 12th year of Henry II.[1] one entry is a perfect monument of wholesale justice, shewing that 34 ordeals, 14 defacements, 14 hangings, and 5 duels cost £9 11s. 3d. Similar debits occur all through the following reigns so late as the closing year of Edward I.,[2] and probably the original exchequer records have examples later still.

Such items as these formed a part of the income and outlay in the very many courts—county court, hundred court, and baron court—in which, within their respective limits of jurisdiction, as well as in the justice eyres, the duel was practised. It thus bulked large in the judicial finance of its time.

CHAP. 14.—*The Approver.*

A REMARKABLE feature of the legal system of the 12th and 13th centuries was the use made of men who betrayed their accomplices and became king's evidence. When battle was a mode of defence which any criminal might claim, when most crimes required

1 Madox, 256, 12 H2.

2 Madox, 256, 13 H2 and 1 R1; p. 257, 2 H3, 49 H3 (9 duels) 14 Edward I. (4 duels), 35 Edward I. (in duellis armandis).

a private prosecutor, and when failure involved fine whether there was a duel or not, it or imprisonment for false appeal[1] was natural that men should shrink from the thankless and dangerous office of making the appeal. Hence, it may be, arose a certain readiness of the law to turn the approver, tainted though he was, into an officer of justice. He had to prove the truth of his charge, and presumably also the sincerity of his own repentance, by fighting his quondam companion in crime.[2]

King's evidence.

So far little objection on any score is admissible, but all the approver's functions were not so legitimate. Bracton says[3] that the king might grant life and limb to a confessed criminal contingently on his ridding the land of a given number of malefactors by his body. He then gives a form of a pardon dependent on the condition that the recipient should conquer in five duels. Possibly Bracton's form was taken from an actual case in 1221, in which a horse thief 'became approver to fight five battles.'[4] Often enough such successive battles were fought. In Staffordshire, in the 4th year of Henry III., Hobbe-the-Werewede, an

1 Bracton ii. 405, 445.

2 For much information as to this see Madox, 255. One wonders if there was any relation between trial by battle and a custom of which there were traces in Northumberland in 1256 where a pursuer recovered his stolen goods on beheading the thief caught red-handed.—Bain's Cal. i. p. 395. It seems the complement of justice personally conducted from appeal to execution.

3 Bracton ii. 521-3.

4 Crown Pleas, No. 140.

approver, defeated Walter-in-the-Grove, but Hobbe soon had to face another opponent, and was vanquished in the second duel.[1]

In the 13th century England was far from orderly. It was, indeed, a terrible century, if the sombre tints in a great picture of English crime[2] are not by many shades too deep. By means of approvers—a system which may have been convenient, but was certainly neither safe nor creditable—ramifications of crime may frequently have been tracked, and lawless gangs broken up. At the same time there is reason to fear that this method led to not a few false accusations. It is a fact admitting no question that the crown for many years kept numerous approvers in the prisons of the various shires, where a large proportion of them died,[3] and one suspects that the approver was deliberately put forward to appeal where no better prosecutor could be got. Such seems a fair inference from the extraordinary recurrences of approvers in criminal prosecutions in the extant reports,[4] as well as from the many payments made to approvers, and to fit them out for duels.[5]

Large use of approvers.

1 Cal. Rot. Pat. p. 12.

2 Pike. It humbly seems to me that they are too deep. The criminal calendar is a bad glass through which to view civilization.

3 Pike i. 481.

4 What other conclusion can be drawn from such a string of accusations as were made by William Smalewud in 1220? He laid charges literally against all and sundry; but Adam, the priest's son, proved too much for him, so his epitaph is—'Victus est et susp.' Crown Pleas, No. 190.

5 Pipe Rolls, 8 H2 pp. 11, 26, 37, 45. 9 H2 p. 72. 11 H2 p. 40.

Charges for shields and armour for the latter purpose are frequent in the reign of Henry II.[1] One entry of the kind is suggestive: it is for the costs of the arms of an approver, and it shews that the fates had been against him in the duel, for it includes the cost of hanging him at its close.[2]

The approver's neck was in no small danger until he finished the last of his battles. If one of his five appeals broke down without battle at all, his life was the forfeit, and this was often the case where the appellee chose to be tried by assize, and not by battle. If in the battle itself the approver pronounced 'that odious word recreant'[3]—if he owned himself defeated—death was equally the penalty. And if, with a cat-like tenacity of life, he had the luck to survive to claim his pardon and permission to go into exile, carrying the scars of his five victories, it is doubtful if the hard-fought-for freedom was always his after all. For there is a faint touch of expostulation in Bracton's tone when he says that when an approver has done what he promised, faith ought to be kept with him.[4] It is certain that at times the approver, although victorious, was hanged.[5]

1 Pipe Rolls, 12 H2 p. 72. Madox 255.

2 Madox, 256. 20 H2. Et in liberatione Willelmi de Bellavalle probatoris, et armatura ipsius, et in custamento suspendendi eum. 11s. 3d.

3 So called by Bracton ii. 531.

4 Bracton ii. 533.

5 Dugd. Orig. 79.

CHAP. 15.—*The Champion.*

AN inevitable product of the system of trial by battle was the champion. But for him it may be doubted if it would ever have been so fully developed; without him it certainly would not have subsisted so long.

No champions in criminal cases.

Broadly speaking, the champion had no place in criminal law, for the appeal of felony had to be conducted, with rare, if any exceptions, by the accuser and accused in person. Clerics, until 1176,[1] seem to have been liable to it. After that date there grew up the 'benefit of clergy,' which saved them from trial in the secular court.[2] Women, in virtue of their sex, were not subject to battle, and appeals by them were disposed of by a jury 'per patriam.'[3] Men past sixty years of age, though sometimes found offering battle by a near relative,[4] were exempt if they chose,[5] as were also men who pled 'mayhem,' that is, inability to fight

1 Radulf de Diceto, R.S. i. 410. M. Paris Hist. Maj. ii. 298. In that year Henry granted his letter to the Pope. 'Concedo etiam quod clerici non cogantur facere duellum.'

2 Bracton ii. 299.

3 Bracton ii. 449. But see Crown Pleas, No. 105.

4 For example, in 1199 a son, Bain's Cal. i. No. 280; in 1201, a son-in-law, Crown Pleas, No. 19; in 1267, a freeman, Bain's Cal. i. No. 2452. The Conqueror's laws provided for this—'Si autem Anglus infirmus fuerit inveniat alium qui pro eo faciat.' Stubbs' Charters, 84. It seems to have been practically disallowed in the 13th century, but may have been permitted in the 12th.

5 Bracton ii. 451. Age was often pled, Crown Pleas, Nos. 19, 165. Till 1219 the ordeal was an alternative in such cases.

by reason of broken bones, or the loss of a limb, an ear, a nose, or an eye.[1] Bracton raises the question whether a fracture of the teeth constitutes disability, and he decides that fore-teeth broken make mayhem, 'for teeth of that kind help greatly to victory,'[2] a fact already illustrated in these pages, and to be illustrated again.

Champions in writ of right.

In civil cases on the writ of right these exceptions had no place. The champion, in a plea of land, dates back to Domesday Book, and in Glanvill's time it was competent for the defender or tenant to fight either in person or by an unobjectionable witness as his champion.[3] But after a time, for a special technical reason,[4] it became the law that both parties must fight by champions. This rule applied to all sorts and conditions of men and women.

By the very nature of things champions, like the gladiators of Rome, were liable to degrading influences, and the law kept a sharp eye on these judicial prize-fighters. On the Continent a defeated champion had his hand cut off.[5] Had not defeat proved him a perjured scoundrel? In England quite the same severity was not shewn; but infamy, the loss of his law, and

1 Bracton ii. 451, 468. Glanvill xiv. ch. 1. Mayhem pled. Crown Pleas, Nos. 4, 9. Bain's Cal. i., No. 2332.

2 Bracton ii. 468. Fleta i. ch. 40.

3 Domesday Book ii. 176. Glanvill ii. ch. 3.

4 Stated later. See ch. 27, last note.

5 Du Cange, *voce* Campio. He had sworn the claim he fought for was true. Defeat proved it false. Therefore he was perjured.

the stigma of recreancy, as well as the pecuniary mulct attendant thereupon—these were serious inflictions.[1] A taint of fraud might infer a punishment worse still.

In appeals of felony the appellant, in all cases except murder, that is, secret homicide, made oath as a witness that he had seen and heard the deed. Originally, also, the champion was a witness, and only as a witness could he intervene. This for long was of the essence of his office.[2] In England, when records of cases begin, he possesses, nominally at least, that character, and in his oath swears in that capacity. In a plea of land he swears to having seen the seisin[3]—that is, that he or his father saw such and such a person in possession of the impleaded lands. How far this was a legal fiction from the outset is not easy to say, but fiction or not, the anomaly remained until 1275.[4] Hired champions were forbidden,[5] nevertheless much hiring, direct and indirect, went on. Championship, in spite of the law, became a regular occupation, notwithstanding its dangers. Where the hiring was proved, things went hard with the champion. Thus, in an early 13th century case, when a certain

Hired champions forbidden.

1 Already noted. See ch. 12.

2 Glanvill ii. ch. 3. The same principle in appeal of felony appears in Brac. N.B., Nos. 723, 1597. The appellant required to be a witness.

3 Brac. N. B., No. 895 in 1224. In the first statute of Westminster ch. 41, it is said, touching the oath of the champion, 'he sweareth that he or his father saw the seisin.'

4 The statute named in last note abolished the cited part of the oath.

5 Glanvill ii. ch. 3. Bracton ii. 517. Fleta i. ch. 38 § 8.

Elias Piggun appeared to vouch to warrant a stolen mare, it was pled that he was a hired champion, to whom money had been paid to undertake the warranty. The court made enquiry. Elias admitted that he was a teacher of sword-play, a fact which no doubt weighed with the jury, who found him guilty of fraud, and he was sentenced to lose a foot, being told at the same time to thank his stars he got off so well.[1] That amputated foot has given Elias Piggun immortality, for Bracton has nailed it up for ever as a practical illustration of English law.[2]

Hiring of champions common.

The objection to a hireling was often pleaded and over-ruled,[3] for it was an objection not easy to prove. But it is easy for us to draw an inference from one charter towards the close of the 12th century, by which two virgates of land were given because of a duel which the grantee had fought for the grantor.[4] It is impossible to resist a still stronger inference when, again and again, the same champions reappear, fighting each time for a different master, frequently not clear of one contract to fight till they took up another.[5]

1 Crown Pleas, No. 192.

2 Bracton ii. 517. Bracton says he lost not only his foot but his fist.

3 Crown Pleas, Nos. 126 and 202 in 1220.

4 Charter of date 1180-1200 by Stephen de Nerbona to William, son of Ralf, 'propter duellum quod fecit pro me.' Hist. MSS. Com., 11th Report, app. part vii. 128.

5 Crown Pleas, No. 202 in 1220. Brac. N.B., No. 185 in 1222, 551 in 1231, 400 in 1230, 328 in 1229. Nos. 328 and 400 give a bit of the history of a Scotsman—Duncan the Scot, a professional champion in the south of England.

Nor is the conclusion weakened by the fact that the subsidiary founts of justice themselves, the local courts, had their champions to maintain the accuracy of a questioned record or the like.[1] In the same direction tends a case of the year 1225, wherein one of the litigants 'produced no champion because, as he alleged, his champion had deserted him for a bribe which his adversary had given.'[2] Were these facts not of themselves enough, proof positive might be found where least looked for, in the records of the church. At this time all churchmen—bishop, abbot, and prior,[3] no less than the ordinary priest—were prone to disregard the canon law which forbade such things as the deeds of men of blood,[4] and were wont to avail themselves of that very secular arm, the champion.

CHAP. 16.—*Some Churchmen's Champions.*

THE benefit of clergy did not extend to pleas on the writ of right. It is therefore scarcely to be called a reproach to churchmen, that they preferred to incur some small taint of deeds of blood by using champions, rather than sacrifice their lands and goods. The church was never equal to the effort of such a self-denying ordinance.

[1] Brac. N. B., No. 40 in 1219. [2] Brac. N. B., No. 1038 in 1225.

[3] Brac. N. B., Nos. 551 and 1672. Year-books 32-33, Ed. I. R.S., pref. p. xl.

[4] Corp. Jur. Canon ii. 623. Edict of Innocent III. in 1216.

Bishop Swinefeld's 'Household Expenses'[1] is as uninviting a volume as any dryasdust ever raked from the ashes of an extinct age. But in those dull pages, which tell of the purchase of eels and salmon, mutton and pork, oats and hay, and other refreshments for man and beast in the year of God 1289, there appears a termly payment of 6s. 8d. to the bishop's 'pugil,' or champion, Thomas of Brydges.[2] There, too, is the very document,[3] dated Tuesday next after the day of All Saints [8 November], 1276, whereby the bishop makes it known to all the faithful of Christ that he has agreed to pay Thomas of Brydges 6s. 8d. a year 'so long as the said Thomas is able to perform the functions of champion'; that the said Thomas has sworn to fight for the bishop against all and sundry when required; and, finally, that the bishop, whenever the said Thomas has to fight, will fully satisfy him on such terms as may be agreed upon, not only regarding his stipend, but also regarding his sustenance and other necessary matters. Whence it is to be concluded that the 6s. 8d. a year (which in 1289 was 6s. 8d. a half year) was a retaining fee, and that other payments were made over and above whenever the champion's services were in request.

A bishop's champion.

'Thrice is he armed that hath his quarrel just,'

said Shakspeare, and there was something in the aphorism. Still it was wise to supplement an honest

1 Publication of Camden Society. 2 P. 125. 3 P. 201.

cause with a stout champion. Truth and justice were apt to rest with the side which preponderated in fighting weight. Have we not read that, in the reign of Edward I., the prior of Lewes lost an advowson because his champion was over-matched and struck down?[1]

The prior of Tynemouth.

The priors of Tynemouth had some experience of champions. This Northumbrian priory, of which the ruins still front the breezes of the North Sea, was a cell of the monastery of St. Albans, and it is from a St. Albans chronicler that this story comes. When Ralph Gubiun was prior, sometime between 1214 and 1235, he was much annoyed by Simon of Tynemouth exacting two monks' corrodies—the maintenance of two persons in the priory. He disputed Simon's right, and as the question was to be deraigned by duel, he took with him a 'magnus pugil,' a big champion, by name William Pygun. The Piguns were a large and fighting family. William[2] was

[1] Year Books 32-33, Edward I. R.S., preface, xl.

[2] William Pigun appears as a champion in a case in 1237—Brac. N.B. No. 1226. Possibly he was the same man. 'And even when vanquished he could argue still'—in some other district where his former defeat was not known. Pigun recurs so often as a surname of champions that Professor Maitland tells me he suspects it to be descriptive. I hazard the suggestion that it means swordsman or fencing master—See p. 49, *supra*. 'Pugio,' sword or dagger, is closely allied to 'pugil,' champion. An old Eng. Gloss. gives 'Pugio, pijon'—Wright's Old Vocabularies, ed. 1884. Perhaps 'pigun' is to 'pijon' as 'pugil' to 'pugio.' It must be said, however, that the Latin form of 'pigun' is 'pigo,' and Schilter's Antiq. Teut. iii. 659, has 'Pigo, acerbus.' 'Fierce' would be a good surname for a champion.

a brother in misfortune of him of whose amputated foot Bracton made a note, for the annalist of St. Albans ruefully ends his story with the words, 'Our big champion was vanquished, and Simon, our adversary, won his case.'[1] More than a century later we shall hear of a prior of Tynemouth and his champion again.

CHAP. 17.—*Another Champion's Contract.*

SELDEN, in the 13th chapter of the Duello, cites a charter, the full tenor of which has been found in another work.[2] By that charter, dated 28th April, 1258, Henry of Fernbureg, called the marshal, bound himself as champion to the Abbot of Glastonbury at all times against the bishop and chapter of Bath and Wells for payment of thirty marks sterling. Here was a paid champion sure enough. Ten marks were payable at the time of waging the duel, five on his being shaven—'in tonsione mea quinque marcas'—and the balance, on the day of battle, was to be placed in the hands of some good man who was to pay it over to Henry if he struck so much as one blow in the duel. If he did not strike a blow the fifteen marks were to be restored to the abbot forthwith.

The device on the signet of Henry must rank

1 Gesta Abbatum, R.S. i. 272-3.
2 Upton's De Re Militari, Bisse's Notes, 36.

amongst the curiosities of seals.[1] Encircled by the name of its owner, it bears a bare-legged and bare-headed champion, with a rectangular curved shield on his left arm, holding in his right hand a weapon, the head of which is like a narrow wedge-shaped hammer pointed at one end. This, no doubt, is the baton tipped with horn which Britton[2] assigns as the arms of offence for the duel on appeal of felony. The seal leaves little doubt that Henry was a professional champion, and that he is the same 'Henry le mareschal'[3] whom the Abbot of Ramsey put forward in 1263 as his champion for the duel in a plea with John de Balliol and Dervorgilla his wife, father and mother of the most miserable of Scottish kings.

A seal and a picture.

Highly popular as an illustration of all books touching on trial by battle is the picture of a duel in an appeal of theft between Hamo le Stare and Walter Bloweberme, contained in a plea-roll of Henry III. Its most glorified version is that of its first presentation in a note to 'Upton's De Re Militari.'[4] It is there so sublimated as almost to defy recognition. Madox gives a good copy.[5] Kendall for his preface gave it less accurately. Last of all,

[1] It is figured in Upton, Notes, 37.

[2] Britton, book i. ch. 23, § 14—known as a ram's horn later. This use of horn is possibly a link to carry the pedigree of trial by battle back to an age before iron.

[3] Bain's Cal. i. No. 2330.

[4] Upton, Notes, 37.

[5] Madox, 383.

photolithography has exactly reproduced it, and made it the frontispiece to the Selden Society's 'Crown Pleas.' The shields of the combatants are very like that on the seal of Henry the marshal, and the weapons of their mutual vigorous assault are likewise much the same, save that the tip of horn is pointed at both ends. Hamo le Stare was vanquished in the duel, and in the background of the picture there stand two upright forked poles—the *furca* of many a charter—surmounted by a crossbar, from which there dangles by a rope the lifeless form of the luckless Hamo.

In Kendall's variant the head of Walter Blowe-berme, the victor in this *cause célèbre*, is represented as close shaven, a fact due, however, to the nineteenth century engraver—not to a thirteenth century barber—for in the autotype reproduction neither of the heads is shaven. What then is the meaning of the phrase *in tonsione mea* in Henry the marshal's contract? Was it the wont of English champions to have their heads shaven before the battle?

A tonsorial question.

Selden does not answer this question, but his hint is broad.[1] To repeat and add to his facts will afford a clear ground of judgment. By the assize of Jerusalem,[2] the head of a combatant was shaved round to his ears—"rongnés a la reonde." In 1190 Richard I., setting sail for the Crusade, ordained, as

[1] Duello, ch. 8, 13. [2] As cited in Du Cange, *voce* Campio.

one of the rules of the fleet, that any convicted thief was to be tarred and feathered and set ashore whenever the ship touched land, but first he was to be 'shaved after the fashion of a champion.'[1] There are instances in England, in much later times, in which the judge ordered a champion to have his head 'razed' or shaven,[2] and occasionally the phrase is that he is to be 'deschevilé,'[3] which means the same thing.[4] Britton says the parties in an appeal of felony fought 'a tetes descouvertes,'[5]—words which have been rendered as meaning 'with uncovered heads.' 'Uncovered' is so far a correct translation, but in a very special sense. In an old law book 'covered' is the antithesis of 'rayed' or razed.[6] Britton plainly means that the uncovered head was shaven. Despite the pictorial witnesses to the contrary, therefore, the question is to be answered in the affirmative. The whole circumstances point to a complete shaving of the head, a much more extensive affair than the clerical tonsure. That this

1 Benedictus Abbas ii. 110, 'tondeatur ad similitudinem campionis.' Hoveden iii. 36, 'ad modum campionis.' Brompton in Decem Script. 1173.

2 Que le teste doit etre rasé. 1 Henry VI. and 9 Henry IV., cited in Duello, ch. 8.

3 6 Edward II., cited in Duello, ch. 13. See also Dugd. Orig. 68, where it is 'deschevele.'

4 Descheviller, Oter les chevilles. Littré. See Discapillare in Du Cange.

5 Britton i. ch. 23, § 14.

6 Sir John Davies in the Manner of Gaginge Battail, written in 1601, says:—'The appellant's head was ever covered, but the defendant's rayed.' Cited in Kendall, 159-60.

strange custom had some religious and ceremonial origin there can be little doubt. The idea that it was simply to hinder the hair from being grasped in the combat is manifestly inadequate.

This tonsorial disquisition would be incomplete did it not tell the story of the dream of a monk of St. Edmundsbury in 1182, when the fraternity in the abbey was in great excitement over the election of a successor to Abbot Hugh then lately dead. In his dream the monk saw three of the candidates standing before the altar in which the body of St. Edmund lay. There was Roger the cellarer, and there was Hugh the third prior, but 'in the midst stood Samson, head and shoulders above the others, clad in a long robe, and all bound about his shoulders, as he stood like a champion ready to fight a duel.'[1] When in a monk's dream a prospective abbot appears in the guise of a fighting champion, one must suppose that the dreamer was familiar with the wager of battle. Surer still is the inference when we read the interpretation of the dream given by his fellow monks. They concluded that the tall Samson, who seemed pointed at as their future abbot, would be a great mover of controversies about pleas of the crown and scutages and purprestures, and that as a champion he would, with a will, fight for the overthrow of his adversaries, and do

A dream about Abbot Samson.

[1] Brakelond, 15. Carlyle in Past and Present, book 2, ch. 8, rather misses the fine point of the words here, 'stantem quasi pugilem ad duellum faciendum.'

his utmost to restore the rights and liberties of his church.[1] All which very exactly came to pass, for Samson did indeed become abbot, and as a Norfolk man should,[2] a decidedly litigious abbot to boot.

Little thought had that monk that his dream would be cited, after seven hundred years, to eke out the evidence on a detail of the judicial duel. But when we know, as we do, that Samson was bald,[3] does not the fact bear directly on the shaving of champions? It would lend to the analogy of the dream a sly piquancy in the gossip of the cloister.[4]

CHAP. 18.—*Three early Duels*, A.D. *1096-1163*.

FROM the time of its introduction trial by battle was competent in cases of treason.[5] It had a wide field before it in appeals of felony, and in civil cases on the writ of right. It was to a qualified extent in unison with the warlike spirit of the time when, as an aid to devotion, psalters were adorned with pictures of tilts and single combats, sometimes very

[1] Brakelond, 15.

[2] They called him a 'barrator de Norfolch.' Brakelond, 9, 31.

[3] Brakelond, in the facsimile, and on p. 29, 'fere omnino calvus.'

[4] Whence came the expressive Yankeeism of Lowell's Pious Editor?

I scent wich pays the best, an' then
Go into it bald-headed.

Is it faintly possible (or is it a question brought in *par les cheveux*) that there is here a transatlantic echo of trial by combat and the shaven champion?

[5] Glanvill, xiv. ch. 1.

incongruously fitted into the text.[1] As might be expected, many memorials of judicial battle exist in the chronicles. English history has many examples, sometimes with detail and circumstance far fuller than purely legal records themselves furnish. In the chapters which follow some account is given of duels and duel incidents illustrative of history between the Conquest and the death of Edward I. They are isolated facts—one of them is, perhaps, an isolated fancy—but it may be that the reader can detect a stream of tendency which connects them all, with here and there the symptoms of a reactionary eddy.

In 1096 William of Eu, charged with treason, was defeated in the duel which followed.[2] As punishment he had his eyes torn out, in pursuance of the principle laid down in the Conqueror's laws that the mutilated trunk should remain as an evidence of treason and iniquity.[3]

Orgar and Godwin.

About the same time, or soon after, must date the occurrence for which Fordun is a not-altogether satisfactory authority. Orgar, an Englishman, to curry favour with

[1] For example, see Humphrey's Illum. Books of Middle Ages, 1849. A facsimile page of a thirteenth century psalter has at the bottom a tilt. At the end of the verse, 'Sit nomen domini benedictum ex hoc nunc et usque in seculum,' a man in chain-mail is fighting with an unarmed jester.

[2] Hoveden, R.S. i. 151. A.S. Chron. R.S. i. 362. Duel here called 'orreste.'

[3] Ancient Laws, England, i. 494.

William Rufus, accused Edgar the Atheling of saying that he and his children were the rightful heirs to the crown. The case was sent to the duel for trial. Edgar was now advanced in years, but an Englishman, Godwin of Winton, fought on his behalf. 'And when silence had been proclaimed by a herald, the gages of both[1] were thrown into the place of combat by the judge, who cried aloud that God, who knows all secrets, would declare the truth of this cause.' There was a bloody combat. When Godwin had nearly gained the victory his sword broke from its hilt, and Orgar plied him hard. But managing to pick up his hiltless blade, and grasping it with two fingers, Godwin pierced Orgar in the eye, cut his head open, and so sorely wounded him that he fell. The old Scotch chronicle says that when Godwin set his foot upon his prostrate foe the treachery and perjury of Orgar were disclosed; for though he had sworn to bear no weapons save such as became a knight, he now drew a dagger which had been hidden in his boot, and strove to stab his enemy. The dagger was wrenched from him, and he then confessed the falsity of his charge. But his confession availed him little; he was stabbed again and again until 'the deep wounds drove out his ungodly soul.'[2]

[1] A reference to the gloves or gauntlets by which the challenge was given and accepted. These were at a later date, as Fordun here represents, thrown into the lists. Fordun, however, is possibly tinting the story with the colour of his own time. Still it was his wont to follow his original very closely.

[2] Fordun, v. ch. 22-23, Bower v. ch. 27-28. Turgot is cited as the

The next story is a well-proved fact of history. Henry, Earl of Essex, royal standard-bearer of England, was charged with treason in 1163. In the Welsh war of 1157 he had been with Henry II., and at a critical juncture threw down his banner and cried that the king was slain. This act of panic, if not of treachery, nearly resulted in the overthrow of the English army, which at the time was in a dangerous pass of the Welsh hills. The standard-bearer had many rivals and enemies, and after long murmuring they had their will when Robert de Montford in Parliament appealed him of treason and a duel was adjudged. They met at Reading and fought in an island[1] of the Thames near the Abbey. Years afterwards Henry of Essex was wont to tell the story of the battle; how, when it was at its height, he discerned the glorious king and martyr, Edmund, in armour, hovering as it were in the air, with frowning countenance, shaking his head at him, full of wrath and indignation. And by the side of the angry saint the conscience-stricken Henry saw a knight whom he had murdered, and who now glared at him with vengeful eye. Unnerved by the sight of these dread onlookers, he made a furious attack on his adversary, but his blows were warded off, and he was struck down. They thought that he

Henry of Essex.

authority for this story in the Scotichronicon, but the work in which it appeared is not extant.

[1] Apud Radingas pugnaturi in insula quadam satis Abbatie vicina.

was dead, and his body was given to the monks of Reading for burial. But he revived, and by the king's grace was allowed to become a monk himself. In the abbey of Reading he told his strange story—time, perhaps, improving its flavour—to our old friend, Abbot Samson of St. Edmundsbury, by whom the tribute to the glorious king and martyr, Edmund, was fitly appreciated.[1] Carlyle[2] has retold the stirring tale, and in his burning page the unjust standard-bearer has become a type of a lamed soul, which, in its extreme need, cannot so much as fight.[3]

CHAP. 19.—*A Hibernian Hero.*

THE Annals of Ireland record a very characteristic duel story of the year 1204. It shall be repeated here in all the pomp of capitals with which Camden's translator[4] endowed it :—

'A Controversy arising between John, King of England, and the King of France about a Lordship and certain castles the King of France offer'd by a

1 Brakelond, 50-2.

2 Past and Present, book 2, ch. 14.

3 In 1177 a great suit between the kings of Castille and Navarre was submitted to Henry II. as arbiter, and each of the contending monarchs sent a man 'of marvellous worth and valour' to undertake the duel in the court of the King of England if it should be adjudged.—Bened. Abbas, R.S. i. 139.

4 Annales Hiberniæ in Camden's Britannia, 1695. Quoted by Selden in Duello, ch. 2. Speed's History (1627), 502. See also Holinshed, vi. 236. As to John Courcy, see Giraldus Cambrensis, R.S. v. 344.

Champion to try his right. Upon this the King called to mind his valiant Knight, John Courcy, whom he cast in Prison upon the information of others; so he sent for him and ask'd him if he were able to serve him in this Combat? John answer'd He would not fight for him but for the Right of the Kingdom with all his Heart; which he undertook to do afterwards; And so refresh'd himself with Meat Drink and Bathing in the meanwhile, and recover'd his Strength. Whereupon a day was appointed for the Engagement of those Champions namely John Courcy and the other. But as soon as the Champion of France heard of his great Stomach and mighty Valour he refus'd the Combat, and the said Seignory was given to the King of England. The King of France then desired to see a Blow of the said Courcy. Whereupon he set a strong Helmet full of Mail upon a large Block; and with his Sword, after he had look'd about him in a grim manner, struck the Helmet through from the very Crest into the Block, so very fast that no one there was able to pull it out, till he himself at the request of the two Kings did it easily. Then they ask'd him why he look'd so gruff behind him before he struck? So he told them If he had failed in giving it he would have certainly cut them all off, as well Kings as others The Kings made him large presents and the King of England restor'd him also to his Seignory viz. Ulster.'

A grim Ulsterman.

It is to be confessed that this gruff and grim

Ulsterman, who was so willing to fight for the right of the kingdom, has features which put him somewhat apart from the high seriousness of history. Nevertheless, to suppress him might savour of another injustice to his country.

CHAP. 20.—*Charters and Charter Stories.*

Charters of exemption.

THE concession made to the citizens of London early in the twelfth century by Henry I., that none of them should do battle, did not long stand alone. In the same reign it is known that Newcastle-on-Tyne possessed an approach to the same privilege.[1] Once this began there could be no stopping. Every burgh strove to obtain the exemption, and one by one the number of exemptions grew — now acquired by favour,[2] oftener by purchase from the necessities of kings and nobles, sometimes through latent humanity stirred to the quick. Even although it was compurgation, or its successor the wager of law, and not trial by jury which the burgesses desired and obtained, the change was a decided benefit. Battle involved a risk from any bully, from which compurgation with all its faults was free. In every view the abolition of battle was an advance. The large towns could not long mono-

[1] Stubbs' Charters, 112. Scots Acts, i. 39, 40.

[2] Norwich got its exemption in 1112 on account of the reception it gave to William the Conqueror's youngest son. James Thompson's English Municip. Hist., 114, 115.

polise so great a boon. The hope of being free is an expansive feeling which cannot be hemmed in. Neither can freedom herself; her shackles are soon shaken from her, and with radiant untiring wing she pursues her resistless course.

The charter of London was the beginning, the end was still far in the future; yet that charter was the beginning of the end. Before the century closed it had many companions,[1] and each place on which the favour was conferred became a centre of hope to its less fortunate neighbours. The privileges of London, or Oxford, or Winchester were models for other grants which fill the Rolls of the charters. A decisive tendency had set in against the duel, as evinced by the marked success of the grand assize.

When a duel was in progress it was an offence severely punishable for any onlooker to speak or do anything to hinder fair-play.[2] In 1213 King John pardoned Roger de Parles the banishment he had incurred by aiding his brother Henry in a duel at Tothill.[3] An early instance of help coming from a very unexpected quarter, proving that litigation did not necessarily dry up the springs of generosity in opposing breasts, shows at the same time humanity

[1] For example, Charters of Winchester (1190), Lincoln (1194), Northampton (1200). Stubbs' Charters, 266, 267, 310. Many such are in the Rotuli Chartarum, especially in the reign of John. See vol. i. 54, 130*b*, 135,138*b*, for examples.

[2] In Bracton ii. 443, and Fleta i. ch. 34 § 31, the punishment was imprisonment for year and day.

[3] Bain's Cal. i. No. 582.

at work for the abrogation of the judicial combat. It is one of the most touching of twelfth century traditions, but it must be remembered that it is a tradition, although it was recorded in 1255. By an inquest at Leicester[1] in the 39th year of Henry III. it was said that in the time of Robert the Medland (or de Mellent—a favourite of Henry I.), then Earl of Leicester, it happened that two kinsmen—Nicholas, the son of Acon, and Geoffrey, the son of Nicholas—had waged duel on a plea of land.[2] They fought from the first to the ninth hour, each conquering by turns. Then one of them fleeing from the other till he came to a certain little pit, as he stood on the brink of the pit and was about to fall therein, his kinsman said to him, 'Take care of the pit; turn back lest thou should'st fall into it.' Thereat so much clamour and noise was made by the bystanders and those who were sitting around that the Earl heard these clamours as far as the castle, and he inquired of some how it was there was such a clamour, and answer was made to him that two kinsmen were fighting about a certain piece of ground, and that one fled till he reached a certain little pit, and was about to fall into it when the other warned him. Then the townsmen, being moved with pity,

A generous act.

1 James Thompson's Essay on Municip. Hist., 39-41. Green's Short Hist. (1875), 189.

2 Parties here fight in person, not by champion. The whole story is not improbable, but traditions are never reliable in details and dates; and Leicester under Henry III. might well have hazy ideas of Leicester under Henry I.

made a covenant with the Earl to give him threepence yearly for each house in the High Street that had a gable, on condition that he should grant that the twenty-four jurors who were in Leicester from ancient times should, from that time forward, discuss and decide all pleas they might have amongst themselves.

Not very long after the year 1182 that Abbot Samson whose bald head provoked a base comparison made a change in the judicial procedure in his abbey lands. By the liberties of the town of St. Edmundsbury the burgesses were exempt from the duel. Not so the abbey's tenants outside the burgh gates. Hence when Ketel, one of them, was accused of theft, he was tried by duel, vanquished, and hung. As the man was believed innocent, sarcastic comments were made in the burgh on his fate. Had he lived within the gates, they said, he would have been acquitted by the oaths of his neighbours. These criticisms so moved the abbot that he abolished the duel by a merging of the jurisdictions.[1] The initiative here plainly came from the town. Reforms which tended to extinguish barbarism, promote commerce, and widen the bounds of freedom, then as now received their impetus in the market-place, the burgh moot, and the workshop.

An extant case in 1200 shows how the citizens of Lincoln valued their privilege of exemption, and pled

[1] Brakelond, 74. Green's Short Hist. (1875), 91.

that 'they needed not to do battle in any appeal,' and the Liber Albus shows how London did the same.[1]

Foul play.

Bystanders were not always like the bystanders of Leicester and St. Edmundsbury. Sometimes the partisans of parties mustered in strong force, with results not tending to the maintenance of the fair field and no favour which were of the essence of trial by battle. In a case on a writ of right during the reign of Henry III. at Northampton, when the duel was being fought outside the walls, the friends of the one side broke into the place of combat, caused their horses to trample on the champion of the other side, and when he was helpless proclaimed him craven. A complaint subsequently made to the king relieved this ill-used champion from the disabilities of recreancy.[2]

CHAP. 21.—*An Incident, A.D. 1267.*

In war time.

DURING the civil wars of Henry III. the revolted barons, in 1267, were occupying the Isle of Ely, and laying waste the whole country-side.[3] The chartulary of Barnwell, near Cambridge, tells a curious tale of the time.[4] Daily the ministers of iniquity came to the priory, and there ate and drank and did much damage. The canons

1 Crown Pleas, No. 82. Liber Albus i. 109. The London case was in 28 Henry III.

2 Pike i. 205-6, 467. 3 Rishanger (Camden Soc.) 58.

4 Quoted in Rishanger, App. 147.

shewed them a cheerful countenance, lest a worse thing should befall. But early one morning a certain man of great stature, by name Philip the Champion,[1] raised the prior from his bed, and demanded for his master the key of the grange and larder. Hereupon two other men, servants to a friend of the prior, said to Philip, 'These goods belong to our master.' Philip replied, 'I shall carry them off in spite of you.' 'By the wounds of God,' was their rejoinder, 'you shall do no such thing!' And so there arose a contention between them, and they drew their swords to slay each other, so that the bystanders could scarce make them keep the peace. Finally, they retired in great wrath to determine the question in the Isle[2] in presence of their lords—carrying off nothing, as the chartulary with some satisfaction observes, that time.

'Champion' was now becoming, indeed had already become, a well-known surname;[3] but there are examples of considerably later date (such as that of John Champion of Biddell,[4] a priest wounded on the head with a sword by a layman in 1311) to show that the name carried with it into private and clerical life some tradition of turbulence.

1 Philippus le Champion.

2 'Recesserunt ergo cum furore magno ad determinandum questionem in insula coram dominis suis; nihil hac vice asportantes.' At first blush this might seem to refer to holmgang, the island fight, but 'insula' must here mean the Isle of Ely, a district.

3 Bain's Cal. i. 2365, 2367. Manorial Pleas (Selden Soc.) 16.

4 Registrum Palatinum Dunelmense, R.S. i. 79.

CHAP. 22.—*Reactionary Signs.*

MEANWHILE the duel was falling rapidly into disuse, but the contact with France in the continental wars of Edward I. occasioned some reactionary symptoms. In 1294, before the Deputy-Justice of Ireland, William de Vescy appealed John Fitz Thomas for defamation, on the ground that he had accused him of having made overtures for a treasonable bond against the king.[1] Denouncing Fitz Thomas as a liar and a false traitor, he offered battle and delivered a 'wad' or gage in the hands of the judge, who accepted it. A duel was then awarded, which ultimately the king transferred to Westminster and before himself. On the appointed day William de Vescy came, 'appareled as a knight with knightly arms, viz., charger and coverture, lance and shield, poniard and breastplate, and other knightly weapons.' But Fitz Thomas, solemnly called, did not come. The annals of Ireland[2] reverse the facts in saying that Vescy would not fight.

An appeal quashed, 1294.

Yet, although he claimed judgment by default against Fitz Thomas, again and again the case was delayed, and at last the king quashed the appeal on

1 Rotuli Parliamentorum i. 127-33. Cal. Ireland, 1293-1301, No. 147.

2 In Camden, sub anno 1294. A somewhat similar account is given in Holinshed (1807) vi. 240-1. A natural national predilection doubtless explains the perversion. Fitz Thomas was an Irish nobleman, Vescy an English official.

the technical ground that the wager had been made before battle was adjudged, 'which,' says the royal deliverance, 'was quite against the law and custom of the realm.'[1]

There is some confusion, if not mystery, about this case, but unless inference strays, Edward had other reasons than mere technicality. His strong good sense made him dislike such duels, and he would allow no dangerous precedent for them in his courts. He was too great a statesman to let chivalry as chivalry find a footing in English law. That was the real issue, and, chivalrous though he was, he had too clear a conception of order to confound chivalry with law. There was better work for his knights to do than for the one to meet the other, 'appareled as a knight with knightly arms,' for empty points of honour.

Edward I. and chivalry.

Chivalry could not be allowed to thwart the progress which the law had made—not if Edward I. could hinder it—as Sir Nicholas Segrave found to his cost. He had been defamed by Sir John Cromwell, and finally, in proceedings before parliament, challenged him to combat. The king disallowed the battle, and when Segrave, in defiance of the prohibition, crossed the channel to achieve the forbidden purpose, he was promptly arrested, tried, and condemned to death. That sentence the great old Plantagenet was with difficulty persuaded to relax,

[1] Rot. Parl. i. 133.

and Segrave was only pardoned after a strong representation that his anger against Cromwell, and not any contempt of the king, had led to his forgetfulness of duty.[1]

CHAP. 23.—*Review and Prospect.*

THE judicial duel which had come in with the Conqueror as an alternative to the ordeal had outlived it. But long before the ordeal was abolished in 1219, a rigid line had formed around the duel which it could not pass. Charters of exemption were being obtained on every side, and in burgh after burgh it passed away. In the other courts in which it was competent, the judges more and more found reasons, and made them, for disallowing a mode of trial in which they could have little faith, and which the people at large by no means loved. The growth of trial by jury, the wonderful development which jurisprudence made before the middle of the thirteenth century, the gradual restriction of private jurisdictions, and the consequent improvement in public justice, all helped in the same direction. When the century ended, trial by battle was far advanced on the high road to extinction. It had become uncommon before the close of the reign of Henry III.[2] In the time of Edward I. it grew more uncommon still, and when a

[1] Roll of Carlaverock, ed. Nicholas, 123. Rot. Parl. i. 172-4. M. of Westminster (ed. 1570) 450.

[2] Professor Maitland, pref. to Crown Pleas, p. 24.

chivalric reaction began, the English Justinian met it sternly. Chivalry was useful to aid in conquering other countries; he would have none of it to upset the law of his own. By the year 1300 the judicial duel had still some vogue in appeals of felony, chiefly in those made by approvers. In pleas on the writ of right it had almost become a form.

Such is a brief summary of what has been set forth in the previous pages. Looking to the pages which are yet to come, it cannot be without misgiving that, after long sojourn on English soil, the Scottish student turns towards his native heath. In England, notwithstanding periodic upheavals, the advance of the law and the constitution was a majestic progress, unique in human annals. In Scotland—although they say that German scholars are in search of some profound generalisations which, it is to be hoped, they will find—it is scarcely safe to assert that the nation ever realized what a constitutional principle was. The records of England teem with orderly, full, and generous illustrations of 12th and 13th century law, in which precise expositions, in statute, ordinance, and treatise, are checked by actual cases decided in the courts. The expositions of Scots law for the same period are voluminous indeed, but there are no decided cases, dates are few and far between, and chaos and doubt sit joint-umpires over the whole collection.

Nevertheless it is believed that an attempt to trace the law and practice of the Scotch judicial duel would be a service to the national history and the national law. The humble hope animates the following chapters, that they may at least lead to better studies of a neglected theme.

PART IV.—SCOTLAND TILL 1300: LAW.

CHAP. 24.—*In Early Scotland.*

ALTHOUGH Craig in his Jus Feudale[1] declares that the duel was part of the law of Scotland as well before as after 1066, although its practice in an islet of the Tay in 1124 is certain, although in 1216 a pope declared it to have existed *ab antiquo* on the border, and although a Carlisle jury in 1294 testified to its prevalence under the name of 'handwarcel' from a time beyond the memory of man, it cannot be affirmed that it was indigenous in Scotland. There, as in England, the verdict must be Not Proven, and the presumptions favour a Norman origin.

It is indeed said that about the time of the Conquest, King Malcolm, the dethroner of Macbeth, offered battle to one of his nobles who was plotting his death.

> Gyve thow thynkys to sla me
> Quhat tyme na nowe may bettyr be?
> Forthi do as suld a knycht
> Ga we togyddyr; God dele the rycht![2]

Such are the words of challenge which Wyntoun,

[1] Jus Feudale, i. dieg. 7, § 24.

[2] Forthi, therefore. 'God defend the right' were the traditional words with which in later times a treason trial was committed to duel by the kings of Scotland.—Pitcairn i. 186*.

following Fordun, puts into his mouth. But to say nothing of the fact that Abbot Ailred was fond of stories which were passing strange, and that it is to his pen[1] that this one is ultimately traced, this one example is not proof. A single unaccepted invitation to fight a duel is no voucher of the duel as part of a legal system.

Charter of Scone, 1124.

What is believed to be the earliest unquestionably authentic mention of trial by battle in Scotland is found in a charter of Alexander I. One of the witnesses to it was Robert, bishop-elect of St. Andrew's, a fact which dates it early in the year 1124.[2] In 1122 the queen had died, and, for the good of her soul and his own, Alexander had granted to the abbey of Scone an islet in Loch Tay.[3] By the subsidiary charter in 1124, he conferred on the abbey and its monks a full baronial jurisdiction, with right to exercise both duel and ordeal. It granted them the privilege of holding 'their own court, that is to say in duel, in iron, in foss, and in all other liberties to the court pertaining.'[4] The duels were

[1] Wyntoun vii. ch. 1; Fordun v. ch. 10; Bower v. ch. 12; Ailred in Decem. Scrip. 367. Wyntoun gives the challenge a much more chivalric ring than it has in Ailred: 'God dele the rycht,' is a poet's license. A tale like this is told of King Edgar of England and King Kenneth of Scotland.—Palgrave's Documents, i. 108; William of Malmesbury's Gesta Regum, i. 177.

[2] Scone Chart. (Mait.) 4.

[3] Scone Chart. 3.

[4] Scone Chart. 4. Suam propriam curiam scilicet in duello, in ferro, in fossa, et in omnibus aliis libertatibus ad curiam pertinentibus.

fought on an islet in the river, not far from the abbey. In 1164, King Malcolm IV. confirmed to the monks 'their court in duel, iron, and water, with all other liberties thereto pertaining.'[1] Before the close of the 12th century, perhaps about 1180, William Vniot, in making a grant of certain lands and fishings, incidentally described them as bounded 'on the north by the island in which the duel of Scone is wont to be fought.'[2] Better contemporary evidence than this it would be hard to find.

Scots Acts.

But there is a great mass of other evidence, often dateless, and always difficult to assort, although most of it has been patiently gathered into the first volume of the Scots Acts of Parliament by the two greatest Scotch record antiquaries of the present century. Upon that volume, which is only a fraction of the services rendered to their country by Thomas Thomson and Cosmo Innes, the attention of the student must concentrate to make his searches into the early law of duel of any avail. Nor will it do altogether to ignore the work of Sir John Skene in the time of James VI., although some of his successors in his impossible task have treated his labours and himself with a disparagement which was certainly ungenerous and by some is deemed unjust.

The system, of which there are a few signs in the

1 Scots Acts i. 365. Scone Chart. 6.

2 Scone Chart. 36. Ab insula qua solet fieri duellum de Scone versus aquilonem.

reign of the first Alexander, assumes a fuller shape in the laws which are ascribed to his brother David I. In passing to his reign an enquiring glance may be cast at the framework of the law then in vogue. Compurgation was a large part of it—a man's oath receiving effect if corroborated by the oaths of a certain number of others. There was no examination of witnesses as such, and the visnet, a kind of jury—who were in many cases witnesses as well as jurors—was only beginning to struggle into existence. Various passages in the assize of David[1] and in his burgh laws[2] show compurgation to have been emphatically regarded as "the law" or "law of burgh." It bulked largely too in the march laws on the borders of England and Scotland.[3] There is strong reason to suspect that it was a very ancient institution of Galloway in the south;[4] and the same inference may be drawn amongst the thanedoms of the north.[5] On these considerations is rested the supposition that compurgation was the prominent characteristic of the native Scotch system before Norman influence brought in the duel.

Compurgation.

1 Scots Acts, i. 317-21, ch. 2, 11, 16, 19.

2 Scots Acts, i. 335-54, ch. 11, 22, 26, 29, 38, 76, 96, 107.

3 Scots Acts, i. 413-6.

4 Scots Acts, i. 482. The charter of Robert the Bruce, with its allusion to purgation by the entire acquittance of Galloway, seems to refer to compurgation. See also ch. 26, *infra*.

5 Scots Acts, i. 320. Ass. David, ch. 16, mentions compurgation by 27 men and 3 thanes. Regiam Majestatem iv. 22.

The ordeals of water and iron appear but seldom in the records of Scots law. There is not extant, it is believed, the account of a single case in which they were applied. Although a charter by King David names them, they are not once mentioned in the two great bodies of law of his time. In these, the oldest code of Scots law extant, it may be said that the sole alternative to compurgation—to the oath of a 6th or 12th or 24th or 27th hand, as the case might be—was the duel.

Ordeal.

CHAP. 25.—*Under David the First.*

BY the assize of David a person who was appealed of theft in the King's Court, or in any other Court, had his choice between battle and compurgation.[1] In a charge of larceny, robbery, arson, or other misdeed out of which a duel might arise, if the accuser claimed not only for his actual loss, but for the shame he had suffered,[2] the defender gave wads (or found bail) to cover the loss only, not the shame. In the appeal of larceny the pursuer's injury was divided into three parts; for two-thirds the defender's money was answerable if he happened to be slain, in which case it is grimly stated that his

The wads.

1 Scots Acts, i. 317, ass. David, ch. 2.

2 This was common in England in some cases. Crown Pleas, No. 87. Some old Scotch forms of writs provide for a claim both of shame and skaith.

body remained upon the 'place' for the third part.[1] A person accused of being art and part or accomplice in a theft might, if a freeman, defend himself by his own hand;[2] indeed, he appears to have had no option, for the words are precise, 'he shall defend himself by duel.'

When duel competent.

By the burgh laws, in the case where a rustic—that is a villein and unfree—had a burgh holding, if he accused a burgess of any crime inferring trial by battle, the burgess was not bound to fight. He could clear himself by compurgation. On the other hand, if he accused the rustic, the rustic could defend by battle.[3] A burgess accused within the burgh by a stranger was not liable to the duel unless on a charge of treason or in a case of 'theme,'[4] that is, where he was vouched to warrant. A burgess might not fight a stranger unless he went outside the burgh,[5] a term which probably implies a kind of renunciation of the freedom of the burgh. The burgess of a royal burgh might claim battle with the burgess of an abbot's, prior's, earl's, or baron's burgh when he was suing, but was not bound to fight when he was

[1] Scots Acts, i. 318-9, ass. David, ch. 8. Si reus fuerit occisus corpus vero ejus remaneat in platea pro tertia parte pecunie. 'Platea' is here technical; see index.

[2] Scots Acts, i. 321, ass. David, ch. 20. Se defendet per duellum.

[3] Scots Acts, i. 335; Burgh Laws, ch. 11.

[4] A good instance of 'theam' (as it is more commonly spelt) is given in ch. 41. See also Scots Acts, i. 742, frag. ch. 5. Stubbs' Charters. 70.

[5] Scots Acts, i. 335; B.L., ch. 12. Compare case in Liber Albus, R.S. i. 109.

sued.[1] Inhabitants of burghs of lower grade than royal, the burghs of barony, were thus put on the same footing as strangers who were not burgesses of any kind. They were of lower status than royal burgesses. Generally it was the defender's domicile or his status which determined the jurisdiction. Great importance attached, as will be seen, to the 'divers conditions of men.'

If an accused burgess had passed the age of fighting, if he was 'passit elde to fecht,' he could establish his innocence by compurgation.[2]

This statement of the law in cases to which battle applied in King David's time may conclude with the mention of the duel in one of those many grants to the church which some of his successors rued. The great charter of Holyrood,[3] granted in honour of the Holy Cross, the Virgin Mary, and all the saints, conferred upon the Abbey, in addition to certain lands, teinds, and churches, 'the ordeal of duel, water, and hot iron, so far as pertains to the dignity of the church.'

Holyrood charter.

1 Scots Acts, i. 335; B.L., ch. 13.
2 Scots Acts, i. 336; B.L., ch. 22.
3 Scots Acts, i. 358, Holyrood Chart. 3. Examen duellii aque et ferr calidi quantum ad ecclesiasticam dignitatem pertinet.

CHAP. 26.—*Under William the Lion.*

DURING this reign several important provisions emerge respecting the legal duel. The year 1174 must be regarded as a red-letter date in Scots law, for it witnessed the capture of the king by an English force under Ranulf de Glanvill, that great English lawyer whose work was so often cited in previous chapters. A marked English influence is traceable in the law subsequent to this date. The Regiam Majestatem, the most decisive evidence of that influence, still remains a battle ground for antiquaries. In 1175, immediately after his release, William made a law for the repression of theft after the English model, but much more drastic. It was, in terms of the assize of Clarendon in 1166, enacted by Henry II. that any man defamed as a malefactor by the oath of twelve lawful men of the hundred and four men of any vill was to go to the ordeal of water.[1] William's enactment was a stronger measure. Whoever was accused of theft or theft bote—that is, compounding with a thief or sharing his plunder—might, on the oath of the bailie or grieve and three other leal men of the vill, be taken and made to underly the ordeal of water. But if to these four oaths the oaths of three old men[2]

English influence.

[1] Stubbs' Charters, 143. This was confirmed and supplemented in 1176 by the assize of Northampt., ch. 1. Stubbs, 151.

[2] Prepositi. Legalium hominum. Seniorum hominum. There may

were superadded, instant execution followed without either ordeal or battle. 'Thruch na batal sal he pas na to wattir na yit to yrn bot hastily he sal be hangyt.'[1]

By an assize made at Stirling 'the Mononday next before the fest of sanct Margaret the madin next eftir the first crounement of schir Philip King of France' [7th July 1180], regulations were made for bringing the local courts of the barons under a certain degree of control by the Crown. Neither bishop nor abbot, earl, baron, nor freeholder was to hold his court unless in the presence of the king's sheriff or his sergeant. Here was a healthy germ of centralisation which, had it grown, might have consolidated the power of the throne, enabled it to keep a fretful baronage in awe, and altered the whole course of national history. But the baronial courts retained their powers and practical independence, and their existence until 1747 has long been recognised as one of the most potent of the causes which helped a turbulent nobility so often and so easily to defy the royal authority. This statute of 1180 closed with the clause that no baron might exercise jurisdiction of battle, water or iron—might hold court of life and limb by duel or ordeal—unless the sheriff

The assize of Stirling.

Baron Courts to be controlled.

be a technical meaning in the last phrase which the Scotch version renders 'thre lele men of eld'—perhaps aldermen.

1 Scots Acts, i. 371. Ass. Wm., ch. 2. The same swift justice was done on a thief taken with hue and cry. Ch. 7.

or his sergeants were there to see law and justice done.[1]

In another assize, probably near the same time, at Perth, the bishops, earls, barons, and thanes, and the whole community swore that they would neither maintain nor harbour thieves, manslayers, murderers, robbers, nor other evildoers, but would do their best to bring them to justice. They would maintain, they said, to the utmost the justice of the land, and after judgment of water or iron or duel was given, they would take no money for the setting aside of justice.[2] The whole tenor of this oath is significant of rampant crime and bribery. In perfect harmony with the state of things which called it forth was that singular enactment that if the king, through ignorance, pardoned a homicide without the consent of the slain man's kin, the kinsmen were, despite the pardon, free to 'tak vengeance of thaim that slew their kyn.'[3]

Assize of Perth.

Hitherto no word has been said about the regulation of the actual battle, but there happily survives an ordinance made in this reign by the judges of Galloway, a province which then reached as far as Lanark and Dumfries, and included a wide tract of the west country no longer embraced by the term. The judges of Galloway, sitting at Dumfries, decided that if any one

Ordinance of Dumfries.

[1] Scots Acts, i. 375; ass. Wm. ch. 12. Curiam belli, aque vel ferri.
[2] Scots Acts, i. 377; ass. Wm. ch. 20.
[3] Scots Acts, i. 375; ass. Wm. ch. 15.

were convicted, whether by the duel or otherwise, of a breach of the king's peace, 'the king sal haf of him xii^{xx} ky and iii gatharionis, or for ilk gatharion ix ky;'[1] that is 267 cows, a tremendous and unintelligible fine. The ceaseless rebellion of unruly Galloway may help to explain it.[2] Possibly it dates about the time of the pacification of Galloway in 1186.

Whatever its date, the ordinance further declared that no Galloway man ought to have visnet unless he renounced the laws of Galloway, and claimed visnet,[3] an example by no means singular of the tenacity with which old customs are adhered to. Visnet was undoubtedly a marked advance upon compurgation; it was a step towards trial by jury. The visnet, having heard the talk of the neighbourhood, was well qualified to judge of a prisoner's innocence or guilt. Possibly the men of Galloway, like the burgesses of England, and, as we shall see, of Scotland also, preferred the old partisan method of compurga-

Law of Galloway.

1 Scots Acts, i. 378; ass. William ch. 22. Gatharion is 'caturius' in the Latin version. What either word means the present writer does not know. No existing dictionary clears away his ignorance. Sir J. Skene thought it was for 'cautherius' a horse. He also reduces the 'kye' to 'twentie-twa'—a reasonable figure. Skene's version of Quon. Attach. ch. 72.

2 Prior to 1175, Gilbert of Galloway, for his brutal murder of his brother Uchtred, offered to pay by way of fine a tribute of 2000 marks, 500 cows, and 500 swine per year to Henry II. Hailes' Annals, sub anno 1186. Cattle were thus current coin in Galloway.

3 Scots Acts, i. 378; ass. Wm. ch. 22.

tion,[1] which looks like a direct product of the clan system so dear to Celtic races. The judges of Galloway at the same time prescribed a penalty upon any one who ventured to raise his voice in the barras[2] or lists when the judicial battle was going on. They ordained that from the time when all men ought to hold their peace, if any man spoke save those whose duty it was to keep order in the field, 'the king sal haf of him x ky in forfalt,' and if any man put-to his hand he should be in the king's mercy for life and limb.[3]

CHAP. 27.—*Writ of Right.*

An anomaly.

IT is worthy of note that Glanvill never describes the procedure in the field—the actual fighting of a duel—in an English plea of land on the writ of right. Bracton promises to treat of the duel in such a plea,[4] but, to the regret of legal antiquaries, seems never to have fulfilled the promise. Britton contains a similar unredeemed pledge,[5] and Fleta, like Bracton and Britton, describes the duel in a plea of felony only.[6] The result is

[1] In 'Scotland under her Early Kings,' i. 283-4, 436-7, Mr. E. W. Robertson thought that the 'law of Galloway' was the law of battle. I venture to differ; see note p. 78.

[2] In palacia, rendered in the Scottish version 'the palice.'

[3] Scots Acts i. 378; ass. Wm. ch. 22.

[4] Bracton ii. 438.

[5] Britton i. ch. 23, § 14.

[6] Fleta i. ch. 34, § 26, et seq.

that in England no extant treatise in the early centuries describes the battle in such a case.[1] In Scotland there is such a description.

The proof for the judicial duel in a plea of land in Scotland is very indefinite, yet there is such a body of floating provisions on the subject that in spite of the poverty of testimony it is reasonable to believe that it had at least some short existence there. Meanwhile, assuming this to be the case, and reserving the argument for a later stage, the reader is invited tentatively to accept as probably the law of Scotland about the year 1200 the account of a plea of land given in this and the next chapter. The whole authority for it is contained in the first volume of the Scots Acts, in that varied section appropriately titled *Fragmenta collecta.*

Battle on writ of right.

Where any one had lost his land[2] by default, not by judgment, he might seek it by writ of right against the holder, unless his default was after he had placed himself upon the assize or had waged duel. In either of these cases the writ would not avail him, as he and his heirs had then lost their right for ever. But where no such bar existed the pursuer in court[3] stated his claim, which he closed by saying that if defender should gainsay it he was ready to deraign or prove

[1] It is described in sundry law reports, not in treatises.

[2] This and next nineteen lines from Scots Acts, i. 742, frag. ch. 9.

[3] From this point the Scots fragmenta adapt Glanvill ii. ch. 3, as commented on later in this chapter. The full tenor of the passage is not given in the text, but all the omitted sentences are in Glanvill ii. ch. 3. The nature of the writ of right is touched on at p. 35, *supra.*

by his freeman N, and should harm befal him by such and such substitutes. Only one of these was to fight, as a man who by his own sight and hearing could testify to the verity of the pursuer's claim. Or pursuer might offer to deraign by his freeman G, whose father in his last hours enjoined him by the fealty which a son owes to his father—if ever he should hear of a plea about that land—to deraign the pursuer's right as what his father had seen and heard. Thereupon it lay in the defender's choice to declare whether he would defend by battle or put himself upon the assize or vouch to warrant. If he neither wished to vouch to warrant[1]—in other words, to fall back upon some other person from whom he acquired the impleaded ground—nor to submit the cause to the assize but declared for battle, he either in person or by a fit prolocutor denied pursuer's claim word by word. Wads[2] were next given in the hands of the justiciar, and these being afterwards repledged by two pledges on either side a day was fixed for doing battle. 'Also it falls to be noted,' says the authority cited, 'that after the duel has been waged the defender cannot in future put himself on the assize nor *ex converso*.'

After certain essoins (or excuses) and delays it was necessary for the pursuer to appear in court before

1 Scots Acts, i. 746, frag. ch. 28. It is quite evident that this tacks on to frag. ch. 9 on p. 742. Deraign, prove or disprove; here, to prove.

2 'Vadia,' probably the gloves of parties. They were redeemed by the 'vadii' or 'plegii,' personal 'wads' who stood bail.

the duel was fought. And he was bound to have his champion there ready to fight, nor would it suffice for him to put forward any champion except one of those by whom he had offered to deraign, nor could he exchange or put another in place of him who had made the wager at first. But if he who had waged battle died by a natural death during the suit, and this were proved by the visnet, then the pursuer might have recourse to one of the substitutes upon whom he had placed his offer to deraign, or if he had named no substitutes then to any other fit person who was a fit witness, and so the plea might begin anew. If the champion had died by his own fault, his master lost his plea. 'Note,' says our authority, 'that the champion of the pursuer ought to be one who knows and can therefore be a fit witness. Neither shall it be lawful for a pursuer to prosecute his appeal in his own person, because that cannot be done save by a fit witness who saw and heard. But the defender can defend himself either by himself or, if he choose, by another fit for the purpose.'

Before battle.

These passages from the Fragmenta are to be found almost word for word in the 3rd chapter of the second book of Glanvill, but the following question and answer are not verbally borrowed from the English author. 'Why cannot a man deraign his right by his own body? Because he cannot from his own sight and hearing speak as to the seisin of his ancestor. Because he cannot bear suit to himself.'[1]

CHAP. 28.—*The Battle*.

'Concerning the champions before the justiciar.'

The champions[2] appearing in court in presence of the justiciar in due manner on the last day of plea armed with the due arms for battle, the pursuer offers himself as ready to deraign by his servant, and the defender shall declare himself ready by his servant to defend his right. Then the champions shall swear in this manner—the champion of the defender shall, with his left hand, hold the champion of the pursuer by the right hand, a person standing between so that he may not hurt it,[3] and he shall hold his right hand over the book, saying, 'Thou hearest this, O man whom I hold by the hand, who makest call thyself by the baptismal name of A or B or C or D, that such a man by name so-and-so,—that is to say, the master of said champion—has no right in

[1] Scots Acts, i. 747, frag. ch. 30. The first of these answers is of course implied in the passage previously cited. This was the original English reason for not allowing the pursuer to fight in person. At a later time the books say neither could fight, on the ground that if either were killed the suit would still be undecided—a far-fetched and unreal reason. Coke upon Lyttelton, 294*b*. Blackst. iii. ch. 25.

[2] This chapter is a full literal translation from Scots Acts, i. 746-7, frag. ch. 29. See note on p. 110.

[3] Quod non distringat ipsam. Similar rule in England—'Quil tensist swefe sanz de strendre ou grever lui.' Case in 3 Edw. III. in Dugd. Orig. 70.

that carucate of land or in such a piece of land with the pertinents lying in such a place, whereto thou makest thyself witness; and that such a one, his ancestor, was never vest or seized therein in the time of such and such a king in time of peace. Nor took he therefrom crops of corn or grass nor other issues of the land to the value of half a mark. Neither did thy father see or hear this, nor did he when he was dying enjoin thee to deraign thereupon.[1] So help me God and these holy Evangels.'

First oath.

Then the other shall take him by the hand in the same way, and in the like words which the first in denying swore, he shall swear in affirming that the truth is as he asserts. Next they shall be delivered to four knights of each side, to be safely guarded and taken into the field. Two knights, who took the batons of the champions whilst they were swearing, shall carry the batons to the field and retain them until the oaths shall have been made there.

And this shall be the oath—'Thou hearest this, O priest, that I have not this day to my knowledge[2] eaten nor drunk nor done aught whereby the law of God may be set aside or

Second oath.

[1] In England this clause was expressly struck at by the first statute of Westminster, ch. 41, in 1275. See ch. 15, *supra*.

[2] 'Secundum intellectum meum.' This oath in the appeal of felony in Bracton is, Hoc audite justiciarii quod ego non comedi nec bibi nec aliquis pro me nec præ me, propter quod lex Dei deprimi debeat et lex diaboli exaltari, sic me Deus adjuvet. Bracton, ii. 442. Fleta (allowing for misprint) is the same, i. ch. 34, § 30.

the power of the devil[1] advanced.' And the other shall swear the same.

Then shall one of the sergeants of the justiciar cry with a loud voice over all the field, commanding, in name of the king and the justiciar, that no one shall either stir or say aught whatever he shall see or hear between those champions, and that if any one do so he shall be seized and sent to the king's prison, there to remain for a year and a day. All which being done, if their masters cannot in the meantime make a concord whilst the champions pray,[2] the battle shall proceed.

Touching the positions of the champions,[3] note that the appellant shall take his station in the field on the east side and the defender on the west.[4]

When the duel is finished[5] the victor shall have from the vanquished, in name of recreancy, sixty shillings, and if the appellant shall be vanquished in the duel his master shall lose his plea, and besides he shall lose the law of the land. And if the defender shall be vanquished his master shall lose the piece of ground with the

Vae victo.

1 See Hailes' note on Canon at Perth in Annals (1797), iii. 173, appx.

2 Dum campiones orant.

3 De stallis pugilum, words of rubric in Edinburgh Univ. MS.

4 English 14th century practice generally made the defendant's champion stand north, plaintiff's south. East and west were the positions in the chivalric duel. Here 'appellans'—the wrong word—takes the place of 'petens.' There was no 'appeal,' and consequently no 'appellant' in the writ of right.

5 From this point the passage cited copies Glanvill ii. chap. 3 at end. No previous part of this chapter is from Glanvill.

fruits and other easements found thereon at the time of seisin never to be heard in court again, for those things which are once determined by duel in the king's court are secure for ever. Then the Sheriff shall be ordained by brieve to let the victor have seisin of the land and recover it with its fruits.[1]

CHAP. 29.—*An Argument.*

THE date of the mysterious account of the duel in a plea of land contained in the two preceding chapters is a matter of some interest because of its possible bearing on the much-debated Regiam Majestatem. As has been seen, the Scotch manuscripts from which it is taken owe much of their inspiration and language to Glanvill. This makes it certain that the account dates not earlier than 1187. A comparison with Glanvill displays a close but not absolute verbal similarity. This remark does not apply to one large and important section, that, namely, which forms the bulk of the last chapter, and describes the appearance of the champions in thc field, their oaths, and the procedure at the battle. No original for this section has been found in Glanvill, Bracton, Fleta, Britton, or any other work.

If it be of English origin, or amplified from

1 Chapter does not end here, but goes on to describe procedure where assize adopted. The rest is a tolerably close copy of Glanvill ii. chap. 6, *re* grand assize, concluding with a part closely resembling a passage in Glanvill ii. ch. 17. Its final sentence is from Glanvill ii. ch. 19.

English practice, it must be of earlier date than 1275, for the champion makes oath expressly as a witness—a practice abolished by the first statute of Westminster. It is true that the oaths and pro-

Significance of ch. 28.

cedure differ little, *mutatis mutandis*, from those used in criminal appeals, as set forth in Bracton, but the differences are sufficiently marked to make it plain that we have here no copy or adaptation of Bracton. The oath against magic scarce differs at all from that of Bracton, but the concluding words of the Scotch version, 'secundum intellectum meum,' are a noteworthy feature of caution.[1] There does not appear on the surface any reason why this account of the duel should not be at least as old as Bracton. It is just such a statement of the law as Glanvill might have penned had he detailed the procedure in the field. May it not have been a Scotch adaptation of Glanvill in the reign of William the Lion?

But was the plea of land ever tried by battle in Scotland? Extrinsic grounds for believing that it was are certainly slender, when analogies are set

Query.

aside; but the analogies are powerful, and the account in question is found in nearly a dozen of the oldest and best manuscript sources of early Scots law. It is difficult to account for this seemingly independent adaptation on any other footing than that of authenticity.

[1] The words are persistent in the Scotch MSS.

Yet no clear evidence from practice has ever been adduced. Here it will suffice to point to a couple of fragments of law of very uncertain date. One of these assigns, amongst other just grounds for the exercise of the feudal privilege of recognition, that is, for the superior taking his vassal's lands into his own hands, one which certainly looks confirmatory. If two men strive, it says, and litigate at arms about the possession of any land, the overlord can recognosce it until it shall be clear to him which is the lawful owner.[1] Is it extravagant to see here an allusion to the judicial duel in a plea of land?

Considerations.

A leading feature of the duel in such cases, alike in the English books and the Scotch fragments, was the finality of it, a circumstance which makes lucid another passage in the flotsam and jetsam of the Fragmenta. Proof or purgation in the absence of one of the parties to a civil case is said to be 'as the striking of battle and the end of the plea.'[2] So correct an application of

[1] Scots Acts i. 733, frag. ch. 22. 'Si duo certent et cumulant ad arma circa possessionem alicujus terre.' This is not greatly unlike the law as stated in Fleta v. ch. 1 § 8. It is, however, only too evident that this may mean mere strife, not litigation. As the writ has been ascribed to the reign of Robert III., the latter is a probable interpretation.

[2] Scots Acts i. 741, frag. ch. 2, 'quasi ictus belli et finis placiti.' In the Scotch, 'the deid of batail and the end of the mut.' Compare passage on p. 93, *supra*. This finality was the very reason why in England the form of battle on the writ of right was retained so long after the thing was dead.

the doctrine could scarcely have come by chance. In England battle remained an essential part of the procedure on the writ of right in pleas of land for five centuries. Scotland imported the writ of right from England. Is it too much to suppose that it necessarily imported with it the duel element?[1] On the whole, the acceptance which Cosmo Innes seems to give to the provision under examination as evidence of 'a very curious Scotch custom of duel'[2] appears well founded. There is but small anomaly in the fact that in 13th century England the duel on a writ of right to land existed, but was never described by any legal text writer. The anomaly would be great were it found that in Scotland such a duel was described but never existed. The natural conclusion is that it did exist in the reign of William the Lion,[3] and probably before, but that it was in little favour, and soon became extinct. If a case could be established for the Regiam Majestatem as a product of the opening years of the 13th century, some difficulties would be removed.

Opinion.

[1] Certain fragmentary provisions for the evidence of jurors seem to have been distinctly moulded by the requisites of a champion's oath. Notably Scots Acts i. 753, frag. ch. 32.

[2] Scots Acts i. 52, Note 5. [3] See ch. 38, *infra*, p. 134.

CHAP. 30.—*Exemptions from Duel.*

WHETHER the duel in pleas of land existed under William the Lion or not—whether it was in his reign or a successor's that it was abolished—this much at least is certain, that its abolition in such cases would have been in harmony with tendencies of the time capable of easy proof. It is in William the Lion's reign that a Scotch burgh charter, following in the wake of similar charters to English towns, first expressly exempts the citizens from trial by battle. To the burgesses of Inverness and their heirs he gave, granted, and confirmed freedom from the duel for ever—the perpetual liberty that never amongst them should they have battle,[1] and that no other burgess nor any other man of all the realm should have battle against his said burgesses of Moray or against their heirs. Henceforth there was to be compurgation only, for in Scotland as in England it was compurgation, the old law, that the soul of the burgess hankered after. This exemption is attested by extant charter, but there is some ground for thinking that the privilege was extended to other towns. A remarkable fragment which, by its mention of the 'law of Winchester,'[2] bears intrinsic signs to confirm its

William the Lion's grants.

1 Nunquam inter eos bellum habebunt. Scots Acts i. 89.

2 In King John's charters the 'law of Winchester' and the 'liberties of Winchester' were frequently cited. The phrase defined certain burghal rights. See Rotuli Chartarum i. 130 b, 135, 219 b 54.

nominal date, enumerates certain privileges which 'King Wilyame of Scotlande grantit to the burgess of his said kynrik,' and specially states that 'he hes grantit to thame that nane of thame do batale bot of the mutis that fallis to the kingis croune.'[1] This clause has rightly enough found a place in the Fragmenta, but in the same manuscript from which it came there is a Latin variant, which, though not printed in the Fragmenta, is worth quoting here. 'No burgess,' it says, 'shall do battle, even in pleas

Collateral.

pertaining to the king's crown, if he can deraign according to the custom of burghs, that is, by the purgation of twelve leal men.'[2] No very positive conclusion can rest on such an unstable base as these fragments lend, though many negative facts give colour to them. They prove, however, that as in England under King John, so in Scotland under King William, exemptions from the duel and rumours of exemption were in the air.

[1] Scots Acts i. 720, frag. ch. 8.

[2] Colvil MS. described in preface to Scots Acts i. 198. It is now in Edinburgh University Library. The passage cited is ch. 19 of the Omne gaderum. 'Nullus burgensis faciet duellum in placitis ad coronam domini regis pertinentibus si possent disracionari se secundum consuetudinem burgorum hoc est per purgationem xii legalium hominum burgi. Et omnis burgensis et eorum heredes de gilda mercatoria quiti sunt de tolloneo stagio pontagio et passagio tam infra quam extra per omnes portus maris omnium terrarum domini regis.' This clause is plainly inspired by English charters. See Rotuli Chartarum *passim*, charters of King John in vol. i.; especially charter of Lincoln in 1199, at p. 5; Merleberge in 1204, p. 135; and Newcastle-on-Tyne in 1216, p. 219b: 'Stagio' is an evident error for lastagio, lastage.

CHAP. 31.—*Regiam Majestatem.*

Assit principio Sancta Maria meo!

THE invocation of the scribe who wrote an ancient legal MS. now in the Advocates' Library at Edinburgh[1] may well be his who girds up his loins to deal with the subject of this chapter and attempt a step out of chaos. But the Regiam Majestatem cannot be ignored. First regarded as a *corpus juris* of David I., next declared a poor copy of Glanvill, then boldly pronounced the original of which Glanvill was the copy, once more proved to be a copy of Glanvill, but stated to have been purposely disguised so as to hide its origin, conjectured to be a compilation made by English judges under the order of Edward I., suggested as the work of King James I. of Scotland,[2] and last of all attributed to a private hand in the 14th century—its mere history has been matter of no less debate than its authority for early Scottish law.

In 1425 the Parliament of Scotland enacted that the king's lieges were to live and be governed 'undir the kingis lawis and statutis of this realm alanerly,' not by particular laws or special privileges, and 'be na lawis of uther cuntreis nor realmis.'[3] The same Parliament passed an Act that six wise and discreet

[1] MS. 28, 6, 1. A second scribe repeats the prayer of the pentameter. 'Amen dico vobis quod Jhon'—echoes a third.

[2] See notes to Wyntoun vol. iii. p. 265.

[3] Scots Acts ii. 9.

men who knew the laws best 'sal se and examyn the bukis of law of this realm, that is to say Regiam Majestatem and Quoniam Attachiamenta, and mend the lawis that nedis mendment.'[1] This process naturally led to some confusion, and the year 1465 witnessed an early step towards codification when the stringent remedy was devised to gather the whole extant laws into a single book and destroy all other copies, 'the kingis lawis, Regiam Majestatem, Actis, Statutis, and uther bukis to be put in a volum, and tobe autorizit, and the laif to be destroyit.'[2] Under such circumstances there is little wonder that there should survive only three or four 14th century copies of the Regiam, that there is only one MS. collection of our early laws of any kind written before the days of Robert the Bruce, and that there is no 13th century copy of the Regiam at all. The fact is no argument against the possibility of the Regiam having been framed in the 13th century; if it were, very many so-called statutes of Scotland not to be found in the Berne MS.[3] would have to be ruthlessly expunged.

The Acts of 1425.

No 13th century MSS.

The authority of parliament, given in 1425 and consistently corroborated, strongly supports the Regiam as a 'book of law of this realm.' It is a libel upon

[1] Scots Acts ii. 10.

[2] Scots Acts ii. 97.

[3] For information as to this and the other MSS. see preface to Scots Acts, i. 177 *et seq.*

our forefathers to believe lightly that they accepted a work foisted upon the country by Edward I., or written by a half-informed contemporary compiler belonging to their own country. It is a grotesque conception that distinguished English judges in 1305[1] deliberately concocted a code for Scotland out of an ingenious combination of Glanvill, written in 1187, with the statutes of King David and King William passed prior to 1214. Nor does the probability of such a process readily commend itself even when attributed to a Scotchman writing after the war and grievously straitened by lack of authorities for his guidance.[2] Admittedly there is much to be said for the last theory—notably one tell-tale sentence now to be considered.

Theories for a 14th century origin.

So far, the one overwhelming argument adduced against an early 13th century origin for the Regiam is that of Chalmers,[3] founding on a fact of which Sir John Skene was quite cognisant.[4] Chalmers pointed out that a part of the Regiam as printed—the sub-section concerning idiots in the chapter 'concerning wardship given by the king'—is almost verbatim et literatim from a provision which once appeared in the English statutes of the realm as the Act 17 Edward II.[5] That so-called

A tell-tale clause examined.

1 The theory of Chalmers, Caledonia i. 732.

2 The theory of Cosmo Innes, Scots Acts i. 48, not strongly urged.

3 Caledonia i. 731.

4 As shewn by his marginalia on this clause, forming ch. 46 of the second book of the Regiam in his version.

5 That is to say, the second half of ch. 40 in Regiam book ii., as in

Act, the Prerogativa Regis, now, however, occupies a very disputable place in the statute-book.[1] Critics roundly deny its authenticity as a statute. Some think its true date much earlier than the 17th of Edward II., and are even disposed to assign its compilation to the reign of Edward I. The difference between Edward II. and Edward I. is not material here. Either date is fatal to the hypothesis contended for. If, therefore, all the copies of the Regiam which contain the chapter on wardship alike contain the sub-section concerning idiots, the question will be virtually closed, and the book cannot possibly date earlier than the end of the 13th century. On that very point the chapter in question has been collated in fourteen copies of the Regiam in Edinburgh, and although twelve of them contain this chapter and sub-section, yet in two good and quite independent manuscripts,[2] the oldest known Scotch versions, the chapter does not contain the crucial sub-section. The case, therefore, against an early 13th century Regiam is not yet closed.[3]

Opinion that case not closed.

It is impossible here to hammer out the endless argument, but the last paragraph will have served to show that, in spite of the labours of Thomas Thomson

Scots Acts i. 617, giving the ward of 'natural fools' to the King, is all but word for word the same as the so-called Act 17 Edward II. ch. 9.

[1] See the Statutes Revised, vol. i. p. 80. My information regarding the criticisms I owe to the kindness of Professor Maitland.

[2] MSS. Advocates Library W. 4 ult. and A, 1, 32.

[3] Because these two copies are copies of copies older still.

and Cosmo Innes, the text of the Regiam as given in the Scots Acts cannot be accepted as definite and final. Varied though the learning of these great antiquaries was, it was not enough to enable them to edit an immaculate text or to justify them in dispensing with variorum readings. Such an edition is perhaps a task awaiting a generation more interested than the present in the study of early law, but until that task is undertaken the obscurity which enshrouds the Regiam will not be dispelled or its paradoxes explained. The questions it raises call for every scrap of evidence the manuscripts can give.

No final text of Regiam as yet.

After a fair consideration of various criticisms, notably those of Craig,[1] Hailes,[2] Chalmers,[3] and Cosmo Innes,[4] and after some examination into the original manuscripts, the opinion has been arrived at that the antiquity of the Regiam has not been disproved. The fact must count for something that it embodies several of the statutes of King David I. and King William, but (after deducting one highly questionable exception)[5] does not embrace the provisions of a single Scottish statute of later date. This fact becomes of more moment when viewed in the light of the English influences at work in and after

[1] Jus Feudale. [2] Examination of the Regiam. [3] Caledonia i. 727-34.
[4] Scots Acts, i. 48. Compare Robertson's Index, introd. 28-38.
[5] The exception is the De confugientibus, Regiam iv. ch. 53. A similar provision is inserted in Scots Acts i. 401 in statutes of Alex. II., but no old MS. so ascribes it. Good MSS. assign it to David I. See Scots Acts i. 224-5.

William's reign. Not unconscious of serious objections to the following opinion, an alternative working theory has been adopted. Either the Regiam was compiled in the first half of the 13th century, say between 1200 and 1230, a view which Walter Ross countenanced in his great historical lectures on the Law of Scotland,[1] or it was compiled from materials of the law of that period. In either case its place in Scots law would fall to be assigned to the opening years of the 13th century as the time to which its contents most nearly apply, when Scotland and England were on terms of friendship and ruled by monarchs who in Scottish chronicle are called the 'kings of peace.'[2] As of that date, therefore, its law is tentatively treated in this work.

An alternative conclusion.

CHAP. 32.—*In the Regiam.*

THE contents of the Regiam divide easily into three classes. The first, about two-thirds of the entire work, consists of clauses adopted without alteration from Glanvill. The second consists of clauses which, while differing from Glanvill, have been distinctly suggested by it. The third class consists of entirely independent statements of law. To these three classes varying values must be attributed. Of the third class, forming much the greater portion of the fourth book, several

Degrees of value.

[1] Vol. ii. 60-4. [2] Wyntoun vii. ch. 9.

chapters are from statutes of King David and King William, and the remainder generally bears a native character so distinctive that for the whole fourth book a degree of authenticity may be claimed. In the second class the alterations of Glanvill are deliberate, and are certainly in harmony with proved tendencies of the 13th century. It is impossible to conceive the purpose of these changes except on the supposition that they were made in course of an honest, though not wholly successful, attempt to edit Glanvill into accord with the early 13th century law of Scotland. The first class, one is constrained to admit, while it contains many provisions equally true in both Scotland and England, provides for a more elaborate machinery of justice than has ever been proved to exist in Scotland in either the 13th or 14th centuries. Still, the Regiam was written by a man who, whatever may have been his knowledge of law, was at least a scholar with very definite ideas. Probably he does not lead us far astray in what he states regarding trial by battle.

A comparison of Glanvill with the first three books of the Regiam, as brought out below in parallel columns,[1] discloses certain interesting facts,

[1] Table contrasting the duel in Glanvill and in the Regiam :—

GLANVILL.	REGIAM.
II. Ch. 3.—In plea of land pursuer offers battle, and defender has his choice either to accept it or to claim an assize.	I. Ch. 9.—Differs radically. In plea of land on writ of right pursuer puts himself on God and the assize, unless the case is changed by allegation of sale or gift—nisi

the most important of which is one obscured rather than otherwise by the collation prefixed to the first volume of the Scots Acts. Wherever Glanvill dealing with the ordinary plea of land on a writ of right

	quod causa mutatur scilicet si terra data sit vel empta. [A reference to III. ch. 25.]
II. Ch. 3.—Concerning champions, as in a large part of ch. 27 and a small part of ch. 28 of this work.	Omitted.
II. Ch. 7.—Eulogy of grand assize and its superiority to battle.	Omitted.
II. Ch. 19.—Notandum that there can never be duel unless assize competent, and *vice versa*.	I. Ch. 13.—Incorporates chapter, but stops short at notandum, which is omitted.
III. Ch. 5.—In plea of land defender who might vouch to warrant chooses not to do so and defends the case himself 'sed jus petentis per se omnino defendit.' If he lose that land 'per duellum,' he can never recover in future against his warranty. The same rule applies if he defends 'per assisam.'	I. Ch. 21.—States first sentence same. In the others omits all reference to the duel.
III. Ch. 7.—In plea of land where defender's lord does not stand to his warranty, defender may adduce any fit witness 'ad diracionationem inde faciendam vel aliam sufficientem probationem juxta considerationem curie faciendam.'	I. Ch. 26.—Much the same but with difference as to proof, 'et hoc ad disracionacionem faciendam per sufficientem probationem juxta considerationem curie legitime probabit. [Glanvill, deraign *or* prove; Regiam, deraign *by* proving.]
IV. Chap. 6.—In claim to advowson tenant may defend by duel.	Omitted.
VIII. Ch. 9.—Third sentence. Clause as to record of duel waged in minor court and transferred to the king's.	I. Ch. 28.—Much the same.

allows a choice to be made between duel and a jury, between battle and the grand assize, the Regiam allows the assize only. The way in which this is worked out in minute details, with a single express

V. Ch. 4.—Notandum that duel has no place in proving or disproving the liberty 'a prima nativitate' of any man.	II. Ch. 8.—Notandum that duel has no place in proving or disproving the liberty of any man.
V. Ch. 5.—Duel competent to prove liberty of a villein made free.	II. Ch. 9.—Omits clause.
VI. Ch. 11.—Duel competent where heir disputes widow's dower.	II. Ch. 13.—Same.
IX. Ch. 1.—Duel competent in dispute concerning service between vassal and lord.	II. Ch. 58.—Same.
X. Ch. 5.—If a 'borh' or pledge denies that he became pledge plea might come to duel.	III. Ch. 2.—Same.
X. Ch. 12.—Debts, like pledges, may be proved by duel or by writ. If debtor disputes his seal it may be proved by duel.	III. Ch. 6.—This chapter in Scots Acts ends with opening sentence of Glanvill x. ch. 12, but wholly omits clauses concerning debts. Singular to say they appear, the same as in Glanvill, in Skene's ed. of the Acts, Reg. Maj. iii. ch. 8.
X. Ch. 17.—General mode of proof of debt, purchase, or loan is either by writ or by duel.	III. Ch. 11.—Same.
VIII. Ch. 9.—Where duel waged in minor court and transferred to the king's, minor court has a record of the claim and defence and of the words on which duel adjudged and waged, but not of other things unless on a change of champions, 'nisi de escambio campionis.'	III. Ch. 20.—Same.

exception, is clear proof of set purpose in the change. Considered alongside of other facts, and particularly of the elaborate account of the duel in such a plea given in a previous chapter —an account taken in the main from passages in Glanvill which the Regiam pointedly omits—does not the significant alteration supply plausible grounds for the belief that it is the record of an actual change in the law?

Writ of right in Regiam.

A statute of undefined date declares that brieves of mortancestry and novel disseisin shall for the future be disposed of, not on the challenge or claim, but only by assize of the good country— not *per calumpniam petentis*, but by the verdict of twelve men.[1] These writs concerned possession, not

VIII. Ch. 9.—Court not bound to defend its record by duel, but bound to defend its judgment. If a fit witness will deraign it may come to duel.	III. Ch. 21.—Same.
XIII. Ch. 11.—In brieve of mortancestry, if defender says pursuer sold, gave, or conveyed to him his holding, matter may come to duel.	III. Ch. 25.—Same. [See I. ch. 9.]
If 'res judicata' by duel, there can be no new case.	Ch. 25.—Same.
XIV. Ch. 1.—(See text, ch. 33). —Plea of felony wont to end by duel.	IV. Ch. 2.—Plea ended by duel or by 'good country.'
'What infamy a recreant incurred has been sufficiently said before,' referring to clause in ii. ch. 3 concerning champions.	Omitted.

[1] Scots Acts i. 325, where it is ch. 35 of ass. David, a most impro-

property,[1] and were therefore not writs of right. It has been supposed[2] that this statute abolished battle in pleas of land. That view would leave little doubt regarding the warrant for the Regiam's pointed change, but it is not tenable.[3]

The testimony of the Regiam to the disuse of the judicial combat is not limited to one particular. True, like Glanvill, it still tells of the duel in cases of disputed dower and pledge, in the proof and disproof of debts and purchases and loans, in quarrels of vassal and lord regarding feudal service, in the maintenance of the judgments of courts, and even in a certain class of cases regarding land. But Glanvill, though he denied it jurisdiction to decide whether a man was born free or bond, declared it a competent tribunal for sending back to villenage a villein who pled that he had been set free. The Regiam, on the other hand, disallows it in both instances, with a broad generalisation that the duel has no place in proving or disproving the liberty of any

bable ascription, making David I. forestall Glanvill's invention of the grand assize. The statute also appears in Reg. Maj. iv. ch. 38, Scots Acts i. 638.

1 Reg. Maj. iv. ch. 40, Scots Acts i. 638. See p. 35, *supra*.

2 E. W. Robertson, 'Scotland under her Early Kings,' i. 283.

3 A better view of the meaning of the Act is that the judge was not to decide the question *de plano* on the petitioner's statement, *calumnia*, or claim. A jury was to pronounce on the facts. Professor Maitland suggests this hypothesis and refers me to a somewhat parallel passage in Bracton iv. 316. In this light the enactment may be deemed the source of the Scotch system of service of heirs as practised from the 13th century until 1847. See Jus Feudale ii. dieg. 17, § 25-41; Stair iii. 5, 29-41; Menzies' Conveyancing 799.

man. One may here see a gratifying sign of the growth of freedom.[1]

The Regiam states, as Glanvill did, that the general mode of proof of debt, purchase, or loan is either by writ or by duel. Deserving to be considered alongside of this clause is one in the Fragmenta which declares that if anyone appeal another concerning anything to the value of 50s. 4d. it may be proved by four due and lawful witnesses. Beyond that value there could be no proof except by writ or seal or by duel.[2]

CHAP. 33.—*Crime in the Regiam.*

THE fourth book of the Regiam deals largely with the law of crime. In such cases where the accused pled not guilty, 'the plea,' we are told both by Glanvill

[1] I cherish a very great suspicion—indeed something stronger—that the account of the duel on the writ of right, quoted before, must at one time have formed part of the Regiam. It is from Glanvill, with additions. So is the Regiam. But the Regiam leaves out *those very passages* of Glanvill, and puts in their stead the present ch. 9 of book I., an independent chapter. It therefore seems highly probable that the Regiam, as it now is, is a revisal of an intermediate work—a first edition in the early 13th century. Ch. 27 and 28, *supra*, in my opinion, supply a new *crux* for the Regiam.

[2] Scots Acts i. 735, frag. ch. 7. In 1405 the court of four burghs holden at Stirling stated the law to be that two men of good fame could prove any sum 'tam excedentem quinquaginta solidos quam infra.' Scots Acts i. 704. Compare with passage in laws of Henry I. in ch. 11, *supra*. If in Scotland the duel in civil cases was abolished in pleas of land first and continued in cases of debt, &c., the fact is singular and the contrast with England very marked. It is preferable to believe that the Regiam was badly revised.

and the Regiam,[1] 'is wont to be determined by duel.' Here Glanvill pauses, while the Regiam continues, 'but it shall be in the choice of the defender whether he will rather undergo the duel or put himself on the good country.'[2] Then the united narrative resumes. From the time when the duel is waged the parties may neither eke nor pare—add to nor take from—the words used at the giving of the wads,[3] nor may they otherwise resile from their first purpose. Whoever does so is to be held as vanquished and judged accordingly. Nor can there be any concord without the King's consent. Every freeman of full age is admitted to make this appeal, but not a woman. The accused can decline on the ground of age—that is, sixty years or more—or on the ground of mayhem. 'Ane manzie' (Sir John Skene's word for *mahemium* in his fine vernacular[4]) 'is called the breaking of anie bane in his bodie or the striking in of his harnepan of his head, or be makin thinne be scheavin of the samine.' In such circumstances the accused was bound to purge himself by the judgment of God, viz., by the hot iron if a freeman, by water if a villein, according to the divers conditions of men.[5]

Age. Mayhem. Ordeal.

Passing over with mere mention various clauses

1 Glanvill xiv. ch. 1. Regiam iv. ch. 2. Scots Acts i. 632.

2 Bonam patriam in se suscipere.

3 So to speak the record was closed, the issue defined.

4 In Skene's Regiam iv. ch. 3.

5 Secundum diversitatem condicionis hominum. Of this whole clause a significant variant is referred to in a note to the next chapter.

which repeat or condense[1] statutes of King David and King William, there may be quoted one of much the same effect as the 56th chapter of the assize of David. It is enacted that after peace is proclaimed in the barras of the king where the duel is fought, no one there shall speak under pain of the king's full forfeiture unless he be the justiciar or the keeper of the barras.[2]

The last point of duel law contained in the Regiam is that the defender ought first to wage battle and afterwards to swear, because in his defence he could elect battle or assize of the country, and ought first to elect, then to wage battle, and after that to swear.[3] This was the natural order of things and was the English practice.

Two facts.

Whatever be the date of the Regiam, whatever its authority in other matters, there need be little hesitation in accepting the fourth book as setting forth with some degree of accuracy the law of the judicial duel in cases of crime between 1200 and 1230. In King David's day the option of an accused was between battle and compurgation. In the Regiam, as in 13th century England, it is between battle and assize of the country. Attention is drawn to two facts, first, that in more places than one it expressly notices the ordeal as in practice,[4]

[1] Regiam iv. ch. 12 repeats ass. David ch. 8 and 20; iv. ch. 14 repeats ass. Wm. ch. 20; iv. ch. 11 condenses ass. Wm. ch. 12.

[2] Regiam iv. ch. 31. 'Barras' in the text is 'palacium' in the original.

[3] Regiam iv. ch. 48.

[4] Regiam iv. ch. 2, 12, 14, and perhaps 53.

and, second, that while the third book sanctions the use of champions in certain civil pleas,[1] the fourth book gives no place to champions in the plea of felony.

CHAP. 34.—*Under Alexander II. and After.*

IN 1216 the Lateran council abolished the ordeal,[2] and in 1219 the abolition was carried into effect in England by Henry III.[3] Eleven years later Alexander II. abolished it in Scotland.[4] Admittedly there are dubieties and variations in the manuscripts, but there is scarcely any doubt that this statute effected an entire abrogation. There are signs of some revisal of the criminal code about this time. To the same day as the statute last cited belongs an important chapter of duel law. Two others made in this reign may reasonably be assigned to much the same date. Roughly classed together these statutes may be designated as the group of 1230.[5]

On the Lord's day next before the feast of Saint Luke the Evangelist [13th October], 1230, 'the King Alysander statut that gif ony man steil ony thing fra

1 Regiam iii. ch. 20.

2 Stubbs' Charters 142.

3 Patent Roll 3 Henry iii. M. 5. The writ is given in extenso in Dugd. Orig. 87. See also Pike i. 467.

4 Scots Acts i. 285, 400. The best reading of this Act is that of the Ayr MS., where an independent chapter, under the rubric 'Deletio legis fosse et ferri et instittutio visneti,' reads as follows:—'De cetero non fiet judicium per fossam et ferrum.' This is the last clearly authentic reference to ordeal in the Scots laws.

5 Viz., statutes of Alex. II. ch. 5, 6, 8, and 13.

men of religioun clerkis wedowis or prebendaris, or ony othir that aw nocht to fecht,' the lord of the fee, or his deputy, with four faithful men of the town, should diligently search out the evildoer, try him by the leal men of the visnet, and, if guilty, inflict just doom.[1]

If one man shall complain against another, says the second provision[2] referred to, concerning any quarrel pertaining to the king's crown out of which duel ought to arise, and if the accused shall fall in the battle, his pledges shall answer to the king for 'ix. ky and a colpyndauch,'[3] and shall satisfy the accuser in respect of his challenge for as much as pertains to him for his escape.[4]

Statute of champions, 1230.

The third Act of this reign[5] to be cited is of peculiar significance. It has been placed by the editors of the Scots Acts, on grounds not unsatisfactory although by no means conclusive, next after a statute of the undoubted date of 1230. 'It was enacted at Scone,' so runs the statute, 'by the king and community of the realm of

[1] Scots Acts i. 399. Stat. Alex. II. ch. 5. On 8th Feb. 1244, an Act was passed authorizing a system of presentment and indictment in all pleas of the crown—Scots Acts i. 403. It was an extension of William the Lion's Act of 1175, noted in ch. 26, *supra*, and of the Act of 13 October, 1230 just quoted. The trace of English influence is here conspicuous, for it was simply an adaptation from the practice in the south. It mentions neither compurgation, battle, nor ordeal.

[2] Scots Acts i. 402. Stat. Alex. II. ch. 13.

[3] Colpyndauch, a quey or young cow.

[4] That is, the mulct for allowing a prisoner of his rank to break out of prison. [5] Scots Acts i. 400-1. Stat. Alex. II. ch. 8.

Scotland that if a knight, or the son of a knight, or any freeholder in a knight's fee, or any other holding his land in any manner by free service or *per fie de hauberk*,[1] or the sons of these, should appeal any man of robbery or manslaughter, theft, rape, or any other misdeed whereby duel might arise, it should be lawful for them, at the bridge of Stirling, in the king's court or in any other, to debel the defender by an interposed person if the appellant said in his appeal in full court that he would prove the defender of his delict, as one who is a freeman, and has men on his behalf to prove him of his delict, since such persons can put forward their men in such cases in their stead. But mailers of rustics born, persons of low birth, or rustics, or any others who have no freehold and are not of free birth, cannot prove their damage except by their own person. But their lords in whose lands they dwell can, for their loss, debel malefactors by interposed persons, and by other persons than those who suffered the damage, because the body of a tenant and all his goods ought by right to be in his lord's protection.'[2]

Such were the terms of the statute which made champions admissible for a land-owning appellant in the plea of felony. In England it was from first to last the central feature of that appeal that the battle

1 'Fief d'haubert,' Norman name for a knight's fee. Latin, 'feudum loricæ.' Craig's Jus Feudale i. dg. 11, § 13. Hallam, Mid. Ages, reprint, p. 809.

2 This statute closely observes 'the divers conditions of men.' Its title is 'De modo duelli secundum condiciones personarum'—almost repeating a phrase of the Regiam. See note 5, p. 111, *supra*.

must be fought in person by appellant and appellee. No custom similar to this statute of champions ever obtained in England. This is the first mention of the champion as a factor in the prosecution of crime in Scotland. Why does the fourth book of the Regiam not name him? Why, on the other hand, does it name the ordeal? These questions admit of easy answer if the Regiam was written before the group of 1230 became law, for this chapter shows that until then there were no champions in pleas of felony, and the ordeal was not abolished.[1]

Points for the Regiam.

For a full hundred years after the reign of Alexander II. there is a great silence in law and chronicle and chartulary on the subject of the Scotch judicial duel; and although the silence is not unbroken, it is believed that the institution was steadily on the wane.

[1] The clause 'De victo in duello,' a fragment of the Regiam out of its place, found in many MSS., supplies instructive evidence of a process of change in the Regiam. It is a version of the Regiam iv. ch. 2, given *supra* p. 111, with which it should be compared. There, as in Glanvill xiv. ch. 1, a person pleading age or mayhem cleared himself by the ordeal 'per dei judicium scilicet per calidum ferrum,' &c. But the clause 'De victo' in some MSS. says that such a one 'tenetur se purgare [accusatus] per veredictum viciniti, quod antiquitus solebat fieri per judicium, scilicet liber homo per calidum ferrum,' &c. Drummond MS., Register House, pp. 98-9. Edinburgh University MS., folio 83. This means that in 1230 ordeal was wholly done away with. It must have been written when men still talked of 'visnet.' Did they do that in Scotland in the 14th century? If not, it is a powerful fact for the age of the Regiam that one of its clauses was undergoing revisal when 'visnet' had not been supplanted altogether by the 'assize.'

CHAP. 35.—*The Duel Described.*

THE man who is happy enough to combine the tastes of pedestrian and antiquary meets wherever he goes with green moot-hills, mostly known as moats; he hears of plea-cairns which once were but are no more; he visits solitary boulders and stone circles reared in far prehistoric time over bronze age graves. In his reading he stumbles upon suggestions of the judicial uses once served by these ancient meeting places; he reads of judgments given on the hill-of-pleas at Scone, at the Standand-Stanys of the Rath of Kingussy, at the Skeat of Crieff, at the Lochmabenstane on the Solway side. Such scenes as these, on bare hilltop or by some river bank, were the seats of justice in early times. Often, too, some knoll beside them—for the alpha and omega of justice were never far apart—bears the ominous name of Gallow-hill.

Moot-hills.

On some such moot-hill, therefore, in presence of the sheriff or some local magnate, took place the preliminary steps of the judicial duel.[1] Apparently, in the appeal of felony, the course of the case was very much the same as in England. Accuser appealed accused, and offered proof by his body. Accused word by word denied the charge and offered the like dis-

[1] This chapter is a mosaic from the Scots Acts and fragments, with a hint or two from Bracton and Fleta, Bracton's Note Book, and the Crown Pleas.

proof. If the court adjudged battle the accused gave his glove to the accuser, and took the accuser's in return. After the exchange of these symbols each party, the accused first, waged battle or found the requisite bail for due appearance.[1] Then the judge appointed the diet of battle.

The challenge.

When that day of dire debate arrived, accuser and accused met once more at the moot-hill before the judge. To prevent the possibility of foul play, or any outburst of sudden rage, they gave up their arms, and a man stood between them to keep the peace as they took the oaths. The accused swore first. Except that it set forth a charge of crime instead of a claim to land, the oath was quite the same as in a duel on a plea of land already described. A priest held out a copy of the gospels, on which the accused laid his right hand, clasping with his left his accuser's right hand. Then the accused swore, so help him God and these holy evangels, that he did not do the deed laid to his charge, and that the accuser never saw him do that deed. Next in the same way the accuser made his oath, that the accused was a perjured liar, that the charge was true, and that he, the accuser himself, had seen the deed.

The morn of battle.

This done the combatants, well guarded, were led into the lists or barras, a ring of palisades not far

[1] That this bail covered the damages is stated *supra*, ch. 25. See also Quoniam Attachiamenta, ch. 8.

away, around which an eager crowd already thronged. No doubt anxious hearts and tearful eyes were there, for men's lives were at stake. The stern decision could not now be long delayed. Entering the barras, accuser and accused—accused again entering first—were set face to face. The accused took his station on the eastern side, the place of the accuser was on the west. Each of them then took the second oath that he had used no magic to aid him in the fight.

In the barras.

An officer of court commanded silence in the field, proclaiming that no one, whatever he might see, should dare, under heavy penalty, to stir or say a word.

The arms of the combatants, spear and sword and targe,[1] were restored; the two men knelt to utter a hasty prayer; the priest bestowed his benediction; and the pulses of the onlookers beat fast as the battle began.

Arma virumque.

> Both stricken stryke, and beaten both doe beat
> That from their shields forth flyeth firie light,
> And hewen helmets deepe shew marks of eithers might.
>
> Great ruth in all the gazers harts did grow,
> Seeing the gored woundes to gape so wyde
> That victory they dare not wish to either side.[2]

Wherein victory consisted is nowhere defined in the Scotch laws. Amongst the old Norsemen he was

[1] There seems to have been great diversity of practice on this point. The text follows the march laws. The law of Clan Macduff mentions the spear. In plea of land the baton or *baculus* was employed.

[2] Faerie Queene, I., v., 7 and 9. Helmets were, however, not

vanquished whose blood first stained the ground.[1] England recognised no such artificial test. Probably Scotland did not either. They fought on until one or other gave in. If that were the luckless accused, his punishment pressed close behind defeat, for he had been fighting all the time with a metaphorical rope round his neck, and a hempen reality in readiness for an emergency. If the accuser yielded he was doomed ever after to wear the calf-skin on his recreant limbs, owning himself a craven, a perjured infamous man. The burden of victory, so to speak, lay upon the accuser; for if he did not conquer before 'the hour in which the stars begin to appear'[2] the maxim *potior est conditio defendentis* applied, and the accused who had defended himself all day long—longer than Falstaff's three long hours by Shrewsbury clock—was held the victor.

Three interruptions.

In Scotland there were three stated exceptions to the necessity of fighting out the duel to the bitter end—three exceptions or interruptions, the character of which is eloquent of age,[3] and not without an unlooked-for touch of humanity. In an appeal of adultery the duel might be stopped if the adulterer owned his fault and paid the 'enach,' a compensation fine for

admissible. Spenser was describing a fight between a knight and a paynim, not a Scotch judicial duel in a plea of felony.

1 Arng Jon. Chrym. 100.

2 Bracton ii. 442; Fleta i. ch. 34, § 32.

3 Skene's version of the Acts assigned them to the reign of William, ch. 27. In the Scots Acts, i. 746, they form ch. 26 of the Fragmenta.

injured honour.[1] Also, by the strange law of Clan Macduff,[2] a duel for the death of a clansman might be stayed if a fellow-clansman of either combatant could pass between the accuser and his spear[3]—a strange archaic provision of mercy, the origin of which it is hopeless to seek. Last of all, where the ground of action was blood drawn below the breath, the defender, after the combatants had fixed their spears,[4] might own the blood, pay enach, and make peace. 'And in no other case,' it is said, 'can the duel be remitted or relaxed.'

The bitter end.

Where there was no remission or relaxation and the battle was fought out, and where its grim issue was the defeat of the accused, short shrift was his, and that night the gallows-hill had a new tenant.

1 Regarding which see Fordun, vol. ii. paper in Appendix, by Dr. W. F. Skene, p. 448.

2 Further details of which appear in Wyntoun, vi. ch. 19; Bower, v. ch. 9. The protest of the Earl of Fife for the rights of the clan in virtue of this law appears in records of Parliament of 1385—Scots Acts, i. 551.

3 Si progenies alterius partis venire poterit in platea inter probatorem et lanceam suam. 'Platea,' the place or field of conflict. 'Probator,' the prover or appellant, does not here mean 'approver.' Scotland apparently did not utilise the approver as England did. His name is never mentioned in early Scots law. But see p. 138-9, *infra*.

4 'In casu sanguinis extracti subtus anhelitum quando fixerint lanceas suas,' &c. 'Subtus anhelitum' is in an early Scotch copy of the laws of the Bretts and Scots, rendered 'under the aand'—Scots Acts, i. 665. The editor or author of Ossian, in the piece titled 'Dar-thula,' states that when a warrior became unfit for battle he 'fixed his arms in the great hall,' as a sign that he was never afterwards to appear in battle. This was called the time of fixing of the arms. Doubts in the Scots

CHAP. 36.—*March Law.*

A FRENCH author, speaking of early customs in Bretagne, has said that churchmen there, notwithstanding the sanctity of their character, fought the duel in person for the maintenance of their rights.[1] The same must have been the case in England, as shewn by the terms of a letter obtained at the instance of the Pope from Henry II. in 1176. It contained this sentence, 'And I grant that no cleric shall be forced to fight the duel.'[2] But this letter did not rule international custom. And on the Borders the duel prevailed, and cleric as well as layman continued subject to its jurisdiction.

An archbishop's letter.

Between the years 1200 and 1202, William Malvoisin, bishop of Glasgow, who had written to the Archbishop of Lyons for information and advice, received a curiously interesting reply from that prelate.[3] 'Clerics,' said his Grace, 'and particularly such as have been promoted to holy orders, ought to be strictly forbidden to prosecute either robberies or thefts in the secular

Acts can scarcely be solved by the eminently debatable Ossian; yet it may be that the passage in the text is a highland idiom for old age. At the same time the indications do not favour that view, for, if so, surely the action could not have arisen. My own interpretation is that 'fixing their spears' means the beginning of the fight. Duels usually began with spears.

1 Coûtumes de Bretagne (1745), i. 5-7.

2 R. de Diceto, R.S. i. 410. Quoted before, ch. 15.

3 Joseph Robertson's Statuta Ecclesiæ Scoticanæ, i. ccxcvi.

courts. If they cannot be altogether hindered, they must on no account dare to go the length of single combat, or the ordeal of burning iron or water, or ordeal of any other kind.[1] If they will not comply with your exhortation, manslaughter and the cutting off of limbs will be perpetrated, and they will incur deprivation of benefice and of the office of the church. The authority of the apostle must be put before them—"Why do ye not rather suffer wrong?"[2] We believe we may well call by the name of wrong that damage which is done to any one by the fraud or malice of another. But all this we have written to you,' diplomatically concludes his Grace, 'without prejudice to your own better and wiser judgment.'

It would seem that the solicitude of the worthy bishop of Glasgow had arisen from the practice of the duel by the clergy on the Border. He was in Rome some years later,[3] and it was probably at his instigation that a papal thunderbolt was hurled against the 'pestiferous custom' in 1216. By his bull—*contra duellum religiosi*[4] —Pope Innocent the Third, greeting with his apostolic benediction all the faithful of Christ throughout the province of York and the realm of Scotland, announces that he has heard that a certain pesti-

A papal bull in 1216.

[1] Usque ad monomachiam vel candentis ferri vel aquæ vel aliquod hujusmodi examen.

[2] Quare magis non fraudem patimini?—1 Corinthians, ch. 6, v. 7.

[3] Melrose Chron. (Bann.) 121, 132.

[4] Glasgow Chart. 94, dated 23rd March 1215-6.

ferous custom, which rather ought to be called a corruption, as quite contrary to the law and honour of the church, had prevailed from of old betwixt Scotland and England.[1] 'Even until this day its observance is so far abused,' he says, 'that if it happen that a bishop, an abbot, or any cleric is prosecuted by any one for any offence for which the duel has been wont to be fought[2] between laymen, he who is prosecuted, religious though he be, is compelled to undergo the duel in person. We therefore,' he concludes, 'utterly detesting the aforesaid custom as hateful to God and the holy canons, strictly prohibit any one for the future from presuming to attempt such things in any manner of way, and this we do, by the authority of these presents, under pain of anathema. It shall be lawful to no man whomsoever to infringe this page of our prohibition, or with rash daring to gainsay the same. But if any one shall presume to attempt it he shall know that he has incurred the indignation of Almighty God and of his apostles St. Peter and St. Paul.'

Neither the Pope's prohibition nor the threatened wrath of the saints was an effectual deterrent. Eleven years afterwards, in 1237, the clergy of England

[1] Ad nostram noveritis audienciam pervenisse quod quedam pestifera consuetudo que corruptela debet potius nuncupari utpote juri ac honestati ecclesiastice prorsus contraria inolevit inter regnum Angliæ ac Scotiam ab antiquo.

[2] Pro quibus duellum inter laicos fieri consuevit.

presented to a papal legate a list of grievances which they wished Henry III. to redress—things which they said were done in England to the prejudice of the liberties of the church.[1] An item in the list declares that, by an abuse which obtained by the will and command of the kings of England and Scotland, not merely simple clerics, but also abbots and priors in the diocese of Carlisle, if they are appealed by any Scot, and *ex converso*, are forced to fight with spears and swords, but otherwise unarmed, the duel which is called *Acra*[2] on the marches of the realms. An abbot or a prior, whatever his dignity or order, must either sustain the duel in person or—himself a prisoner on the scene of the duel—must have a champion. If his champion fall he is slain, and the abbot or prior himself likewise is beheaded. 'Thus in our own time,' ends the complaint, 'the prior of Lide[3] was subjected to this article of the law.'[4] In conclusion, the clergy prayed the legate to stir up both the kings that so detestable an abuse

The persons of churchmen in 1237.

1 Annales Monastici, R.S. vol. i.; Annales de Burton, 256.

2 Read in previous editions of the Burton Annals, 'Aera.' The instance stands alone. Perhaps same as 'Campus,' a well-known name for duel. Compare 'Campus justicie,' a place at Aberdeen, near the gallows. Aberdeen Chart. (Spald.) ii. 279; also 'Dedefurlang' in Raine's North Durham, No. 267.

3 Not satisfactorily identified. Leath Ward in Cumberland, was anciently spelt Lyth. It contains 'Prior's Dale,' under Cross Fell.

4 Si ejus pugil succumbat, ipso interfecto, ipse quoque abbas vel prior plectrum capitis similiter sustinebit; sicut nostris temporibus prior de Lide legis tali conditione ligatus fuit ibidem.

might no longer be allowed 'as regards the persons of churchmen.'[1]

'As regards the persons of churchmen'! As seen in the bull of Innocent, and in this petition, clerical sympathy confined itself very closely to clerical hardship. Notwithstanding, churchmen remained subject to the duel in the Border-code even when, twelve years later, a matured enactment of march law was made.

CHAP. 37.—'*The Lawis of Merchis*,' *A.D. 1249*.

ON 14th April, 1249,[2] there met on the Marches certain representative sheriffs, with four-and-twenty knights of fame, from both sides of the Border. More successful in transacting business than some such previous meetings had been, this convention framed and adopted the great Border statute, the *Leges Marchiarum*, or 'Lawis of the Merchis.' Of these laws battle was no small part, for battle was the remedy for almost every Border wrong.

Border statute of 1249.

Any malefactor of one realm charged with misdeed done in the other, whether robbery, theft, homicide, or aught else whence duel might arise, had to answer for it at the march. Stated places were assigned, Camis-

[1] Quoad personas ecclesiasticas.

[2] The Leges Marchiarum are to be found in Scots Acts i. pp. 413-416. Another version appears in the 'Leges Marchiarum,' by Nicholson, p. 2, but it is very defective. Ridpath's Border History, anno 1249, may also be consulted.

furd[1] for the east march, next the sea ; Reddenburn[2] for the middle march ; Gamelspath[3] for Redesdale and Coquetdale; Sulwath (the Lochmabenstane[4] on Solway side) for Dumfriesshire and Cumberland.

The convention declared that by the custom of the two realms all men dwelling between Totness in England and Caithness in Scotland[5] might be called to do battle, excepting only the proper persons of the kings and of the bishops of St. Andrews and Durham, and no man, save these four, could swear to any charge by proxy.

1 Camisfurd is the one border forum I cannot identify. Opposite Coldstream there is a ford of the Tweed not far from the mouth of the Deday. The Deday divided the East March from the Middle March. Scots Acts i. 414. There are old camps near at hand. I half suspect that Camisfurd (query, Campsford) may have been at this point, but the conjecture is not worth much. I can find, and could hear of, no place answering to the name between Coldstream and Berwick. 'Hamisford' is an alternative reading.

2 In Sprouston parish, Roxburghshire, close to the Tweed, Reddenburn, once Revedeneburn, is now known locally as Carham burn, but still forms part of the border line as it did in 1222. Bain's Cal. i. No. 832. A short way above it is a ford to Birgham, a village known to history since 1290 from the famous treaty of Brigham made there.

3 On the border line at the fountainhead of the river Coquet.

4 This is an inference too long for detailed insertion here. The writer believes he has proved that the Lochmabenstane, a fine old boulder in the angle of the junction of Sark and Kirtle in Gretna parish, was at one end of the ordinary crossing place of the Solway Firth. Sulwath, now Solway, means muddy ford, just as (according to Prof. Skeat in N. and Q. 7 S. vii. 301) Solmonath, the old name of February, means muddy month. The name of the ford came in time to embrace the estuary. In August 1889, the Lochmabenstane stood amidst waving corn.

5 Totness (in Devonshire) and Caithness play a rather important part in Geoffrey of Monmouth. See book i. ch. 15, ii. ch. 15, iii. ch. 5, iv. ch. 16, ix. ch. 1 and 3.

In cases touching life and limb, fifteen days or fourteen nights elapsed between the accusation and the duel, and if in the interval the defender died, the code declares, 'The body of him shall be carried to the march on the day and to the place appointed betwixt the parties, for no man can essoin himself by death.' A stern conception this insistence on the appearing of the 'cited dead.'[1]

The cited dead.

Where the appellant came not, and the defender duly appeared, he crossed the march to take 'handwarsil,' *i.e.*, three persons to witness that he had appeared at the appropriate spot to do battle on his due day, and that he was quit of the claim for ever. If any of these witnesses proved a backslider by refusing his evidence afterwards, if the lost claim happened to be renewed, the person aggrieved might bring defective memories to task by fighting any one of the witnesses, or, if need be, all the three.

If a borderer tracked and found on the other side of the march goods or cattle which he claimed as his, and if the person in whose possession they were found denied the claim, this was a clear case for the duel, for it was a root principle of march law that there could be no proof by witnesses—there could only be probation by the body of a man.

A waif beast

The wads or pledges of a march criminal became security for the accuser's claim. If he had no pledges,

[1] 'Sir Amadace' (one of 'Three Metrical Romances,' Camden Socy.), turns gruesomely on the arrest of a dead body for debt.

and was convicted by duel, all the goods he had on the day of his arrest accrued to the accuser. 'But all such,' says an obscure passage in the code, 'ought to fight as men passing out of prison.' The march laws say that it is a natural result of the restriction of proof to proof by duel that many battles rise concerning records and judges in pleas mooted at the march.

Midstream of Esk and Tweed.

An appropriate close to this account of the code of 1249 is its unique alternative to the duel provided for a man who had at first denied a pursuer's claim to stolen cattle, but afterwards changed his mind, preferring a tardy honesty to a dangerous persistence, and determined not to fight after all. On the appointed battle day, instead of making for the Lochmabenstane or Reddenburn, spear and sword in hand, he went in peaceful guise with the stolen beast. Into the Esk or the Tweed he drove it, and if it passed the midstream in safety, he was free of all claim. But if it sank before the midstream was passed, he was answerable for it, according to the custom of the marches.[1]

Some glimpses of practice of march law at the end of the 13th century add a little to what is known of the system. On 3rd November, 1292,[2] a court was held at Carlisle, presided over by Hugh de

[1] At that time the Esk was the boundary between the realms. In the 13th century the Debatable Land was undoubted Scotch territory.

[2] A date which appears in the extant roll, Stevenson's Hist. Doc. R.S. i. 357, checked by the statement in the Lanercost chronicle (Mait.) 147.

Cressingham, that pompous prelate, hated as bitterly by the English as by the Scots, whose body some five years later lay amongst the dead at Stirling bridge. In the court an inquest stated[1] that if a man did a felony in Scotland he was taken 'to a certain place which is called Sulwat, at the marches of the realms,' and there the accuser appealed him and claimed heavy damages for his goodwill. The captive found wads for the damages, and if in the duel he had the victory he was acquitted, but if conquered the appellant received two parts only—that is, two-thirds[2]—of his claim. If he could find no wads he was wont to be handed over to the accuser to do his will upon him. 'This custom,' said the inquest, 'prevailed until the time of our present lord the king, who repudiated it about the ninth year of his reign.'

Inquest at Carlisle.

There is here an obvious reference to a case of the year 1280, still happily extant.[3] Henry Scot had bought a horse at the fair of Carlisle, and he complained to the sheriff of Cumberland that John of Wyncheles had appealed him of theft by law of march, according to which Henry, if unable to find securities to pay John whatever he claimed as damages, even if it were £1000, must undergo judgment as lawfully convicted. An inquiry was ordered, and the inquest declared

Handwarcel.

[1] Stevenson's Hist. Doc. Scotland R.S., i. 357, *et seq.*

[2] It has been suggested that the other third went to meet expenses.

[3] Bain's Cal. ii. No. 183.

that there had been a custom from a time whereof no memory existed that a Scotch robber must be sued within forty days, and that the pursuer was entitled to 'handwarcel' with spear and sword and targe. The record of the inquest is somewhat mutilated, but its fragments suffice to make it clear that the jurors of 1292 accurately stated what had been the law before 1280, that an accused who could find no securities was liable to be handed over to his accusers 'to do justice concerning him at their will.' Justice in such a case, it is to be feared, would often be after the Jeddart pattern or the law of Lidford :—

I oft have heard of Lydford law,
How in the morn they hang and draw,
And sit in judgment after.[1]

Such a custom could not fail to lead to the grossest injustice, and its abrogation in 1280, which is to be gathered from the inquest of 1292, was an eminently sensible change.

CHAP. 38.—*Recorded Duels from 1155.*

IT may mitigate the severity of the charge of tediousness to which these last few chapters may possibly be open to hint that they contain what is at least an approach to an exhaustive body of the law relative to the duel in Scotland and on the Borders, brought down to the close

Precept and practice.

[1] Cited in appendix to Richard the Redeles (Camden Society's edition). Notes, p. 57.

of the 13th century. But when, after such a series of frequently conflicting enactments, the duels in which they were applied come to be considered, the reader may well be astonished to find that the duels and the enactments bear something like the ratio of Falstaff's bread and sack. The recorded 12th and 13th century Scotch duels make a beggarly array.

The chronicle of Holyrood contains a brief but pregnant passage to the effect that on 3rd March, 1155, 'Arthur, a traitor to the king, died in single combat.' Here evidently was a case of treason tried by battle.[1] The king in question was Malcolm IV. surnamed the Maiden.

In the reign of his successor, William the Lion, it may be remembered that the chartulary of Scone gives decisive proof of the practice of the duel in an island of the Tay.[2]

Hoddom, an ancient parish in Dumfriesshire, rich in ecclesiastical tradition, gave its name to the powerful border family of De Hodelme, holding lands in both countries as vassals of the Bruces, lords of Annandale.

Robert of Hoddom.

Udard, the first steward of Annandale on record, was probably the founder of the family. In the later years of the 12th century, a long dispute regarding the manors of Gamelsby and Glassonby in Cumberland had broken

[1] Anno MCLIV. (1154-5) Arturus regem proditurus iii. Martii duello periit. Chronicon Sanctæ Crucis (Bann.) 32. Hailes' Annals, sub anno 1154.

[2] Scone Chart. 36. See ch. 24.

out between Richard Fitz Troite and Robert de Hodelme, engendering bitter animosities. It is hinted that it was from this cause that in the year 1199 Richard Fitz Troite accused the Annandale baron of treason to Henry II. The case thus falls properly into English law, but its international bearing may give it a place here. The charge was that Robert had abandoned the King of England and allied himself with King William of Scotland, and Richard added that he had already made this appeal before King Henry himself, when Robert had not dared to defend and had therefore been expelled from the court. 'If he shall deny this,' said the appeal, 'Richard offers probation by his body or that of his freeman.'

Richard de Hodelme denied the felony word by word as a man of sixty years and more, or by his son,[1] and declared that the appeal was made out of malice by Richard in hopes of getting him disinherited. In the end the appeal was quashed; Richard Fitz Troite was fined, and the baron of Hoddom acquitted.

Between the years 1208 and 1213 Robert of Line in Peeblesshire granted a charter[2] to the bishop of

[1] Bain's Cal. i. No. 280. This is one of those cases presenting the features of an offer by the accuser to prove by a freeman, and by the accused to defend by his son as champion. No actual and authentic case of this being permitted is known. The doctrine of the treatises is that in cases of age and mayhem the country was their champion; that is, that aged and maimed persons must be tried by assize. See ch. 15.

[2] Glasgow Chart. 76.

Glasgow. On his list of witnesses appears Waldev, the champion.[1] As the champion in the plea of felony was the creature of the statute of Scone in 1230,[2] Waldev is a most valuable witness. The existence of such an occupation as his in Scotland twenty years before the statute of Scone is, in view of English analogies and the floating fragments of Scots law, confirmation strong for the opinion that the judicial duel was still practised in Scotland in pleas of land in the opening decades of the 13th century.

'Waldevo pugile.'

On 19th March, 1230-31, following close upon the statute of Scone, Alexander II. issued a remarkable writ on behalf of the monks of Melrose.[3] It commanded that whenever complaint should be made of malefactors who had theftuously taken the avers (that is, the cattle) or money of the brethren of the convent the sheriffs should pursue the cause as they would one of the king's own, making the requisite appeals and answers, 'and on our behalf finding, if by chance there shall be need, a champion for the foresaid monks and friars.'[4] This curious writ shews the statute of Scone in operation, whereby any holder of lands by charter might

Champions for monks of Melrose.

[1] Waldevo pugile.

[2] See ch. 34.

[3] Melrose Chartulary (Bann.) 161-2. The date is 19th March of 17th year of Alexander's reign. He acceded on 4th December, 1214.

[4] Appellationes et responsiones contra ipsorum malefactores secundum genus cause sue facientes, et pugnatorem si forte opus fuerit ex parte nostra eisdem monachis et fratribus invenientes.

do the fighting by champion in appeals of felony. The brethren of Melrose were to be provided with a champion, if need were, a saving clause glancing sideways at the other statute in the group of 1230[1] which in most cases would dispense with any such necessity.

The swineherd of Coldingham.

Two charters of undetermined date, between 1240 and 1260, are of high interest. The one is a grant to the priory of Coldingham, and the other is a confirmation of it. By the first, John, formerly swineherd of Coldingham in north-east Berwickshire, gave to God and St. Cuthbert and St. Ebba three acres and a-half, with a toft and croft in Great Riston, 'which Richard, the son of Adam of Riston, gave me for a duel which I undertook for him, and in which I conquered.'[2] It was probably at or about the same time as this first charter that the second was granted by which the above-named Roger, the son of Adam of Riston, confirmed to the priory those three acres and a-half which he had given to John, formerly swineherd of Coldingham, 'for a certain duel which he undertook for me and in which he conquered,'[3] and which acres

1 See ch. 34, p. 113-4.

2 Quas mihi Rogerus filius ade de Riston dedit pro duello quod pro eo manucepi et vici. Raine's North Durham, No. cccxcvii. The witnesses were Wm. de Mordington, Alan de Swynton, Thomas de Nesbit, Adam de Prendergest, and Robert de Prendergest. Riston, now Reston, is in Coldingham parish.

3 Quas dedi Johanni Condam *(sic)* porcario de Coldingham pro quodam duello quod pro me cepit et vicit. Raine's North Durham, No. cccxcviii. Only one witness's name is given—Wm. de Lindesay.

John had given to the priory and monks of Coldingham. The ex-swineherd's charter of his field of blood has few companions in Britain. In Scotland it has none.

CHAP. 39.—*A Great Trial, 1242.*

TO the year 1242 belongs the most remarkable trial recorded in Scottish history. Patrick, the youthful and handsome earl of Athole, had been present at a tournament at Haddington—a *hastiludium* which, as Bower quaintly says, ended in a *juguludium*,[1] or cutting of throats. In the course of the tilting Patrick the earl unhorsed[2] Sir Walter Bisset, who it is said bore his defeat so ill that he planned a lawless and cruel revenge. The Lanercost Chronicle states that Sir Walter's wife sent a warning letter to the victim. If so her kindly purpose failed. That night in his inn at Haddington the young earl was drugged and murdered, and to hide the deed the house itself was set on fire. So said some. Certain it is

Sir Walter Bisset.

[1] Bower ix. ch. 59-60-61. Lanercost Chronicle (Mait.) 49-50. Although Matthew Paris is followed in some points, especially in the view that it was Sir Walter and not Sir Wm. Bisset who was concerned in this strange story, it is obvious that both Wyntoun (vii. ch. 9) and Bower were drawing upon extant sources of information. Bower has therefore in the main been relied upon in this account. See further regarding this in Hailes' Annals, sub anno 1242. Bain's cal. i. preface p. xxxvii.

[2] M. Paris, Cron. Maj. iv. 200. Walterus Bisset . . jacturam incurrit prævalente quodam nobili Paterico filio Thomæ de Galeweia.

that in the morning only a blackened corpse was recovered from the smouldering ruin. The guilt of Bisset was loudly proclaimed in the country, and he was brought to trial. He offered to prove his innocence either in single combat against any knight, or by the oaths of whatever worthy knights they wished. In other words, he offered proof by battle or by compurgation. But the earls who were his accusers, and also sat amongst his judges, would accept neither alternative. 'Would he put himself,' they asked, 'upon the visnet?'[1] This he refused to do because of the ill-will of the people and the inexorable hatred of his adversaries.[2] Wyntoun's account of this trial omits the proposal for compurgation, mentioning only battle and assize.

Battle, compurgation, and visnet.

> He profferryd wyth his body
> To put that fra hym apertly;
> Bot he wald on na wys
> Thar-off bynd hym till assys.[3]

Ultimately, 'by the judgment and counsel of all the nobles of Scotland,'[4] Bisset with all his kin was out-

1 Offerens seipsum in singulari conflictu contra militem quemlibet hoc probaturum, vel per juramenta militum emeritorum quorumque vellent se innocentem ostensurum. Comites vero quicquid oblatum fuerat respuerunt, interrogantes tamen si vellet se committere juramentis compatriotarum, et super viciniam se ponere. Bower ix. ch. 60.

2 M. Paris describes Bisset as 'offerens corpus suum ad disrationandum judicialiter coram rege et curia sua innocentiam ejus contra quemcumque armis et viribus præpotentem,' but the accusers would not hear of this, because the manifest enormity of the deed needed no proof. M. of Paris Chron. Maj. iv. 201.

3 Wyntoun vii. ch. 9.

4 Bower ix. ch. 61.

lawed and exiled. He vowed to journey to the Holy Land and to be a life-long pilgrim there for the good of the dead earl's soul. Needless to say, the vow was not kept, and he returned to die in 1251, 'far off in Scotland,' said a Yorkshire jury, 'in a certain island called Arran.'[1] His trial is unique, shewing side by side in one case the three systems—battle, compurgation, and visnet. The mode adopted—the judgment of his peers—was in harmony with a statute[2] of David I. The case may, however, have been the occasion of a clause[3] in an enactment of 1244 to the effect that any knight indicted of crime should pass to a visnet or assize of knights or hereditary freeholders.

CHAP. 40.—*Merse and Kyle, 1264-66.*

THE early records of the Scotch Exchequer must have been a mine of wealth as rich in Scottish law and history as the Pipe Rolls are for England. Alas, that the shreds and patches saved from the 13th century are so few! But though few, they are laden with meaning. A brief entry in 1264 reads thus:—'Item, for the costs of two approvers, 52s. 6d.' This might go to show that justice at the hand of the informer, so prominent in the law of England, was known to

Facts from Exchequer Rolls, 1264.

1 'Araane.' Bain's cal. i. No. 1836.

2 Scots Acts i. 318; ass. Dav. ch. 5.

3 Scots Acts i. 403; stat. Alex. II. ch. 14.

Scots law also.[1] But as it is believed to be the sole evidence on the point, and as the account from which it is taken relates to the Northumbrian Tynedale, then an appanage of the Scottish crown, the conclusion cannot be drawn.

Another valuable item is from a Roxburghshire account of the same year. It relates to the 'wad' or pledge of a man of the Abbot of Jedburgh for a duel fought in the Merse.[2]

Monks of Melrose and the duel.

The monks of Melrose—for whom Alexander II. was so desirous to find champions, if need were—owned lands in many a shire. They had large possessions in Ayrshire lying within the sphere of the influence of the Stewards of Scotland. These ancestors of the Stewart kings already had their seat in that county at Dundonald, which in after years was a favourite residence of their descendants, and is now a massive but fast crumbling ruin. On 25th March, 1266, Alexander the Steward granted to the monks their charter of the liberties of Kyle.[3] It gave them the right to hold courts wherever they pleased within their lands. If in pleas concerning theft or other crimes they wished to take visnet, the vassals of the Steward were to be commanded to attend and make the visnet[4] along with the tenants or vassals of the abbey. Any one convicted of theft or

[1] Exch. Rolls, i. 25. Item in expensis duorum probatorum, 52s. 6d.

[2] Exch. Rolls, i. 29. Plegio cujusdam hominis Abbatis de Jedwoth pro duello facto in Marchia.

[3] Melrose Chart. 286-7.

[4] Ad visnetum faciendum.

other crime for which he ought to suffer death was after judgment to be delivered to the officers to be punished according to the doom given; but the escheat was the abbey's—the brethren were to have the convict's chattels. 'And,' says the Steward, by a special clause[1] of this valuable charter, 'if in the said court the duel shall be adjudged between any, after such adjudication the duel shall be fought in our land, and the chattels and escheats of the slain shall belong to the abbot and convent.'

Nothing could shew better than this that in 1266 the two modes of trial were visnet and battle. As might be expected there is no mention of the ordeal. It had died by statute, and compurgation was passing away.

CHAP. 41.—*Baron Courts of the Bruces, 1292.*

THE power of pit and gallows was common in the border shires in the 13th century. In England the Crown was gradually absorbing all minor jurisdictions and thus strengthening its own central authority. In Scotland there is little to shew that the assize of Stirling in 1180[2] had proved of much avail. The statute law of Scotland occupies a peculiar position. In England a statute is always law until it is expressly repealed; the Act of Parliament Parliament alone can

[1] Et si in eadem curia duellum adjudicatum fuerit inter aliquos, post idem judicium idem duellum fiet in terra nostra, et catalla et escæte occisi erunt abbatis et conventus. [2] See ch. 26.

undo, and statutes do not cease to be law by desuetude. Not so in Scotland; there, desuetude and contrary practice deprive statutes of their force. This contrast in interpretation of legislative enactments not inaptly expresses the relative regard which in the past the respective nations entertained for the idea of law and order. In England statutes were laws; in Scotland they were only laws if Scotsmen chose. Without a strong central executive and system of justice—in other words, with a weak throne—the growth of constitutionalism as it grew in England was not possible.

But in England neither the idea nor its realization was the product of one reign or of one century.[1] Evidence of an early stage in its development is extant concerning Cumberland in the 13th century. Facts regarding local courts in that county—in view of the well-proved kinship and similarity of institutions at that time on both sides of the marches—may without violence be supposed to bear closely on local courts in southern Scotland. It is a point not without significance in this connection that King David, in his first charter to Robert de Brus soon after 1124, expressly gave the lands of Annandale with all the customs of Carlisle and Cumberland.[2]

Powers of local courts.

[1] The victory of the king's court over the feudal courts is interestingly discussed in Manorial Pleas (Selden Society), pref. by Professor Maitland, ch. iv.

[2] Nat. MSS. Scot. i. No. 19. Scots Acts i. 92.

The much-litigated manor of Glassonby in 1199 formed, it was suspected, a part of the ground of an appeal which nearly involved Robert de Hodelme in a duel.[1] In 1292 it had passed by descent to Christiana, wife of Robert de Brus,[2] soon to be known as competitor for the Scottish throne. A great friend both of Brus and his wife was Adam de Crokidaik, their confidential adviser and steward, destined in after years to be an English justiciar. It was the steward's function to preside in the baronial court, and accordingly, in 1292, Adam de Crokidaik was sitting as judge at Glassonby when Gilbert the Goose charged Hugh Bolare with the theft of an ox, and raised the case in the baron court of Robert de Brus.

'And the foresaid Hugh said that he had the foresaid ox by delivery and sale from one William the Long, who was present, and offered to prove by his body that Hugh never had the foresaid ox by delivery from him. And the foresaid Hugh offered himself as ready to prove the contrary by his body. Whereupon it was, by the judgment of the court, decided that there should be a duel betwixt them, which duel was waged, armed, and fought between them in such wise that the foresaid Hugh, vanquished in the duel, was, by the judgment of the said court, hanged.' Such was the pithy record of the facts made to Cressingham,

Bruce's jurisdiction.

[1] See p. 132-3. [2] Bain's Cal. ii. No. 645.

presiding, as has been already noted, in the justice-eyre at Carlisle on 3rd November, 1292.[1]

The duel and execution stirred some question as to the competency of the proceedings. Brus and his wife claimed that, from a time beyond memory, they and the lady's ancestors had been wont to determine such duels in their court. Further inquiry was made. 'Between what other persons may the duel be determined in that court in the like case?' They answered that they did not know of any other; but they said that the custom was the same throughout the whole county.[2]

The experience of Hugh Bolare, when he vouched to warrant at Glassonby and fell in the duel, supplies a very good example of the exercise of the jurisdiction of 'theam' in a baronial court.

Considering the fact that Brus was lord of Annandale, that Adam de Crokidaik was the steward or seneschal of Brus as well in Scotland as in England, and that in general the customs on both borders were much the same, it would not be surprising if, in southern Scotland at this time, especially within the ample liberties of Annandale,[3] the duel was still occasionally practised in the baronial courts.

1 Stevenson's Hist. Doc. Scot. R.S. i. 362-3.

2 Dicunt quod ipsi clamant hujusmodi duella in curia sua prædicta terminare modo prædicto et similiter ipsi et antecessores prœfatæ Christianæ uxoris ejus in curia prædicta facere consueverunt a tempore quo non extat memoria. . . . Et quæsitum inter quos alios duellum in curia prædicta in casu consimili fuerit terminatum, dicunt quod non constat eis de aliquo. Sed dicunt quod consimilis consuetudo est per totum comitatum.

3 Bain's Cal. ii. 1588.

CHAP. 42.—*By 1300.*

THE meagre annals gathered into the last five chapters constitute all that has been found incidental to the duel in practice in Scotland and on the Border prior to 1300. For the years from 1296 till 1307 there is extant a greater body of evidence than for any other period of Scottish history before the reign of Mary. Notwithstanding the fact that law does not flourish in the midst of arms, it is certain that law was not suspended by the war of independence. If the duel had been at all general, if it had prevailed even so much as it then did in England, it is almost a certainty that something would have been heard of it in the great mass of documents which are a fairly faithful picture of Scotland, as well as a record of the foiled ambition of Edward I. But the duel is not once mentioned, and the fact gains a higher significance from the almost equal silence of the next half century on the subject.

Duel believed almost extinct.

In the 13th century the kings and nobles of Scotland were extensive owners of English land. Scotsmen helped to wrest Magna Carta from King John. A Scottish lord and his wife founded and endowed one of the greatest of English colleges. It was a period of much direct intercourse and close sympathy of institutions between the two countries.

The duel had arisen in both about the same time; in both practice was analogous; and in both there are signs of the same tendency to restrict its scope, and of the same effort by the Crown to engross the jurisdiction of inferior courts. The probability that this international sympathy would lead to a contemporaneous decline is borne out by the facts so far as they go. English law was more and more trampling the duel under foot; and Scotland, advancing in civilisation with rapid stride, was little likely to cumber her progress with an institution which the sister realm had left behind. The whole circumstances warrant a hesitating conclusion (for records are indefinite), that by the year 1300 the duel in Scotland was nearer absolute extinction than in England.

Parallel with England.

Chivalry had not yet infected law. In all these voluminous Scottish fragments, in all the varied detail of English law and practice in a previous part of this book, no mention has been made of either constable or marshal. These high officials, who in after times held stately office in connection with the duel, had as yet no place there. The duel of the 12th and 13th centuries was the duel of law. With law as such constable and marshal had nothing to do.[1]

Chivalry not yet affecting law.

[1] Of course their palace jurisdiction is not here referred to. The offices of constable and marshal, as defined in the reign of Henry II., are void of connection with duels. See heraldic MS. in Record Office State Papers, James I., stating practice in time of Gilbert de Striguill,

They were officials of chivalry, and over the legal duel they had no jurisdiction until law had become tinctured with chivalry and the chivalric duel had taken a place in law. That was a future phase.

and referred to in Cal. Dom. 1619-23, 436. It has been searched expressly. See also Madox, 27-33; Dialogus de Scaccario, in Stubbs' Charters, 179-80. The Scotch so-called laws of Malcolm Mackenneth, Scots Acts i. 710, say nothing on the point. Fleta is equally silent, ii. chap. 30, 31, 74, but says that the steward (senescallus) had power to hear appeals and join duels, in the exercise of his palace jurisdiction, like any justice itinerant, ii. chap. 3. I do not find anything of this in Madox *re* Senescallus or Dapifer. Madox, 33-6. This, it will be observed, was a purely judicial function within the limits of the marshal's wand, viz.—over offences committed within twelve leagues of the king's presence. It was entirely different from the function subsequently exercised in chivalry by the constable and marshal. I cannot pretend to say what connexion existed between these functions. See Liber Quot. Contrarotulatoris Garderobæ (1787), 3, 5, 65, 92, 201. Also see note, p. 179 *infra*.

PART V.—ENGLAND, 1300-1603: LAW AND CHIVALRY.

SECTION FIRST.—THE DUEL OF LAW.

CHAP. 43.—*Continued Decline after 1300.*

SIGNS are not wanting of attempts on the part of chivalry to bring back the duel in the closing years of Edward I. But the attempts[1] were fruitless, and the rapid decline which marked its course under Henry III. and Edward I. was not checked in the reigns of their successors. In the 14th, and even the 15th centuries battle was still practised, but it had fallen from its place and the duel actually fought was rare. The process of restricting and disallowing it went on as before.[2] Nevertheless it was still the law. Approvers continued to lead a baleful and unhappy life. The malice of their appeals was often laid bare,[3] and juries much dis-

In felony appeals.

[1] Knights offering and accepting battle 'as a knight,' in plea of trespass or case of abduction; Court 'had no warrant to receive such an issue.' Year-Books, 32-33 Edward I. R.S. 318-9.

[2] *E.g.* see the Act 6 Rich. II. ch. 6, forbidding it in cases of rape.

[3] For example in 1309 two Scotch prisoners in Nottingham Castle were accused of robbery by an approver. Charge dismissed as malicious. Bain's Cal. iii. No. 86. Earlier instances, nnder Edward I., occur in Rot. Hundred. Of these the case in ii. 22b. is a good type.

liked to convict on charges made by such attainted accusers. Scores of them died in prison, and the death of many was not left to the slow process of nature. It has been stated in so many words that persons accused by approvers were almost always acquitted, and the approvers almost always hanged.[1] The approver had been found out, and the system which used him was the object of an increasing suspicion which steadily led to its abandonment.

It will be convenient to deal first with the pure duel of law—that is in ordinary appeals of felony, and in the writ of right. In the latter the duel was still a part of the procedure, but in most cases the judges took the matter in hand, a concord was effected, and the impending battle was stayed. The minuteness with which every preliminary step is detailed in some cases, is sure proof that the thing had become uncommon.

A report of a suit in 1329[2] tells how each champion with his coat ungirt, with shaven head, bare legged, bare armed,[3] and kneeling, handed his glove, with a penny in every finger,[4] to the judge. When the duel was awarded the gloves were restored to their owners, and by command of the court exchanged. Thereafter

[1] Pike i. 481. [2] Dugd. Orig. 68.

[3] Et le champion fut vestu, de sa cote desoynte, et deschevele et deschauncee des soulers, et ses maunches reverses issint que ses bras furent nuds. The shaving of champions was dropped afterwards, see Maynard's Year-Books, 1 Henry VI. p. 7, but continued in the case of approvers.

[4] For other instances of this see S. W. Beck's Gloves, their Annals, 207; Maynard's Year-Books, 30 Ed. III. p. 20; 1 Henry VI. pp. 6-7.

the parties were ordered to take their champions to two separate churches, and 'to offer there the five pennies which were in their gloves, in honour of the five wounds of God, that God might give the victory to him who was in the right.' This case terminated in a concord, and its only other notable feature is that, in the arrangements for the projected battle, the judge made the champion of the defendant stand to the north and the champion of the plaintiff to the south. For the pleasure of the court the two champions made a few passes of fence with their shields and batons,[1] the latter minus its tip of horn. After they had 'played for two turns' the court rose.

North and south.

CHAP. 44.—*The Prior of Tynemouth's Champion.*

THE romance of trial by battle on the writ of right was not dead under Edward III. Not very long before 1346, Thomas de la Mare (who became abbot of St. Alban's in 1349) was prior of Tynemouth, which, as there was occasion to remark in an early chapter, was a cell of the abbey. To the priory belonged the manor of Hawkslaw,[2]

Gerard de Widdrington.

1 Ove lour Escues et Bastons sanz Crok. I suppose the 'Crok' was the crook or tip of horn of which Britton speaks. See Maynard's Year Books, 1 Henry VI. pp. 6-7 for a writ of right case, in which it is said that the baton ought to have a knob at the end of it.

2 See charter by King John in Dugdale's Monasticon, ed. 1846, iii. 314. It also appears in 1212 and in 21 Ed. I. as priory property, iii. 316-8.

but the prior had a covetous and dangerous neighbour. Gerard de Widdrington was a scion of a border family known in song and story, descended from that Bertram de Widdrington, whose right to the vill from which the surname came had been challenged early in the reign of Henry II. by William Tasca. But after battle was duly waged on the plea, neither the envious Tasca nor his champion Alan of Driridge put in an appearance on the battle day, and the court adjudged Alan a craven, and confirmed the right of Bertram to the vill as his own proper inheritance.[1] Gerard de Widdrington laid claim to the manor of Hawkslaw.

The prior.

Not a day passed without some outrage. He kept the prior and his people in constant bodily fear. He went so far as to attempt the prior's life, and seized and tortured some Augustine friars returning from Tynemouth, under the mistaken belief that his victims were monks of the priory. Naturally the feud ended in a lawsuit about the manor.

The prior, says our gossipy chronicle, had a 'nose delicately aquiline,'[2] adding to that aristocratic endowment a pertinacity not easily outdone. He was well connected, and amongst his high-born friends included a lady of the house of Percy, who sent him jewels to defray the costs of the litigation. Besides, she sent

[1] Hodgson's Northumberland, vol. ii. part ii. p. 224. Tomlinson's Comprehensive Guide to Northumberland, 283.

[2] Vultum cum naso gratiose deducto. Gesta abbatum (St. Albans) R.S. ii. 372.

him a knight, Sir Thomas Colville by name, of great repute at the time in consequence of an encounter of his in France. A French knight on the further bank of a river had boasted that no man in all the army of England durst cross to try his mettle. And in sooth none dared to tempt the dangerous passage save Colville. He, putting his lance in rest, set spurs to his horse, swam the stream, and reached the bank in safety. Then he rode at the Frenchman, pierced him through and through, turned his horse's head and swam back—famous.

The knight proved good-at-need to the prior. When the case with Widdrington came before the court, Colville stood forth to champion the prior's cause. His unlooked for presence occasioned no little consternation. His renown had spread through all the northern shires and so great was it that none durst encounter him to test the validity of the prior's pleading. 'Wherefore,' says an annalist of St. Alban's, 'the prior's adversaries losing heart, he gained the wished for termination of the aforesaid suit.'[1]

A good champion.

A predecessor of the aquiline nosed prior had been less fortunate in his selection of a champion, but the bloodless victory of the doughty Colville may be counted a fair set-off to the defeat of William Pigun a hundred years before.[2]

[1] The foregoing narrative is from Gesta Abbatum, R.S. ii. 375-6.
[2] See ch. 16.

CHAP. 45.—*Magic*, A.D. 1355.

IN 1355 the Bishop of Salisbury brought a writ of right[1] against the Earl of Salisbury for the recovery of a castle, and battle was waged. On the due day the champions appeared. Robert Shawel, the bishop's man, was arrayed in white leather, with a red surcoat of sendal,[2] bearing the arms of the bishop. A knight carried his baton and a varlet bore his shield. The earl's champion was arrayed and attended after the same fashion, and his red surcoat of sendal was decorated with the earl's shield of arms. But when the justices examined the accoutrements, they reported that they had found some defaults in the harness of the champions, and the case was continued. It was said that in the coat of the bishop's champion they had found several rolls of prayers and charms. In the interval of continuation a concord was effected, and the castle became the property of 'Our Lady of Salisbury' for the substantial payment of 1500 marks. When the bishop died his epitaph commemorated his achievement. The figure of a champion was cut in memorial brass, and the inscription records how, like a gallant champion, *ut pugil intrepidus*, the bishop had recovered the castle, which

Prayers and charms.

1 Reported in Maynard's Year-Books, Hilary term, 29 Ed. III. p. 12.

2 Sendal, sandal, or cendal, a kind of hin rich silk. S. W. Beck's Draper's Dictionary.

had been forcibly withheld from his church for 200 years.[1]

Teufel hilf mir !

The precaution against charms in this case afforded a convenient pretext for delay when compromise was imminent. There was a very thorough belief in such magical aids and in their efficacy. On the shaven crown of the champion on the Continent characters of power were sometimes traced. A frequent form of charm was a formula of various epithets of God. In Germany invocations were at times addressed to a different quarter. 'Teufel hilf mir!' 'The Devil help me,' are the opening words of one.[2] The grave and reverend chartulary of Glasgow preserves amongst its writs and evidents, alongside of a prescription for certain famous pills, *famosæ pillulæ*, which Pope Alexander used every day[3]—a direction for the cure of a colic. The suffering brother is advised to wear a ring inscribed with the mystic words, 'Thebal Guth Guthani,' which a gloss explains as names of the deity.[4] On the fly-leaf of a MS. volume of the time of Edward I. or II., there is a copy of a charm also containing a list

1 Meyrick, ii. 43, gives the inscription. 'Pugil' had early acquired a figurative meaning. The Peterborough chronicle speaks of Bishop Gerard as 'sanctæ ecclesiæ fortissimus pugil.' See (ed. Giles) p. 86, sub anno, 1132. Used of a Scotch Bishop by Bower vi. ch. 46.

2 As to Continental charms see *Cornhill* article, 734-6.

3 Papa Alexander qualibet die eis utebatur. Glasgow Chart. 610.

4 Thebal Guth Guthani, Hoc est Deus princeps conditor conditorum, Theos enim deus, Bal princeps, Guth conditor, Guthani conditorum. Glasgow Chart. 610.

of the names of God, to be recited in cases of emergency, one of them being when in fear of a wound.[1] When Tresilian, the hated Chief-Justice of England in the time of Richard II., was dragged to execution, it is said that there were found upon him certain mystic experiments and signs, 'after the fashion of carectes,' and a devil's head and many names of devils written, and it was not until these were removed from his person that he was hanged.[2]

CHAP. 46.—*The Last Approver's Duel, A.D. 1456.*

THE approver meanwhile had fallen into great disrepute. An Act of Parliament[3] passed specially for his correction had not whipped the offending Adam out of him. A case of the year 1455 or 1456, as related in the entertaining pages of William Gregory, mayor of London in 1451, is very significant, and not without a certain rude pathos.[4] This may not be in truth the last approver's duel, but it was amongst the last; and in any event the title of this chapter will be justified by the fact that Thomas Whithorn is the last of the approvers with whom this book takes any concern.[5]

1 Pur doute de plai. Year-Books, 32-33 Ed. I. R.S. pref. 16, 17.

2 State Trials, i. 117-8. Checked with original authority.

3 5 Henry IV. ch. 2. 4 Gregory, 199-202.

5 The gradual disuse of the system is noted in Barrington, 158-9. See case under Edward III. in Rot. Parl. ii. 296. For hatred of

Whithorn, a thief, was imprisoned at Winchester. To save his life he made a series of appeals against honest men, some of whom were hanged. 'And that fals and untrewe peler hadde of the kynge every day i. d. ob.' So this false 'peler' continued for almost three years drawing his three halfpence a day and making false appeals. At last one that he appealed said he was false in his appealing, and that he would prove this with his hand, 'and spende hys lyfe and blode apone his fals body.' The judge, according to Gregory's report, laid down most peculiar law. Full courteously instructing the parties as to the conditions of an approver's duel, he explained that if the 'peler' prevailed he would go back to prison, but would fare better than before, as he would be allowed twopence a day during the king's pleasure. The combatants, he said, must be clad all in white sheep's leather, both body, head, legs, feet, face, hands, and all. The staves, three feet long, were to be of green ash, 'the barke beynge apon.' At one end each staff was to have 'a horne of yryn, i-made lyke unto a rammys horne,[1] as scharpe at the smalle ende as hit myght be made.' Then they must fight fasting. And indeed, as Gregory says, it is too shameful to rehearse all the conditions of this foul conflict. But, most singular of all was

The false 'peler.'

approver see Pike, 286-7, 481. Some law on the subject is laid down in Maynard's Year-Books, 21 Henry VI. pp. 19, 20.

[1] The 'crok' of note 1 on p. 149.

the judge's law, when he told the defendant that if in the duel he slew that 'peler,' he was to be hanged for manslaying, 'by soo moche that he hathe i-slayne the kyngys prover!' Nor should the slain man have Christian burial; he should be cast out as one that wilfully slew himself.

James Fisher, the accused, the 'meke innocent,' as Gregory sympathisingly calls him, did not shrink from battle even on these hard terms, and the day was fixed. 'Hange uppe Thome Whythorne,' said the people, for he was too strong to fight with James Fisher, the true man, with an iron ram's horn. But although the judge had pity, the battle must needs be fought.

The meek innocent.

Duly appareled in sheepskin, and armed with their formidable staves, appellant and appealed entered the place of battle near Winchester — the 'peler' entering from the east side, the other from the south-west. Full sore weeping, as the touching account of Gregory records the duel, the defendant entered with his weapon and a pair of beads in his hand, and he kneeled down upon the earth towards the east and cried, 'God marcy and alle the worlde,' and prayed every man's forgiveness, 'and every man there beyng present prayde for hym.'

Then the approver cried out, 'Thou fals trayter, why arte thou soo longe?' The defendant rose, and with the words that his quarrel was faithful and true, and that in it he would fight, he smote at the 'peler,' but broke his own weapon with the blow. One stroke only was the approver allowed to make at the defendant, then the officers took his weapon away too. A long time they fought with their fists and rested, and fought again and rested again, and then in Gregory's expressive phrase, 'they wente togedyr by the neckys.'

With their teeth they tore each other like dragons of the prime, soon their leathern coats and the flesh beneath were all 'to-rente,' and the end seemed to have arrived when 'the fals peler caste that meke innocent downe to the grownde.' But in the deadly wrestle more by hap than strength, 'that innocent recoveryd up on his kneys, and toke that fals peler by the nose with hys tethe,[1] and put hys thombe in hys yee, that the peler cryde owte and prayde hym of marcy, for he was fals unto God and unto hym.'

So the duel ended, and the judge pronounced sentence upon the approver, whose fate Gregory piously recorded thus—'And thenn he was confessyd ande hanggyd, of whos soule God have marcy. Amen.'

The victor was set free, but the memories of that terrible hour seem to have darkened his life. He became a hermit, and ere long he died. Gregory's moving story, with its warm sympathy for the accused and its hearty detestation of the accuser, is a good

[1] Fine illustration of Bracton and Fleta, that front teeth help much to victory. See ch. 15.

index to public feeling on the subject at the time. The prayers of the people were not with the approver.

CHAP. 47.—*An Elizabethan Scene, A.D. 1571.*

As far back as the 14th century battle on the writ of right had become a sham, the name of it, or little more, remaining to lend formality and finality to litigation. It had ceased to be fought, or if fought at all, the cases were exceedingly few. But all through the 15th and 16th centuries the form continued.

Paramour's case.

In Queen Elizabeth's reign it cropped up to the no small perturbation of the legal profession,[1] when Paramour, defendant in a writ of right, chose trial by battle.[2] The wager was made by the defendant's champion casting down a gauntlet[3] which the other champion took up. Duel was adjudged to take place at Tothill on 18th June 1571. Lists 60 feet square were made, and scaffolds were set around for onlookers. Defendant's champion, George Thorne, 'a big, broad, strong-set fellow,' came first. About seven in the morning plaintiff's champion, 'a proper slender man, and not so tall as the other,' by name Henry Nailer, a fencing-master, came next, heralded by drum and

[1] The phrase is Spelman's. See his Glossary, *voce* Campus.

[2] The following account is a combination from Dyer's Reports, 300-302, and Stow, 668-9.

[3] Incorrect form.

fife, and with Thorne's gauntlet carried in front of him upon a sword's point.

When the lord chief-justice was seated the champions entered the 'place,' Thorne at the north-end, Nailer at the south. They were appareled in red sendal over armour of leather, bare-legged from the knee downwards, bare-headed, and bare-armed to the elbow. Their arms were red bastons an ell long, made taper-wise, tipped with horn, and shields of hard double leather. On the appearance of the champions, Thorne passing to the south side of the 'place'—the right side of the court—and Nailer to the north, proclamation[1] was made for order and silence.

'And then was the prover,' says Stow, 'to be sworn as followeth:—This hear, you justices, that I have this day neither eat, drunk, nor have upon me either bone, stone, ne glass, or any enchantment, sorcery or witchcraft, where-through the power of the Word of God might be inleased or diminished, and the devil's power increased, and that my appeal[2] is true, so help me God and his saints, and by this Book.'

But this oath was not needed. The case had been compromised, as the justices knew, the day before. The defendant himself did not appear, and so the court gave judgment against him. Then the lord chief-justice commanded Nailer to give back to

[1] Given in full in Stow.

[2] Wrong form again. This was not an appeal.

Thorne his gauntlet. 'Whereunto,' says the ever-interesting Stow, 'the said Nailer answered that his lordship might command him anything, but willingly he would not render the said gauntlet to Thorne except he could win it; and further, he challenged the said Thorne to play with him half-a-score blows to shew some pastime to the lord chief-justice and the others there assembled, but Thorne answered that he came to fight and would not play. Then the lord chief-justice, commending Nailer for his valiant courage, commanded them both quietly to depart the field.'

An extra-judicial challenge.

Over 4000 persons were spectators, and proclamation was made that all should go home, every man in the peace of God and the Queen. Henry Spelman, then a boy of ten, was one amongst the crowd which dispersed with a shout of 'Long live the Queen.'

SECTION SECOND.—THE DUEL OF CHIVALRY.

CHAP. 48.—*A French Edict*, A.D. *1306*.

IN France as in England the duel of law had very greatly declined from its pristine importance. Philip the Fair wished to abolish what remained, but the time was scarcely ripe for positive abolition. His edict in 1306, however, allows it the narrowest limits for a duel of law.[1] For a duel of chivalry its limits were wide enough and were probably not too strictly construed. To entitle a case to be tried by combat, there were four requisites under that famous ordinance:—1. The homicide treason or other serious crime must be notorious and certain. 2. The crime must be capital, not mere larceny. 3. The combat must be the only means of obtaining conviction and punishment. 4. The accused must be notoriously suspected of the deed. A specific charge was necessary, appellants were to guard against 'saying aught villainous against the accused' which did not concern the immediate quarrel. After the appeal was made the accuser threw down his glove for a gage.[2] When the battle was adjudged the glove was lifted by the defendant. Sure pledges were found for due appearance of parties in the lists on a certain day and hour under pain of being reckoned recreant and vanquished.

Ordinance of Philip III.

The lists were made ready, and when the day of combat came it was for the appellant to be first in the field. The combatants might ride to the place of battle with visors raised and with their arms carried in front of them. It is hinted that as they rode to the scene of their deadly argument, it would shew most convincingly that they were true Christians, if as they rode they crossed themselves, or carried a

1 Quoted in full in Du Cange *voce* Duellum.

2 Doiht jetter son gaige de bataille.

crucifix or a banner with a picture of our Lord, our Lady, an angel, or a saint.

In due season the parties were summoned by a herald. Five proclamations were made for order and silence in the crowd around the barriers. No one was to bear sword or dagger—to be on horseback—to enter the lists. All were to sit down. None should dare to utter word or cry, give signal, or do the like under heavy penalty. These proclamations made, the knights, after further formality, rode into the lists through opposite gateways, crossing themselves as they did so. They were escorted to separate pavilions, that of the appellant on the judge's right—that of the other on his left.

Then came the triple oaths. Before the judge stood an image of the passion of Christ, and the appellant kneeling, with visor raised and gauntlet removed, swore on the sacred symbol that his accusation was true, and that his quarrel was holy and just, so aid him God, our Lady, and the good chevalier St. George. In like fashion the defendant swore to his innocence.

The first oath.

A second time, with their right hands on the crucifix, both knights swore together—by the sovereign joys of Paradise, which they would renounce for the pains of hell—upon their souls and honour that the quarrel was just; and again the oath closed with an appeal to God as their true judge, our Lady, and the good

Second oath.

chevalier St. George. At the same time each swore that he carried neither upon himself nor upon his horse, words, stones, herbs, charms, carectes, conjurations of devils, wherein he hoped for aid, and that he placed his sole reliance on the justice of his cause, his body, his horse, and his arms. Then they kissed the cross.

Third oath.

The third oath they swore holding each other by their right hands. Each again called God, our Lady, and the good chevalier St. George to witness the justice of his cause. They kissed the crucifix once more, and thus deeply sworn, returned to their pavilions. The solemn sanction of Christianity had been sought by an imposing ritual, and the cross was removed from the lists.

Laissez les aller.

To God and St. George the cause now stood committed. Three times the herald cried *Faites vos devoirs*, and the combatants made ready to mount. When both were fairly in the saddle, the marshal, who throughout was master of the ceremonies, rode into the centre of the lists carrying the glove which had been the gage of battle. Thrice he cried, *Laissez les aller!* The end of the long and striking ceremonial had come, and he gave the signal for action when he flung down the glove. The mailed horsemen spurred their steeds; there was the shock of splintering spears, followed, if need there were, by hand to hand battle with sword and dagger afoot; and then one of the two lay bleeding, a vanquished traitor, who had invoked in vain the aid of God, our Lady, and the good knight St. George.

CHAP. 49.—*The Rise of Chivalry.*

THE struggle of chivalry to make its way into the law has been detected in the reign of Edward I.[1] Perhaps before that time some recognition was given to knighthood in allowing a knight the privilege of defending himself as a knight when charged with felony or treason, as William de Vescy claimed in 1294. But beyond that the privilege did not go if it went so far, and even in that case the trial had arisen in the ordinary courts and under the common law. Examples from the 12th century had long ceased to be precedents. Before Edward died there were many signs of the growing influence of chivalry, of which his own fantastic vow of the Swan and his bequest of his bones for the conquest of Scotland were remarkable manifestations. Edward II. was too much of a weakling to feel the charm of

The three Edwards.

[1] See ch. 22 and 43 *supra*. Edward was himself the subject of an appeal of felony before the court of France in 1274 at the instance of Gaston of Bearn, a Gascon. The English king sent five knights across the Channel, each ready to accept battle on his behalf, but the appeal was dropped. Annals of London in Chronicles of Ed. I. and II. R.S. i. 84-5.

chivalry, and the troubles of his reign gave England other things to think of. His policy, like his father's, wisely repressed the inclination for chivalric duelling.[1] His son Edward III., however, felt the full force of the current of the time. Coming to the throne in 1327 a mere child, the half-century of his reign saw great things. It was an age in which a man of individuality in high place could not fail to wield a vast influence on contemporary manners.

Edward III. to the business capacity of his grandfather added a chivalric tendency born of the time. The young king was emphatically a man. In prosecution of his claim to the throne of France he went to war with King Philip VI. On 26th July 1340, when in the midst of the siege of Tournay, he wrote a letter[2] to Philip of Valois, as he named the French king, denying the royal title. 'To avoid the death of Christians, and as the question concerns us and you alone, the discussion of our challenge should be made between our two bodies.' This was the avowed motive of a challenge to fight Philip in single combat, or in a combat of 'a hundred persons, the most sufficient' on either side.[3] The historians who record the

A royal challenge.

1 See fines for challenges cited in Borthwick on Judicial Combats in Remarks on Brit. Antiquities, 1776, p. 16. 2 Rymer, v. 199.

3 'Pur eschuer mortalite des Cristiens ensi come la quere est apparaunt a nous et a vous que la descussion de nostre chalaunge se fesist entre nos deux corps; a la quele chose nous nous offroms.' An alternative was—'Par bataille de corps de cents persyones de plus suffisauntz de vostre part et nous autre tauns de noz gentz liges.'

challenge paraphrase its aim to have been 'the avoidance of the oppression, devastation, and slaughter of the people.'[1] But Philip accepted neither alternative, and after a while he fought and lost Creçy instead.

Saint George.

The English people, swearing terribly in Flanders and elsewhere, had begun to swear by St. George.[2] Under his banner, ranged side by side with those of St. Edmund and St. Edward, the army of England had marched in 1300 to the Scottish war.[3] But now St. George stood far in front. Of the seven champions of Christendom he was the favourite. It was St. George whom Edward himself invoked[4] again and again when engaged in that terrible single battle of his at Calais with Eustace de Ribaumont, whom at last he made his prisoner.[5] Nor was this a mere single invocation in an hour of need, for it was in honour of this saint whom he styled the protector and patron of England, that Edward had instituted the famous Order of the Garter, caused the chapel of Windsor to be consecrated, and established the Table Round.[6] To chivalry England owes her tutelar St. George, the soldier saint whom the French

1 Hemingburgh, ii. 361. Walsingham, i. 229.

2 Froissart, i. 180. This in 1349: later instances numerous. Henry V. had good precedent for his cry of 'England and St. George.'

3 Roll of Caerlaverock (Wright) 35; Liber Quot. Cont. Garderobæ (1787) 64. The ship St. George was at that time carrying engines for the siege of Caerlaverock. Lib. Gard. 70.

4 Walsingham, i. 274. Froissart, i. 180. Selden's Titles of Honor, part ii. ch. 5, § 40. Camden's Remains (1674) 443.

5 Froissart, i. 181.

Selden's Titles of Honor, part ii. ch. 5, § 40 and 43.

knights called to witness in the ordinance of Philip the Fair. It were superfluous to insist further on the potency of the chivalric tendencies of England and Edward III.

In the wake of these influences, which were to reach a climax under Richard II., there came a revival of the duel—what for lack of a better phrase may be termed the treason-duel of chivalry. It was so far a continuation of the older law. Treason had been tried in that way before, but that was long ago, and the chivalric duel differed essentially from the duel of law. It was not in the ordinary courts, and constable and marshal had duties there unknown before. At first the institution received little recognition, chivalry did not truly force its way into law until the following reign; but this chapter and the following shew the spirit of chivalry taking legal form, and the court of chivalry already in the making.

Treason duel of chivalry.

England, as Hallam has well said, did not, except from the reign of Edward III. to that of Henry VI., offer a congenial soil to chivalry as a military institution.[1] It had always been more popular on the continent, where it had bloomed earlier, and where far later it continued in flower. But in the reign of Edward III. the tendency had set strongly in, gaining power and volume from the contact with France and the personal character of the king. The appear-

[1] Hallam's Middle Ages, ch. 9, part ii. (reprint 823-4).

ance of a knight as a champion in a writ of right was an omen of danger to law. The heraldic blazons in the Bishop of Salisbury's case,[1] too, were portentous. Duels were talked of[2] and even fought[3] by the royal leave over coats of arms. These were straws marking the force of the stream. With insular restrictions the ordinance of Philip the Fair was to become the basis of English and Scotch practice. Everything foretold a renascence of the judicial duel under chivalry.

CHAP. 50.—*Precedents*, A.D. 1350–52.

ONE of the most famous of English duels took place on 4th October 1350, between two foreigners before Edward III. Sir John de Visconti, a Cyprian (an Yprian[4] according to some) challenged to single combat[5] Sir Thomas de la Marche, bastard son of that king of France whom Edward had challenged ten years before. The accusation was that Sir Thomas had taken bribes and had betrayed a Christian army to the infidel Turk. The reputa-

[1] Ch. 45 *supra*.

[2] In the case between Nicholas Lord Burnel and Robert de Morley in 1346 for the arms of Burnel, Peter Corbet in Lord Burnel's retinue challenged Morley at Calais, but the king effected a compromise. Pennant's Tour in Wales, ii. 419.

[3] Duel fought at Berwick before Edward III. between Sir John de Sitsilt and Sir John de Faukenham for the arms now worn by the Cecils. Kendall, 165-6. Neither reference nor date given.

[4] Walsingham, i. 275. Ypres in Flanders.

[5] The following account is taken from Galfridus le Baker, 208-9-10; Stow, 251; Meyrick, ii. 32.

tion of Edward for valour and chivalry explains the adoption of that prince as the judge of two foreigners. It was a compliment to England bitterly resented in high quarters in France.

At Westminster the battle was fought within the bounds of the royal palace. A trumpet blast was the signal for attack. At the first shock the spears were shivered against the shields without unhorsing either knight. Promptly alighting they drew their swords and fought on foot. But after a time, victory declaring for neither side, the swords of both were rendered useless, and the knights grappling fell in fierce wrestle. The visors of their helmets were guarded with small bars of steel. At all other points the combatants were girt with impenetrable armour. When they rose the Frenchman, with certain short, sharp pricks of steel fastened on the knuckles of his right gauntlet—'pricks,' says a contemporary writer,[1] 'which the moderns call "gadelinges"'—struck through the helmet bars at the face of his opponent, who, having no gadlings,[2] could not return the blows. Repeated wounds on the face forced the Cyprian to yield. King Edward threw down his baton, the marshal[3] cried 'Ho!' and the combat ceased. The vanquished knight became the prisoner of the victor, but Sir Thomas chivalrously

The value of gadlings.

1 Galf. le Baker, 208.

2 See S. W. Beck's 'Gloves,' 72.

3 I take the facts in this sentence from Meyrick. He may have had authority for them, but I have not traced it.

gave his captive to the Prince of Wales, and devoutly made an oblation of his armour to St. George in the church of St. Paul's.

The Prince of Wales at once set the vanquished Cyprian free, and English history hears of him no more. On the other hand, it is painful to record that the gallant and victorious Sir Thomas, on his return to his own country, where a jealous brother reigned, was beheaded for high treason to France, because of his fighting the duel in the court of the English king.

Dangers of perjury.

In 1352, Henry, Duke of Lancaster, a high-spirited soldier, learnt that Otto, son of the Duke of Brunswick, had purposed to take him prisoner when he was journeying 'against the enemies of Christ.' He therefore in public repeated this charge of a treasonous plot. Otto wrote giving him the lie, and offering to maintain his honour, body to body.[1] Lancaster at once accepted the challenge, and in the lists before the French king he and Otto met. Knyghton says that before Otto took the oath there was not to be seen a knight handsomer or more gallant than he, but no sooner had he sworn than his countenance fell and his cheek grew pale and he could hold neither shield, nor sword, nor lance. Such, according to Knyghton, were the dire effects of a false oath! In fact Otto either was ill, or as some

[1] Knyghton, 2603-4, gives terms of challenge. Accounts of the duel are given also by Galf. le Baker, 220-2; Stow, 254; Walsingham, i. 279

chronicles have it, feigned illness. This was observed, the king took the case in hand and stopped the duel, but 'Otto was commanded first to depart the lists, and so went his way.'

Precedents at home and abroad were multiplying for English practice.

CHAP. 51.—*Transmarine Treason, A.D. 1380–84.*

HUMAN nature, Walsingham truly if tritely observes, delights not only in changes but in unwonted things. In the year 1380, says that fluent St. Albans historian,[1] whose words will be often closely quoted in this chapter, a new thing was seen in England. In the reign of Edward III. Sir John Annesley, a knight, made a charge of treason against his squire, Thomas Katrington, who had been keeper of a castle in France. The squire, so the knight asserted, had sold and surrendered the castle to the French in the year 1375, when neither men nor stores were lacking for its defence. He therefore challenged him to battle. On this charge the squire was imprisoned for a time, but when Edward lay on his deathbed he was set free. The knight in vain sought redress, 'some asserting that it was against the laws of the realm that any Eng-

Knight and squire.

[1] Walsingham, i. 430-4. All the annalists record this celebrated case, but Walsingham gives a particularly good description.

lishman should fight in terms of any such law.' After several years, however, early in the reign of Richard II., it was settled, against the better judgment of the lawyers and older knights of the land, *coactis juridicis et senioribus militibus regionis*, that for a foreign plea in a cause arising beyond the realm and across the seas—a case of transmarine treason[1]—the duel was quite lawful on being duly notified to the constable and marshal and fought before them.

The 7th of June 1380 was the day of battle, and wooden lists were made at Westminster, 'as strong as if they had been meant to last for ever.' An immense body of people flocked to the spectacle. So great was the multitude that it far exceeded the number of those who had gone to witness the coronation a few years before.

Early in the morning the king took his seat. And soon, 'as the manner is, the knight in his armour rode up on a charger decently caparisoned, for the appellant must enter the place first to be ready for the coming of the defendant.' In an hour's time the squire was called with three trumpet blasts, 'Thomas Katrington, defendant, appear to defend thy cause for which John de Anneslee, knight and appellant, has appealed thee in public and by writ!' At the third trumpet blast the squire rode forward, armed, on a charger royally caparisoned, and with his horse-cloths bearing the

Entry of the combatants.

[1] Note terms of Act 13 Rich. II. cited in next chapter.

arms of Katrington. As he neared the lists he dismounted, lest in accordance with the customs of battle the constable should claim the horse if it entered the lists. But as the rather unfriendly historian remarks, 'his astuteness availed him nothing, for the horse, prancing near the lists, thrust its head and neck a little over the barriers, whereupon the constable, Sir Thomas of Woodstock,[1] claimed the horse and swore he would have its head at any rate, viz., as much of it as had come within the lists.'[2] The horse was adjudged the constable's.

Points preliminary.

The squire entered the lists on foot, and the indenture previously made containing the articles of accusation and defence was read. The squire's conscience pricked him, and he tried to take some objection. But he was sharply told that unless, according to the conditions of the duel and the laws of arms, he owned the accuracy of the indenture he would be reckoned a traitor and hanged without parley. On this he bluntly said that he durst fight with the knight, not on that plea only but in any quarrel in the world—a remark which suggested the

1 Uncle of the king, author of the Ordinance of Battel, often cited hereafter.

2 By the Ordinance, 'The Mareschall's fee is all the wepyns, horses, and armures, as wele of the appelaunt as of the defendaunt, whereof they have dismyssed theym or letyn from theym after that they ben entred into the lists.' Dugd. Orig. 85. This is not mentioned in the Black Book, i. 300-329. Evidently, as it was the squire who was challenged, the fight was to be on foot.

historian's comment, that he trusted more in the force of his valour than in the justice of his cause, for he was great of stature, whilst the knight was less than middle-sized.

The knight was first to take the oath, 'as is the custom,' and then the squire swore also that his cause was true, that he was not conscious of any magic art by which he might gain the day, and that he bore neither herb nor stone, such as evil-doers used to aid them against their foes.[1] These preliminaries over, prayer was devoutly offered and the battle began.

They fought for a long time, first with spears, then with swords, last of all with daggers. At length the knight disarmed the squire, closed with him, and threw him. Then he prepared to fling himself with all the weight of his armour on his prostrate foe, but a strange mishap, the proverbial slip 'twixt cup and lip, befell. The long fight had completely exhausted him, the sweat running down his brows under his helmet obscured his sight, and instead of tumbling heavily upon his adversary as he intended, he missed him and fell down by his side. The

In dubious strife.

A dead lock.

[1] Quod non erat conscius ullius artis magicæ per quam de adversario posset reportare victoriam nec gestabat super se herbam aut lapidem nec experimenti genus quibus solent malefici de hostibus triumphare. This part of the oath in the Ordinance (Black Book version, i. 317) is 'ne stone of vertue, ne herbe of vertue, ne charme, ne experiment, ne carocte ne other inchauntment by the, ne for thee.' In the French version 'carocte' is 'carecte.' It means a special kind of written mystic 'character.'

squire though sorely exhausted seized his opportunity, quickly raised himself, and threw his body across the knight's.

A great hubbub arose; some cried that the knight was beneath, and was therefore vanquished—others said he would soon rise and gain the victory. The king ordered proclamation for silence and commanded that the knight should be raised. When the officers went to obey the order the knight implored them to let him lie exactly as he was, for all was well with him and he would yet win the day. But he was too much worn out to shake off the dead weight of the squire and he was lifted. No sooner was this done than he ran to the king and asked as a favour to be put back in the same position with the squire over him. He had noticed that the squire was nearly dead in consequence of his extraordinary efforts in the long duel, and the heat and weight of his armour. Meanwhile the squire had been raised also, but could neither walk nor stand unaided, and had been set in a chair in the lists.

Victory.

When the king and his nobles saw how eagerly the knight desired that the battle should be renewed, and how he even offered a great sum of money for that purpose, they decreed that the combatants should be replaced in their former positions, the squire above, the knight below, 'in accordance with wonted custom.'[1] But suddenly

[1] The Ordinance directs the constable and marshal to 'take gode

the squire fell from his chair as if he were dead. Wine and water were promptly taken to him, but they were of no use until he was stripped of his armour. 'Which fact proved the knight the victor, and the squire the vanquished.' After a long delay the squire somewhat revived, raised his head and looked fiercely around. The knight, who had laid aside none of his armour from the beginning of the fight came up to him, and glaring into his eyes called him a false traitor, and dared him to fight again. But there was neither sense nor spirit left to answer; it was proclaimed that the long battle was over; and the traitor-squire was carried home to bed to die next morning raving in delirium. The issue of the duel gave great satisfaction. Walsingham, with a congenial fling at the Earl of Lancaster, says that it occasioned 'the delight of the people and the grief of traitors.' Adam of Murimuth concluded that it afforded great evidence of the truth of the knight's cause, seeing that the death of the squire was the result.[1] Probably Adam's conclusion was sounder than his logic.

The end of the squire.

Walsingham[2] records another duel on 30th November 1384, of the same kind, fought at London.

kepe how they ben departed, so that they be in the same estate and degree in all things yf the Kynge wole suffer or do them go ayen togidir.' Dugd. Orig. 84 (compare also 78), Black Book, i. 323. A very curious instance of this in a feat of arms appears in Hall, 268.

[1] Adam de Murimuth, 239-40.

[2] Walsingham, ii. 118; Appx. to Higden's Polychronicon, R.S. ix. 53.

Martigo de Vilenos, a Navarrese, appealed John Walsh, an Englishman, of treason. Treason was not the true motive of the appeal; it arose out of what Selden slily calls a 'close combat' of a domestic nature. Vilenos was vanquished, and despite the queen's intercession paid the penalty of a false appeal of treason, and was himself hanged and drawn as a traitor. The constable and marshal, one chronicle[1] says, condemned him to be drawn and hanged, and the king consented to the sentence being carried out 'lest such appeals should become too many in the land.'

CHAP. 52.—*The Court of Chivalry.*

THE last chapter records more than the victory of knight over squire, it records a conquest of law by chivalry. In the end chivalry had forced the citadel of law. When Richard II. was still but a lad, his uncle, Thomas of Woodstock, the Constable of England, whom we have already seen in the lists at Westminster, wrote his famous Ordinance containing the rules of the duel in chivalry. Originally written in French, it was an adaptation to English practice of a development of the edict of Philip the Fair. Its forms were very faithfully observed in the trial of Katrington.[2]

Richard II.

[1] The Appx. to Higden.

[2] A very complete idea of the Ordinance may be gathered from a future Scotch chapter titled 'The Order of Combats,' and from foot-

King Richard, in the seventh year of his reign, on 8th September 1383, when in the first blush of youth, made overtures for a duel with Charles VI. to decide their rival rights to the crown of France. He was willing either to submit the question to the judgment of the Most High by single combat, or by a combat in which each monarch should have his three uncles as companions. To stay the effusion of Christian blood and the desolation of the land was the reason assigned in the suggested challenge[1]—a conscious or unconscious repetition of the terms of the challenge of Edward III. to Philip VI. But the suggestion came to nothing, and as the first had not stayed the battle of Creçy the second did not hinder the battle of Agincourt.[2]

The court of chivalry—its jurisdiction.

Richard was fond to excess of tilt and tournament, a taste which led him to cultivate the court of chivalry. The treason duel became an established branch of law, with marshal and constable as officials of law and chivalry combined. The court thus newly

notes to ch. 51 and 53. Two versions have been used: Dugdale's, which belonged to John Selden, and another which got into the Admiralty Black Book through the two offices of High Admiral and High Constable being held by one person. The former version is in Dugd. Orig. 79-86; the latter in the Black Book, i. 301-29.

[1] Rymer, vii. 407-8. Quòd negotium tam arduum in evitationem sanguinis plurimorum foret inter personas quas immediate concernit, Nostri, viz., et præfati Adversarii sub Speculatoris Supremi Judicio terminatum.

[2] The last half of this sentiment is eloquently expressed in Pike, i. 393-4.

established in the opening years of Richard, although it had existed in an inchoate form in the time of the previous king,[1] was regarded with great suspicion by the Commons, who complained that it encroached on the common law. Acts were therefore passed in the eighth and thirteenth years of his reign, narrating the complaint, and restricting and defining the jurisdiction.[2] The second of these statutes declared that to the constable belonged 'the cognisance of contracts touching deeds of arms and of war out of the realm, and also of things touching arms or war within the realm, which cannot be determined or discussed by the common law.' But whilst Parliament misliked the duel, the king had seen within its own walls, a year or two before, a challenge taken up by a whole political faction as if they had been one man.

A challenge in Parliament.

Sir Nicholas Brembre, mayor of London, had had the ill fortune to adhere to the king's party, which for the time was the losing side. In Parliament in February 1388, he was charged with treason in the king's presence. Indignantly denying the charge, Brembre offered to defend himself as a knight by battle against any accuser. His challenge did not wait long for

[1] As I take it the court of chivalry had at first only an unofficial character, something like that which the Jockey Club now exercises in its own sphere. But as is shewn it became a legal tribunal. I regret that my opportunities of historical study do not enable me to trace more fully and formally the gradual rise of the court of chivalry, and to examine its connexion with, and probably origin from, army law. See p. 146.

[2] 8 Rich. II. ch. 5; 13 Rich. II. ch. 2.

an answer; the chiefs of the opposing faction declared their readiness to meet him in the lists by throwing their gloves at the king's feet.[1] 'And on a sudden,' says an old narrative, 'like snow[2] there flew from every side the gloves of the other lords, knights, esquires, and commons, crying with one voice, "We also will accept the duel to prove these things to thy head."'

But Parliament resolved that battle did not lie in that case. There was a shorter road to judgment, and without duel Brembre met a traitor's doom.

CHAP. 53.—*In Chaucer.*

IT was at this time of tilt and tournament, in the hey-day of the court of chivalry in the England of Richard II., that Chaucer lived and transferred to his page of 'English undefiled' his bright, true, and unfading descriptions of life. The 'Canterbury Tales' were not written before 1386. English antiquaries, from Camden and Selden and Dugdale downwards, have turned to them again and again for light on points of law and history. Need a Scottish pen fear to follow their great example?

Readers of early English verse who are not lawyers, and lawyers who are not readers of early English

[1] State Trials, i. 114-5, checked with original authority.

[2] Tanquam nix, undique in toto volabant chirothecæ. My friend Mr. S. W. Beck, author of 'Gloves and their annals,' will no doubt see in this image a proof that the gloves were white.

verse, may be surprised to learn that it is studded with legal figures of speech. Grossteste gave Adam 'seisine' in the bliss of paradise.[1] Robert of Gloucester distinguished between descent and purchase as accurately as his Scotch copyist did between heritage and conquest.[2] Barbour put the words 'lege powysté' into the mouth of King Robert the Bruce.[3] Chaucer knew precisely what champerty[4] implied, and Gower declared that the three Gorgons held their one eye 'in purpartie.'[5] Wyntoun made Scotland a feudal holding by ward and relief 'off God hymselff immedyate.'[6] The tendency was handed down to later times. Ballad literature, both English and Scotch, abounds in the terminology of antique law.[7] Spenser is not innocent of legal metaphors,[8] while Shakespeare used so many that Lord Campbell[9] deemed them a half-proof, considerably more than a suspicion, that the swan of Avon was once perched in an attorney's office. Last to be named here, a central

Law in the poets.

1 Chasteau d'amour (ed. M. Cooke, 1852) lines 129-31 French, 51 English.

2 Spec. Early English, part ii. 1873, i. (A) lines 505-6; Wyntoun, vii. ch. 2, lines 180-190. See N and Q 7 S, iv. 126, and vii. 117.

3 The Bruce, ed. Jamieson, iv. line 165.

4 Knight's Tale, line 1091.

5 Confessio Amantis (Morley, 1889) 55.

6 Wyntoun, vi. prologue line 20.

7 See examples in Ritson's Robin Hood Ballads (Routledge) 'borwe' 158, 'wedde' 151, 'grithe' 438.

8 *E.g.* livery and seisin. Faerie Queen, vi. canto 4, st. 37.

9 'Legal acquirements of Shakespeare.'

pivot of Paradise Lost turns upon an analogy from the punishment of high treason.[1] When law in general has lent so much to literature, it excites no wonder to find in Chaucer's tales the influence of trial by battle.

Langland, brooding over the iniquity of the time in his Richard the Redeless, draws a dark picture of the institution.[2]

> They constrewed quarellis to quenche the peple,
> And pletid with pollaxis and poyntis of swerdis;
> And at the dome yevynge drowe out the bladis,
> And lente men levere of her longe battis.

But Chaucer, soldier and courtier as well as poet, saw with kindlier if less searching eye than the sombre dreamer on Malvern hills. To him the romantic side appealed, and one of his poems is charged with a technicality which hitherto has escaped full recognition by his editors, but which shews beyond question his minute knowledge of that pleading with pole-axe and point of sword which the author of Piers the Plowman so bitterly condemned.

Langland and Chaucer.

The tale of Palamon and Arcite[3] is to some men's thinking the noblest product of Chaucer's genius. He found as was his wont an old story, but he breathed into it the breath of a new and never-dying life,

[1] Paradise Lost, iii. lines 200-210. For Milton on 'Force and Fear,' see iv. 97; 'Approbate and Reprobate,' x. 758-9.

[2] Richard the Redeless, lines (circa) 331 of passus iii.

[3] Knight's tale in Canterbury Tales. Clarendon Press edition by Dr. Morris has been used, and most of the glossarial notes are from that admirable work.

leaving it instinct with the music of his time, and sounding every note in the diapason of chivalry.

Palamon and Arcite conduct their quarrel on true legal lines from the outset. Arcite in Palamon's view was precluded by bond of fealty and friendship from pretending to the love of Emelye, but Arcite pled that love was free and denied the claim.

'The Knightes Tale.'

> For I defye the seurté and the bond
> Which that thou seyst that I have maad to the.
> What verray fool, think wel that love is fre!
> And I wol love hire mawgre[1] al thy might;
> But, for as muche as thou art a worthy knight,
> And wilnest to derreyne[2] hire by batayle,
> Have heer my trouthe, to-morwe[3] I nyl not fayle.

To this Palamon agrees.

> And thus they ben departed[4] til a-morwe
> When ech of hem had leyd his feith to borwe.[5]

Next morning in the midst of their duel Duke Theseus, whose prisoners they had been, suddenly rode up,

> And at a stert he was betwix them tuoo
> And pullede out a swerd and cride, Hoo![6]

[1] Mawgre, in spite of.

[2] Derreyne, an old term from Latin disrationare, originally meaning to disprove, afterwards either to disprove or prove by battle. The battle element in the word survived the element of proof, and latterly to deraign meant little more than to fight. See glossary to Globe Spenser, and compare with Du Cange, and Barrington on Stat. pp. 21 and 296.

[3] To-morrow I will not fail. [4] Parted till the morrow.

[5] Laid his faith in pledge. This legal metaphor is very common in early literature. It is still used when a man says, 'I pledge my word.'

[6] Hoo, stop.

Nomore, up peyne of leesyng of youre heed!
By mighty Mars, he schal anon be deed
That smyteth eny strook that I may seen!
But telleth me what mester[1] men ye been
That ben so hardy for to fighten heere
Withoute jugge or other officere,
As it wer in a lystes really.[2]

Struck by the wild romance of their quarrel he bade them return after fifty weeks, each with a hundred companions, to fight for the lovely Emelye.

Palamon and Arcite's duel.

Everich[3] of you schal brynge an hundred knightes
Armed for lystes up at alle rightes,[4]
Al redy to derrayne hire by bataylle.

Against the time appointed the lists were prepared and Chaucer's knight tells

Of Theseus that goth so busily
To maken up the lystes rially,
That such a noble theatre as it was
I dar wel sayn that in this world ther nas.
The circuit a myle was aboute
Walled of stoon, and dyched al withoute.
Round was the schap, in manere of compaas
Ful of degrees,[5] the heighte of sixty paas,
That whan a man was set on o[6] degré
He lette noughte[7] his felowe for to se.
Estward[8] ther stood a gate of marbel whit,
Westward right such another in the opposit.
And schortly to conclude, such a place
Was non in erthe as in so litel space.

[1] What sort of men. [2] Royally, before a king.

[3] Each. [4] In all respects. [5] Degrees, steps. [6] O, one.

[7] Lette noughte, hindered not. The steps rose in successive tiers, so that each row could see over those in front.

[8] By the Ordinance it is directed 'that the Lists be Lx pace of length and xl pace of widness . . . . wele and strongly barred all about

For the lists were rich in paintings and sculpture, and an altar to Venus was reared above the eastern gate, whilst on the western another rose in mind and memory of Mars.'

The day approached when Arcite and Palamon with their hundred friends were to return 'the bataille to derrayne.' It were treason to the majesty of Chaucer's verse to render into feeble prose his matchless picture of the preparatory scene, and we must silently follow the crowd thronging towards the lists.

> It nas not of the day yet fully pryme[1]
> Whan set was Theseus ful riche and hye
> Ypolita the queen and Emelye
> And other ladyes in degrees aboute.
> Unto the seetes preseth al the route.[2]
> And westward, thurgh the yates under Marte
> Arcite and eek the hundred of his parte,
> With baner red ys entred right anoon,
> And in that selve[3] moment Palamon
> Is under Venus, estward in the place[4]
> With baner whyt, and hardy cheere and face.[5]

. . . . and a Gate in the Est and anothir in the West, with gode and stronge Barres of vii fote high or more, that an Hors may nat lepe over.'—Dugd. Orig. p. 79.

1 Pryme, the first quarter of the day; nas, was not.

2 Route, company.

3 Selve, self-same.

4 Place, here technical, as before, see index under *place*.

5 Great importance was attached to the order in which the combatants appeared. The appellant, on whom the burden of victory rested, was to be there first. This did not apply here—neither party was, properly speaking, appellant or appealed. Therefore neither came before the other; in the self same moment they entered the lists—eastward and westward. If possible, still more consequence was attached to the order of leaving the lists if the case happened to be settled. Then the

When the two gallant companies had ranged themselves on opposite sides of the 'place,' the gates were shut and the signal of battle was given.

Tho were the yates schet, and cried was loude,
'Doth now your devoir,[1] yonge knightes proude!'
The heraudes lafte here prikyng[2] up and doun;
Now ryngen trompes loud and clarioun.
There is nomore to sayn, but west and est
In gon the speres ful sadly in arest[3]
In goth the scharpe spore into the side,
There seen men who can juste,[4] and who can ryde,
Ther schyveren schaftes[5] upon scheeldes thykke.

Stern was the fight and long.

And som tyme doth hem Theseus to reste,
Hem to refreissche, and drinken if hem leste.[6]

But the end came at last. That morning when Arcite had made his vows at the altar of Mars, the statue of the god had murmured 'Victorie,' and now the augury came true.

etiquette was that they should 'evynly be brought out att the Porte of the Lysts, so that that one go nat before that othir, . . . for it hath ben seide by many auncien people that he that goeth first out of the Lists hath the dishonour.'—Dugd. Orig. p. 84; see end of ch. 50 *supra.*

[1] This signal is in perfect accord with the Ordinance. 'And the Constable sittyng shall sey this sentence with high vois, *Lessez les alier. Lessez les alier. Lessez les alier et faire lour Devoire.* And after that, in the kyng's presence, the Appelaunt shall goe to the Defendaunt and assaile hym vigerously.'—Dugd. Orig. p. 83.

[2] Prikyng, spurring.

[3] In arest, in rest. The rest was the support of the spear when couched for the charge.

[4] Juste, joust.

[5] There the lance shafts are shivered.

[6] Again in accord with the Ordinance,—'And yf the Appelaunt wole te or drynke he shall aske leve first of his adversary.'—Dugd. Orig. p. 83.

For er the sonne unto the reste wente,[1]
The stronge kynge Emetreus[2] gan hente[3]
This Palamon as he faught with Arcite,
And made his swerd depe in his flessch to byte,
And by the force of twenti is he take,[4]
Unyolden[5] and idrawe[6] unto the stake.[7]
And in the rescous of this Palamoun
The stronge kyng Ligurge[8] is born adoun ;
And kyng Emetreus, for al his strengthe,
Is borne out of his sadel a swerdes lengthe,
So hitte him Palamon er he were take,
But al for nought, he was brought to the stake.

. . . .

And whan that Theseus hadde seen this sighte,
Unto the folk that foughten thus echon
He cryde 'Hoo! no more, for it is doon![9]
I wol be trewe juge and nought partye
Arcyte of Thebes schal have Emelye,
That by his fortune hath hire faire i-wonne.'

Nevertheless no taint attached to the honour of Arcite's conquered adversary.

1 Very faithful to the rules. Bracton's hour when the stars began to appear will be remembered. The wager in chivalry was the same, to do the battling between sunrise and sunset. See Dugd. Orig. 78.

2 Emetreus was one of Arcite's hundred.

3 Gan hente, did seize.

4 Take, taken.

5 Unyolden, not having yielded.

6 Idrawe, drawn.

7 A stake placed outside the lists. When taken there he was clearly forced out of the lists.

8 Ligurge, another of Arcite's hundred.

9 'Hoo!' Another correct touch of colour. See duel of Marche and Visconti in a former chapter, also instances *infra.* By the Ordinance constable and marshal were to be nigh 'to take heed if the kyng crye Hoo!' Various of their squires had spears without iron to part the combatants 'whan the kyng cryeth Hoo.' Dugd. Orig. 83. It is the only word that ever calls a halt to the eternal fights of the Morte Darthur.

Ne to be lad with fors unto the stake,
Unyolden and with twenty knightes take
O persone allone, withouten moo,
And haried[1] forth by arme, foot, and too,
And eek his steede dryven forth with staves
With footmen, bothe yemen and eek knaves,
It nas aretted[2] him no vyleinye,
Ther may no man clepe[3] it no cowardye.[4]

The rest of the story does not touch the present purpose, and there is no need here to follow it to its sad, sweet close. The marriage bells, which, with a chastened melody mindful of past sorrow, ring out the end of In Memoriam, had a Chaucerian prototype.

CHAP. 54.—*A Contrast and Conclusion.*

THE duel of law and the treason-duel of chivalry in England may be contrasted.

1. In the duel of law the gloves were handed to the judge before being exchanged. In chivalry the glove or gauntlet was thrown down.

2. The duel of law might take place before any judge. The duel of chivalry could only be fought before the king, constable or marshal, or, very rarely, a special deputy.

[1] Haried, roughly dragged. [2] Aretted, imputed to. [3] Clepe, call.

[4] Chaucer preserves the fair fame of Palamon, who, though beaten, incurred no note of disgrace. In cases of treason the vanquished was dragged with every mark of shame out of the lists to execution—'a corner of the Lysts brokyn up in reproche of hym, whereby he shall be drawen out with horses . . . unto the place of Juyse, where he shall be heded or hanged.' Dugd. Orig. p. 84.

3. The origin of the duel of law as a counter-plea to perjury is manifest in this, that the defendant not only gave the lie to the appellant's charge, but waged his battle first, was first in the field, and swore first. In the duel of chivalry the appellant waged first, was first in the field, and swore first.

Law and chivalry.

4. The oaths, although the same in substance, differed considerably in form.

5. The duel of law was not fought on horseback or in armour of mail. The duel of chivalry was always on horseback or in armour.

6. The weapon of the duel of law was a baton—never sword or spear. The duel of chivalry never lacked sword and spear.

7. The most usual positions of the champions in a writ of right were north and south. The invariable positions in the duel of chivalry were east and west.

8. The judge had no authority to stop a duel of law in progress, for, so to speak, the battle itself was the real judge. The duel of chivalry was very frequently stopped, and arbitrary judgment delivered by the king.

This comparison though not exhaustive will suffice. It shows essential differences in vital points all along the line. There was very little in common between the two duels. The one was a direct tradition of 13th century English law. The other was not linked to the forgotten precedents of the 11th and 12th centuries. It was as much a product of 14th century French influence as the paramount popularity of St. George himself, or as Thomas of Woodstock's ordinance was of the edict of Philip the Fair.

CHAP. 55.—*Richard II.*

STRANGELY the fortunes of Richard are linked with the judicial duel. His proposal to end the long French quarrel in the lists was a promise of energy and worth which the future did not fulfil. His favour for the court of chivalry was a sign of a deficiency in kinglier qualities. The glitter of the tilt blinded him to the truth often pressed upon him that the new court was a menace to the common law.[1] But though he could not see it the fact was not forgotten, and a day of retribution came.

Hereford and Norfolk.

It was a famous treason duel which focussed the fierce light of popular criticism upon him and helped to decide his fate. In spite of the Act of Parliament the court of chivalry, with the king at its head and the constable and marshal as his officers (the constable being his vicar-general in terms of Woodstock's ordinance), had become a tribunal not for transmarine treasons only, but for all treasons.[2] In 1398 Henry the Duke of

[1] Sufficiently evident in the Act 13 Rich. II. ch. 2, quoted, p. 179, *supra*.

[2] This was illustrated in Norfolk and Hereford's case.

Hereford in Parliament, appealed the Duke of Norfolk of high treason in the use of words tending to the king's dishonour. Norfolk denied the charge, and the king who hated Hereford and had good reason to fear his ambition appointed 16th September for a duel;[1]

> Body for body as in sic case
> The oys all tym in Yngland wes.

The two dukes made great preparations. The best armourers in Milan came with armour of mail and plate for the one; arms from Germany came for the other. The news of the coming battle made a great stir. The lists fenced round with a wet ditch or moat were made at Coventry. A great concourse of spectators assembled on the fateful day—little witting that they were to witness a turning point in English history.

At Coventry, 1398.

Hereford as the accuser came first to the barriers of the lists armed at all points, mounted on a white horse barbed with blue and green velvet. He was the people's favourite. Constable and marshal met him at the gate. In answer to their formal question he answered that he, the Duke of Hereford, had come to do his devoir against the Duke of Norfolk as a false traitor. He swore on the gospels that his quarrel was true and just, then sheathing the sword which he held naked in his hand he put down his visor, made the sign of

[1] The following account is drawn from Hall, 4; Adam of Usk, 23, 131; Trokelowe R.S. 225-6. The couplet is from Wyntoun, ix. ch. 18, lines 1807-8; oys, use.

the cross on his forehead, and with spear in hand entering the lists dismounted there.

Soon afterwards the king took his seat on the staging prepared for the purpose. In case of fray or tumult 10,000 armed men were in attendance. The king had it by divination, says one,[1] that Norfolk should prevail and he rejoiced much.

Norfolk meantime 'hovered on horsebacke at the entery of the listes,' his charger barbed with crimson velvet. Like Hereford he took the oath and as he entered the lists he said aloud, 'God aide hym that hath the righte.'

Shakespeare has in his 'King Richard II.' described the scene.[2] When the two dukes faced each other in the lists, it seemed to the king that Hereford would prevail—so one at least[3] explains his strange action. He stopped the duel, and banished both intending combatants. Hereford's exile was to be for ten years, Norfolk's (which it is hinted the king intended to relax) closed with

'The hopeless word of never to return.'

Whatever were the king's intentions Norfolk never did return—ere long he died in Venice. But Hereford came back next year, all England gathered round him, and Henry IV. took the place of Richard II. deposed.

In the long list of articles with which Parliament charged the redeless king, there was one that i

[1] Adam of Usk. [2] Act i. scene 3. [3] Adam of Usk.

violation of Magna Carta persons maliciously accused of treasonable words against the king had been taken and imprisoned and tried before the constable and marshal in the military court. 'In which court,' says the article, 'the said accused lieges could make no answer except that they were not guilty, and could justify and defend themselves only by their bodies and in no other way, notwithstanding that accusers and appellants might be young, strong, and hearty, and the accused old and weak, maimed or infirm.'[1] A vernacular version adds that 'the said aged personnes fearyng the sequele of the matter, submitted theymselfes to his mercy, whom he fined and raunsomed unreasonably at his pleasure.'[2]

The deposition.

An old Scotch historian at a loss for a precedent for Richard's deposition found none so apt—

As ane alde abbote swa put downe
For opyn dilapidatioune.[3]

There was some force in the parallel.

CHAP. 56.—*A Royal Jest,* A.D. *1399.*

'IN the silence of dark midnight, weeping and lamenting that he had ever been born,'[4] Richard was taken away from what had once been his capital. When the tragedy of the unkinged king was hasting

[1] Rot. Parl. iii. 420. [2] Hall, 11.
[3] Wyntoun ix. ch. 20, lines 1981-2. [4] Adam of Usk, 151.

to its last act within the castle of Pontefract, Henry IV. was crowned in pomp. In this ceremonial the champion's challenge was made in accordance with previous custom. The manor of Scrivelsby in Lincolnshire was held by service of grand serjeanty, the lord of the manor being bound to act as the king's champion. It was his function to ride into the hall at the coronation banquet, and flinging down his gauntlet offer proof by his body that the new crowned king was king by right.[1]

The coronation.

At the accession of Richard II. Sir John Dymock, in right of his wife, had been preferred to the office in competition with Sir Baldwin de Frevyle. Each claimed descent from the family of Marmion. One reason for the preference was that the Black Prince in his lifetime had been heard to speak with favour of the Dymock claim.[2]

Again in 1399 at the coronation of Henry, the Dymocks and Frevyles made opposing claims, but again the Dymocks prevailed. A second Sir Baldwin de Frevyle, although he alleged right to the office in

[1] Camden, 470-529. Blount's Jocular Customs (1679), 4, 5, 6. Scott's Marmion, note i. Is there proof for this function before the 14th century? I have searched, but have not happened to meet it. In the absence of better evidence than I have yet seen, I crave leave to doubt. See Testa de Neville 86b, 335. I have considered Dugdale.

[2] Speed's Hist. (1627) 604. See Walsingham, i. 337. Sir Alexander de Frevyle had been champion at the previous coronation. Cal. Rot. Pat. 196b. The fact is utilised in Marlowe's play of 'Edward II.,' in which, at the coronation of Edward III., the champion makes his challenge on the stage. See act v., scene 4.

virtue of his tenure of 'Tamworth tower and town,' was set aside. The hereditary office involved some paradoxes. Sir John Dymock in all due form had offered battle with any man who dared to question the right of Richard II. to the throne.[1] It was by Henry that Richard had been deposed. Yet the son of Richard's champion was the champion of Henry.

The champion of England.

The petition of Sir Thomas Dymock was framed by the lawyer and chronicler, Adam of Usk. It declares the readiness of Dymock, armed as the king himself would be when riding into mortal battle, to proclaim four times within the hall at the time of the banquet that if any one should say that Henry was not of right king of England 'he, the same Thomas is ready to prove by his body, where, when and how the king wills, that that man lies.'[2]

Accordingly in the midst of the coronation banquet Sir Thomas Dymock, fully armed and mounted on his charger, rode into the hall at Westminster, preceded by two others bearing a naked sword and spear. He caused a herald to proclaim that if any man should say that his now liege lord and king of England was not of right crowned king, he as the king's champion was ready to prove the contrary with his body. Adam of Usk, who naturally took a warm interest in his client's performance, records that

[1] Adam of Usk, 34. There was a hitch in the ceremony because the champion came too early. Walsingham, i. 337.

[2] Adam of Usk, 34, 149.

when the proclamation was made Henry IV. turned to the champion, and referring to the terms of his challenge said, 'If need be, Sir Thomas, I shall in mine own person relieve thee of that duty.'[1]

CHAP. 57.—*Some Treason-Duels.*

THE change of sovereigns altered very slightly the court of chivalry.[2] The Act 1 Henry IV., chapter 14, was passed to remedy the 'many great inconveniences and mischiefs' attendant on appeals of treason. It ordained that in future all appeals concerning facts within the realm should be tried by the ordinary laws, and that only appeals on facts out of the realm should be tried before the constable and marshal. 'Moreover,' says the Act with a change in diction made doubtless with a purpose, 'it is accorded and assented that no appeals be from henceforth made or any wise pursued in Parliament in any time to come.' The legislative body thus gave assent and accord to the abrogation of the parliamentary appeal —a form of process which Bracton[3] can scarcely be

Under Henry IV.

1 Adam of Usk, 33. An account of the dispute for the championship at this coronation is also given in Trokelowe, &c. R.S. 288.

2 Several of the most noted heraldic cases were decided about this time. Scrope *versus* Grosvenor by Richard II., Lord Edward Hastings *v.* Reginald Lord Grey under Henry IV., and Henry V. Boutell's Heraldry (1873), 245-6. Adam of Usk, 178-9.

3 Bracton, ii. 264-7. Fleta, i. ch. 21.

said to countenance, but of which the subsequent history of trial by combat has afforded not a few practical examples.

In other respects, in limiting the sphere of the court of chivalry, this statute of Henry IV. only re-enacted the provisions of the Act 13 Richard II. already noted. But the limits assigned by these two Acts were not over-closely regarded in practice. They formed no great obstacle to the 'battle of treason,' provided only that the quarrel was in form or in reality the king's. When neither party pled the objection, and both desired the combat, it was quite natural in that age to allow the duel. A treatise by an official of Henry IV. and Henry V. sets forth the formalities of the duel[1] with even more circumstance than Thomas of Woodstock's ordinance. Many duels were fought. Sometimes it is difficult to tell whether they were real battles of treason or only feats of arms,[2] although the word *duellum* is rarely used in contemporary writings, except for the genuine judicial duel.[3] In the following instances there is no room for doubt.

A writ in Rymer in 1406 orders a duel[4] between

1 'Battle of Treason,' by John Hill; in Hale MSS. described in Pike, 389-92.

2 Very many combats à outrance took place, but the combat à outrance was not a treason duel. For a case of treason between John Kightle and Stephen Lescrop ended without a duel in 2 Henry IV., see Cal. Rot. Pat. 241b.

3 In Rot. Scot. it is never so used, except in the headings which I apprehend are the editor's.

4 Rymer, viii. 440.

two burgesses of Bordeaux to be fought before Henry IV. A second writ[1] gives an account of the fight surprisingly vivid for a legal document. Bertrand Usana had denounced the desperate iniquity of Englishmen in general, and John Bolomer had accused him of treason. The duel was fought at Nottingham on 12th August 1407, before the king. When the combatants were ready, 'armed with divers kinds of arms,' the constable cried 'Lessez les aler, lessez les aler, lessez les aler et fair lour devoir.'

Usana and Bolomer.

Bolomer the foresaid appellant, says the writ, as a valiant and worthy knight prosecuting his appeal against the said Bertrand Usana, fell manfully upon him with various kinds of arms, and the said Bertrand the defendant bravely meeting him, made strenuous defence. They fought for a long time, and then the king, having regard to their reputation and their years, listened to the intercession of 'our dearest cousin the king of Scotland[2] and our own sons' to preserve both combatants from a traitor's fate. Uttering the accustomed word of peace he cried, 'Ho, ho, ho!'[3] and stopped the duel, declaring that neither party had incurred infamy, but rather honour in the battle.

[1] Rymer, viii. 538-40, dated 20th June, 1408.

[2] James I. was then a prisoner in England. Bain's Cal. iv. pref. xxx.-xxxi.

[3] Silentii vocabulo consueto scilicet Ho, ho, ho! (quod est) Cessate, cessate, cessate.

In 1409 there is mention of another duel[1] between one called Gloucester, appellant, and another named Arthure, defendant. It too was stopped by the king after a valiant beginning.

A lawyer in the lists.

A lawyer in the lists is a phenomenon sufficient to justify fuller notice here of a duel in 1430. John Upton, a notary, accused John Downe, gentleman, of treason in that he had imagined or plotted the king's death on his coronation day.[2] Henry VI., who came to the throne a mere infant, had been crowned in the eighth year of his reign on 6th November 1429. On 24th January following, the duel was fought in presence of the royal boy. A writ has been printed in Coke upon Littleton,[3] by which the sheriffs of London were ordered to make the lists and barriers for the battle, to level the ground within the lists sufficiently with sand, and to see that no large stones were left. There was a long fight, but in the end the king took the matter in hand and forgave both parties.

In 1445, Thomas Fitzgerald, prior of the Knights of St. John at Kilmainham accused James Butler, Earl of Ormond, of certain points of treason. The 4th of October was appointed for a duel at Smithfield, but in the interval Henry VI. gave a general pardon to the earl. Nevertheless on the battle day the prior duly appeared at the appointed place armed

1 Stow's Survey (1720) iii. 239.
2 Stow, 371; Cal. Rot. Pat. 275; Gregory, 171.
3 Edition 1817, iv. ch. 17.

and ready with all his weapons, 'keeping the field till high noon.'[1] And in that same year a similar challenge was made between a person named Arblaster and another citizen of London, but the duel was continued, 'and,' says Gregory,[2] in an enigmatical sentence, 'the same Arblastre ranne yn to the contente,' which perhaps means that he fled to the continent. How he 'ran' there is another matter.

Bacchus and Mars.

Any duel may adorn a tale, but there are so few to point a moral that the didactic may turn with satisfaction to a case of the year 1446 tried in the court of chivalry, before the constable and marshal. It arose out of certain utterances or prophecies 'made and imagined' against the king, laid to the charge of a London armourer.[3] 'This yere,' says Hall,[4] 'an armerar's servant of London appeled his master of treason whiche offered to bee tried by battaill. At the daie assigned, the frendes of the master brought hym Malmesey and *aqua vite* to comforte hym with all, but it was the cause of his and their discomforte; for he poured in so much that when he came into the place in Smithfelde, where he should fight, bothe his witte and strength failed hym, and so he beyng a tall and a hardye personage overladed with hote drynkes

[1] Gregory, 186-7. [2] Gregory, 187.

[3] Nichols' Illustrations of Manners (1797) p. 217, has the writ to the barons of Exchequer. By an odd blunder Nichols dates it 1524, though it bears *in gremio* to belong to the 25th of Henry VI.

[4] Hall, 207-8.

was vanquished of his servaunte, being but a coward and a wretch, whose bodye was drawen to Tiborne, and there hanged and behedded.' The grammar of this passage is not of the best. It was not John Davy the armourer's servant whose body was drawn to Tyburn, at least not then. He slew his master William Catur in the duel which was fought on 31st January 1447, and the body despoiled of its armour lay in the field all night. Next day the dismemberment which followed treason was duly inflicted, and the severed head was set up on London Bridge.[1] The exchequer accounts contain a ghastly item[2] 'for the watchyng of the ded man in Smythfelde,' the cloth laid upon the body, the hire of a horse to draw it to the block, and the pole and nails used in fixing up the head.

John Stow's servant.

But that false servant lived not long. He was hanged shortly afterwards at Tyburn for felony. 'Let such false accusers note this example,' says honest John Stow,[3] in a burst of indignant autobiography, 'and looke for no better end without speedie repentance. Myself have had the like servant that likewise accused me of many articles. He liveth yet, but hath hardly escaped hanging since. God make him penitent.'[4]

[1] Gregory, 187.

[2] Item of 12s. 7d. Quoted at large in Meyrick, ii. 149; taken, I am sure, from Nichols' Illustrations of Manners, 218-220. Meyrick is often to be 'aretted of the villanie' of not giving his references.

[3] Stow, 385.

[4] Shakespeare describes this duel in the 'Second part of Henry VI.,'

CHAP. 58.—*The end of Chivalry.*

CHIVALRY was dying fast in the 15th century. The feudal relation was breaking up. The knight was not what he had once been in the battle field, for the centre of military equilibrium was changed. 'In the footmen is all the trust' wrote one.[1] 'A horse is but a weak weapon when men have most ado,' said another, in the press of single battle.[2] The discipline of infantry now outweighed the fiery valour of iron-clad horsemen. With his worth as a soldier the knight lost fibre as a man. Gunpowder put chivalry to flight.

Chivalry in decay.

In England civil war hastened the end. It induces an atmosphere of exasperation in which the spirit of chivalry cannot live. The commons under Richard II. were not querulous without cause. The court of the constable was a menace to the common law. It had not been content with the scope which the Act of Parliament gave; treasons of all kinds came before it. In the common law courts its claims were recognised. There was much disagreement amongst the common law judges as to the precise position it

Acts 1 and 2, scenes 3 and 3. The fight in the play is with staves and sandbags. The Duke of York says to the armourer's servant at its close, 'Fellow, thank God and the good wine in thy master's way.' Shakspeare, like the chronicles, thought the real traitor was the aqua vitæ.

[1] Gregory, 214.

[2] See a future chapter.

occupied,[1] but a positive place for it in the appeal of treason was denied by none. Its arbitrary character made it a danger to public liberty—a danger which became very real when it was turned into a political engine in the reign of Edward IV. To its last inevitable day chivalry had come when its high priest the constable held a royal commission as sole judge of his political opponents, and his court—the bodily form of an institution which was to right the wrongs of the oppressed—became by the irony of fate an instrument for the murder of Lancastrians.[2] The white rose of York grew on the grave of chivalry.

Fuit Ilium.

Chivalry was dead,[3] and, did not things ride over logic, trial by battle had died with it. It was certainly stricken beyond hope of recovery. In the year 1492 occurred what is believed to have been the last judicial duel fought on English soil. It arose out of a quarrel between Sir James Parker and Sir Hugh Vaughan relative to the arms which the garter king gave to the latter. A duel on such a cause was by no means unprecedented in English annals. A great joust was being held at Richmond, and advantage was taken of the opportunity to fight out the question before the king, Henry VII., founder of the Tudor dynasty. In the

The last judicial duel.

1 See case of Paston in Maynard's Year-Books, 37 Henry VI. pp. 3, 20, for a discussion. Contrast Brookes' 'New Cases' (reprint 1873) 150, 30.

2 Stubbs' Constitutional Hist. iii. 282-3. Commission dated 24th Aug. 1467 quoted there. Rymer, xi. 581-3.

3 Buckle, ii. 135.

first course Sir James was slain. His helmet played him false, giving way before the spear of Vaughan, 'and so he was striken into the mouth that his tongue was borne into the hinder part of the head, and so he died incontinently.'[1]

Henry VIII. tried in vain to restore the splendour of knighthood; the spirit had fled beyond recall. As pilot of his people through the stress of a storm which he himself provoked, the bluff King Hal had a more practical task. Considering the personal compass by which he steered his success was remarkable. He left England orderly and strong. He had ruled without the aid of trial by battle and his children did the same.

CHAP. 59.—*A Summary with an Exception.*

THE duel of law was rapidly becoming extinct in the reign of Edward I. It was almost a memory in the middle of the 14th century. But there came then a distinct renascence of the duel under chivalry which had long struggled for legal recognition. The struggle was successful, culminating in the institution of the court of chivalry in the reign of Richard II. It is difficult to avoid seeing in that renascence and in the court of chivalry itself an interruption to what Tennyson has called the increasing purpose of the ages, or what may

[1] Stow, 475-6.

less poetically be termed the natural course of legal and constitutional development. The contemporary parliamentary protest so far bears that out. But England was infinitely less insular then than now, and her adoption of a practice prevalent in France cannot be deemed in every sense a retrogression. Still, Justice masquerading in the livery of St. George was a sign of the times boding danger to the State, as events proved. Whilst chivalry flourished in England the treason duel flourished too. As the one decayed so did the other, and the last actual judicial duel in England was fought soon after the extinction of chivalry. The rise of the private duel did not influence the law of England in the 16th century.

The summary.

Yet in the ashes glowed the wonted fires. On 12th September 1583,[1] under the sway of Elizabeth, in presence of her justices, judges, and council, one of whom was an archbishop, a legal duel was fought. Not indeed in England, but in Ireland, the encounter of the O'Connors—Connor MacCormack O'Connor and Teig MacGilpatrick O'Connor—took place. It was as formidable as the antagonists' names. Teig had charged Connor with treason, trial by combat was adjudged, and Dublin Castle, a place of many strange traditions, but none more strange than this, witnessed

An Irish exception—the O'Connors.

[1] The facts of this duel are from Holinshed, vi. 455; *Cornhill* article; Ware's Hist. Antiq. of Ireland, ed. 1764, 153; Cal. Ireland, 1574-85, p. 468.

in its inner court a terrific duel with sword and target. The end was that Teig got Connor into the awkward defenceless position known to pugilists as 'chancery,' and with the hilt of his sword so pommelled his head that, in the words of a fellow-countryman, he 'knocked the seven senses out of it.' Then beheading Connor with Connor's own sword, and fixing the bloody trophy on the point of the weapon, he presented it to the justices of Queen Elizabeth. Holinshed is good enough to wish that the same fate had rather fallen 'upon the whole sex of the O'Connors.'

This was surely an eccentric experiment in the art of misgoverning Ireland.

PART VI.—SCOTLAND, 1300-1603: CHIVALRY.

CHAP. 60.—*Before Bannockburn.*

AT the outset a critical task is presented. It is necessary to test the evidence of a duel which Perth claims amongst the many fought on the North Inch.[1] Robert the Bruce ordained it, if a document professedly of his granting may be trusted. Hugh Harding, an Englishman, appealed Walter de Seintlowe, a Scot. Both claimed right to the same arms undifferenced, viz., on a field gules, three greyhounds or, collared blue. The Scotsman owned himself vanquished in the duel, and by word of mouth in presence of the king resigned and for ever surrendered the impleaded arms to the 'aforesaid Hugh,' with the whole triumph and victory. King Robert therefore gave his decree in the Englishman's favour.

Alleged combat on a point in heraldry.

Lord Hailes, citing this writ[2] in his Annals, had

1 Gazetteer of Scot. 1843, *voce* Perth; also Ordnance Gazetteer, 1885.

2 Annals, Miscel. Oc. sub 1312. It is from Upton's De re militari, Bisse's notes, 34, where it has figured beside it the shield with the three greyhounds. I quote its tenor from Hailes:—Robertus dei gratia Rex Scotiae omnibus ad quos praesentes literae pervenerint salutem. Cum nos accepimus duellum apud nostram villam de Perthe,

some doubt of its authenticity, and asked, 'Was this Hugh related to John Harding the forger?' Perhaps his lordship had a double meaning in the query, and covertly hinted at a possible relation between John Harding and the document as well as between him and the 'aforesaid Hugh.' The point must be considered.

For an Englishman to go into the heart of Scotland in 1312, to beard the lion in his den, and fight for his armorial bearings against a Scotsman before King Robert the Bruce, would have been an achievement rash enough for the most reckless of knights-errant. But is it probable? No other case is known of a Scottish legal duel over a coat of arms. Nor in England can examples be adduced of such duels prior to the beginnings of the court of chivalry under Edward III. A field gules, greyhounds or, and collars azure are still the arms of a Northumbrian family of Hard-

die confectionis praesentium, inter Hugonem Harding, Anglicum appellantem, de armis de Goules tribus leporariis de auro colloree de B. et Willielmum de Seintlowe, Scotum appellatum, eisdem armis sine differentia indutos. Quo quidem duello percusso, praedictus Willielmus se finaliter reddidit devictum et praedicto Hugoni remisit ac relaxavit et omnino de se et haeredibus suis in perpetuum praedicta arma cum toto triumpho, honore et victoria, ore tenus in audientia nostra. Quare nos in solio nostro tribunali regali sancti patris, cum magnatibus et dominis regni nostri personaliter sedentes, adjudicavimus et finaliter decretum dedimus per praesentes quod praedictus Hugo Harding et haeredes sui de caetero in perpetuum habeant et teneant, gaudeant et portent praedicta arma integraliter absque calumnia perturbatione contradictione reclamatione praedicti Willielmi seu haeredum suorum: In cujus rei testimonium has literas nostras fieri fecimus patentes apud dictam villam nostram de Perthe secundo die Aprilis anno regni nostri septimo annoque Domini 1312.'

ings.[1] John Harding (Hardyng) was of Northumbrian birth, and the talents he used in forging proofs of his country's claims to the over-lordship of Scotland may well have been employed to lend to his own family the lustre of a daring deed. His notorious repute rises up in judgment to attest the likelihood of his so doing.

The record forged.

The document does not resemble in its form the genuine writs of King Robert, but it does resemble the undoubted forgeries of the Northumbrian squire.[2] In several respects it has the trick of Harding's style. Whether a fabrication of his or some other forger's hand it must be branded as a fraud.

More puzzling than fraudulent, perhaps, is the deliverance dated 17th May 1312, attributed to Bernard, abbot of Arbroath and Chancellor of Scotland.[3] The question was whether a boy of eleven was of lawful age to undergo punishment on a charge of life and limb. The abbot is reported to have ruled[4] that there were in law three ages; first, for seven years a boy was the ward of his parents; second, at fourteen he might contract

Pervenire ad duellum.

1 Burke's General Armoury.

2 A general glance at Hardyng's forgeries—Palgrave's Documents, 368-76; Bain's Cal. iv. 1841-48—will satisfy any one of this. It is noticeable that the form of letters patent, the dating 'at our town of Perth,' the *die confectionis praesentium*, and the 'magnates' are each represented in the forgeries.

3 Bower fathers a couplet about Bannockburn on this worthy prelate, xii. ch. 21.

4 Scots Acts, i. 745.

matrimony; third, at twenty-one 'he ought to come to heritage as well as to go to the duel.'[1]

In the light of this decision, and on the doubtful assumption that it is genuine, it is impossible to believe that the duel as waged in pleas of the crown had yet become extinct. At the same time it is safe to regard the abbot's phrase, *pervenire ad duellum*, as a traditional expression to indicate full liability for crime rather than a representation of current and common practice. The absence of records of any such simply legal duels—the fact that in no 14th century case of ordinary crime in the courts of Scotland is there an instance of any mode of trial except by assize—must negative any large general conclusion based upon the letter of the abbot's ruling.

CHAP. 61.—*Before Halidon Hill.*

ON 26th February 1332 King David II. declared by deed that the grant he had made to Sir John Somerville of the 'palatium' or barras at Aberdeen during a tournament should not be held to prejudice the right of the constable or his successors.[2] This charter

1 A closely analogous division of ages appears in the Welsh laws. At seven a boy could commit and receive 'saraad,' *i.e.*, was liable to be fined for insult, and could sue for insult. At fourteen he became a lord's man. At twenty-one he took land and became liable to the duel. That liability ceased at sixty-three. Welsh Laws, ii. 211.

2 Remarks on Peerage Law by Riddell, 114-5. The reference to the whereabouts of the deed is not too explicit—'Copy British Museum.'

is of prime consequence. It proves that so early as 1332 (earlier perhaps than in England) the place of the constable in the duel and in passages-at-arms was recognised—a most substantial token of the spirit of chivalry taking flesh. Whence the influence came it is not possible to say dogmatically, but it may be hinted that the relations of the Scots and French were very close, and that it is highly noteworthy that the armorial bearings of the constable of France and of the constable of Scotland—an arm gauntleted fesswise issuing from a cloud and grasping a naked sword erected in pale—were the same.[1] The perquisite admitted by King David's charter was one which in England, by the ordinance fifty years later, pertained not to the constable but the marshal.[2]

A suggestive charter.

A single combat was no unusual part of or prelude to a battle. Before the English and Scotch armies engaged at Halidon Hill on 19th July 1333, an ominous incident took place. There stepped forth

The great peerage antiquary mistakenly regarded 'palatium' as meaning palace. Some international tilting took place about this time. One encounter took place in 1329 at Edinburgh, and the English knight was defeated. Exch. Rolls, i. 238.

1 Nisbet's Heraldry, part iv. p. 71. In England the arms of the constable appear to have been different. In Castile the office of constable was first introduced in 1382—an importation from France and Arragon, says Mariana, 'more ex Gallia atque Aragonia translato.' De Rebus Hispaniæ (1605) ii. 143.

2 The Mareschall's fee is . . . and the lists, barrers, and scaffolds of the same. Ordinance in Dugd. Orig. 85; Black Book, i. 328-9. This is not mentioned in Philip the Fair's Edict.

from the Scottish ranks, says a contemporary historian,[1] a certain champion[2] of great stature, but like another Goliath trusting more in his valour than in God. Standing in the midst between the two armies he offered single combat to any Englishman. He was named Turnebole from a deed of his, the turning of a bull.[3] Sir Robert de Venale, a knight of Norfolk, kneeling before King Edward III. besought his blessing. Then armed with sword and buckler he advanced against the giant Scot. Meeting by the way a certain black mastiff, which attended on his adversary, he suddenly made a stroke at it with his sword, and severed its spine at the loins. The master of the slain dog fought hard but without spirit, and was vanquished, and the knight cut off his left hand and his head.

Turne-bole and his dog.

The tradition of Rule Water lives in Leyden's verse. It celebrates the fame of William Turnbull, who is said to have bravely rescued Robert the Bruce from the attack of a furious Caledonian bull.[4] But Leyden and tradition alike preserve a stony silence on this story of his fate.

1 Galf. le Baker, 118. See also Stow, 231.

2 I take this word from Stow's version. 'Champion' had become a well-established ideal of valour. Barbour's Bruce (written in 1375) x. 614 makes the Scots in Ireland fight—

at abandoun,
As ilk man war a campioun.

Chaucer's Frere is similarly likened—

Therto he strong was as a champioun.

Prologue, Canterbury Tales, line 239.

3 Qui ab effectu 'tauri versor,' Anglice 'turne bole' vocabatur.

4 Leyden's Scenes of Infancy, part i. See note.

CHAP. 62.—*The Law and Custom in 1354.*

THERE is a strong temptation to touch upon a great joust-of-war in the winter of 1341-42[1] as a sign of the growth of the Scottish spirit of chivalry, but it must be resisted and, instead, attention is drawn to a legal document of the year 1354.

Heron of Ford and his horses.

Annandale was, as it had been for a considerable time previous, subject to Edward III. From 1336 onwards[2] it was in the hands of William de Bohun, earl of Northampton, as its English lord. In his court, doubtless under the walls of Lochmaben Castle, Sir William Heron appeared one day as a prosecutor. Sir William was a Northumbrian. More than once he was associated in active service with Gerard de Widdrington,[3] the enemy of the aquiline-nosed prior of Tynemouth.[4] At the battle of Neville's Cross in 1346 they had been in arms together, Heron had taken one Scottish prisoner, and Widdrington had taken two.[5] Heron had known defeat too in his time,[6] and had varied the

1 Wyntoun, viii. ch. 35; Bower, xiii. ch. 43; Extracta, 173-4; Scalacron. 299; Bain's Cal. iii. pref. xlix. No. 1373; Knyghton, 2580; Hailes' Annals, Miscel. Oc. 1336. Notes on some of the dramatis personæ in Wyntoun, viii. ch. 34, 37; Rot. Scot. i. 517[a], 587[b], 616-7; Knyghton, 2625; Scalacron. 315.

2 Rot. Scot. i. 399[a].

3 Rot. Scot. March 1336-7, i. 487[a].

4 Ch. 44, *supra*.

5 Rot. Scot. i. 678.

6 In 1338. Bower, xiii. ch. 48. He was wounded and defeated by Sir Alex. Ramsay in an engagement at Wark Castle.

life of a soldier by some service as a justice at Berwick.[1] This gallant energetic[2] borderer came before de Bohun's court to pursue John Walayse and William Prudhome for the felonious theft of his horses. The men thus accused answered to his charge that they were not guilty of the felony, 'and this by their bodies according to the law and custom of the land of Scotland, they offered to defend against the said William Heroun or any of his men.'[3] Heron in return declared his readiness with God's help to prove the felony 'in the said land of Scotland' by two of his men if he might have the king's permission. He therefore sought leave 'to make that proof in the form aforesaid,' and on 28th October 1354, special license was granted at Westminster to that effect.[4]

'Law and custom.'

This may have been a Border duel, for Annandale though in English hands was under Scots law, and therefore the case may have been amenable to jurisdiction at the Lochmabenstane on the Solway side. But it is more probable that there is here a late instance of the duel purely legal, not at all chivalric,

[1] In 1350. Rot. Scot. i. 733a.

[2] Rot. Scot. i. 627a.

[3] Rot. Scot. i. 774b; Rymer, v. 808. The thieves pled that they 'culpabiles non fuisse et hoc per corpora sua juxta legem et consuetudinem terre Scotie se contra dictum Willelmum Heroun seu aliquos de suis defendere optulerunt.'

[4] Last reference. Heron being a knight was not liable to fight in person with those low-born horse thieves.

claimed and allowed. It is however vain to speculate. No further record survives to tell what fortune the doughty Heron of Ford had in his appeal. The sequel is silence.

CHAP. 63.—*Three Half-told Stories, 1362-95.*

THE relationship between chivalry in Scotland, in England and in France, was close. It must have been strengthened by the stay of David II. in France from 1334 till 1341, and by his captivity in England from 1346 to 1354, as well as by his many subsequent visits to the English Court. Therefore, it is not surprising to find in Scotland under his rule examples of duels analogous to those which were taking place in France and England about the same time.

Keith and Mar, 1362.

In 1362 King David besieged and took Kildrummy Castle which belonged to Thomas, Earl of Mar. Bower obscurely states that this was 'on account of some discord' between the king and him,[1] and Wyntoun casts no light upon the point.[2] But the Scalacronica says that it was to a great extent because of an appeal of battle made by Sir William Keith, marshal of Scotland, against the earl in the king's court. The earl and the

[1] Bower, xiv. ch. 24. Mar was exiled for a time, 'de regno recessit.' Wyntoun says the same—

For the Erl off Mar Thomas
Past out off the kynrike wes.

[2] Wyntoun, viii. 46.

marshal met armed in lists at Edinburgh—for the making of which an entry appears in the Exchequer Rolls.[1] There the matter was taken into the hands of the king, who apparently stopped the duel and banished Mar. It is hinted that the king favoured Keith although Mar was his own near kinsman.[2] Still the connection between the duel and the siege of Kildrummy[3] is not very apparent.

Douglas and Erskine, 1367.

In 1367 James, heir of William Douglas of Dechmont, presented a petition to King Edward III., craving that whereas a duel had been waged and was to be fought between him and Thomas de Erskyn,[4] 'according to the law of Scotland, for certain causes,' his servants might have license to buy in London certain arms and armour, a pair of plates, a habergeon, a pair of gauntlets, a helmet, bracers and greaves, long arms

[1] Exch. Rolls, ii. 129. 'Pro meremio ad clausuram palicii, pro duello 3l. 6s. 8d.' Moneys also were given 'ad solvendum harraldis.' Perhaps these payments had something to do with the duel. Further items, 'pro factura palicii,' and 'pro barreris factis,' probably referring to the same duel, also appear in the Exch. Rolls, ii. 177 and 222.

[2] Quel movement mult sourdy pour un apel de batail qe William de Keth appella le dit count en la court le dit roy, sure quoy furent armez en lices a Edinburgh, la querel illoeqes pr...n mayn du roy, qi plus sembloit bien voillaunt au dit William qe au dit count, tout estoit il son cosyn prochein. Scalacron. 202.

[3] David granted several charters at 'Kyndromy' in September and October 1362. Reg. Mag. Sig. i. pp. 21 and 23.

[4] Sir Thomas Erskine had on 26th October 1367, received a safe conduct into England. Rot. Scot. i. 916a. He was the son of Sir Robert Erskine, chamberlain of Scotland. Sir Thomas was keeper of Edinburgh Castle and Sheriff of Edinburgh in 1371. Exch. Rolls, ii. 364.

and coverture for two horses, two daggers, the head of one lance, and 'certain other armour needed for the said duel.' He also desired permission for his servants along with Robert of Erskynshawe to take the armour to Scotland. On 8th December 1367 the requisite permission was given.[1] A month later, on 5th January 1368, the adversary of Douglas received license to buy in London in person, and to take back with him to Scotland a somewhat similar assortment of the essentials of knightly argument. These comprised plates, basnet, bracers, cuisses, greaves, a chaffrein for one horse, a dagger, a long sword, a short sword, and a pair of gauntlets 'for a duel waged in the parts of Scotland.'[2] As is too often the case in the history of Scotland the intimations of the English records serve only to tantalise. One hears of duels which are to be, but lacks the satisfaction of knowing the event. The story ends with the beginning.

Such was the case in the duel of Douglas and Erskine under David II. A similar disappointment is experienced in regard to the account of the projected encounter of Robert Mercer and John Gille, both esquires of Scotland, in the reign of Robert II. John Gille was a

Mercer and Gille, 1381.

1 Rot. Scot. 916 b. Rymer, vi. 582.

2 Rot. Scot. i. 917 ab. Rymer, vi. 583. Bracers guarded the arm, cuisses the thigh, greaves the shin. The basnet was a helmet. The short sword hung without sheath on the wearer's left side from a ring; the place for the dagger was on the right side. See Archæologia, 1824, vol. xx. p. 499, article by Meyrick.

member of Parliament and a burgess of Perth.[1] A meeting in the lists had been ordained, and on 8th April 1381 the Scottish Lyon-herald received from Richard II. license to take back with him into Scotland certain armour which he had bought for Mercer, 'to arm him at all pieces,' for the approaching duel.[2]

These stories, which chronicle and State paper have left half told, are yet told fully enough to warrant conclusions which will be stated by and bye.[3]

CHAP. 64.—*Border Duels till 1396.*

THE appeal to arms which formed so large a part of march law in 1249—the pure duel of law—had still no doubt some force on the Borders in the 14th century. But the long war, the shifting uncertainty of the Border line, and the irregularity of courts, must have occasioned much interruption and tended strongly towards entire disuse. The tendency of things in both countries at the time was against it, and cannot fail to have hastened its decay. The surmise is hazarded that it had become very uncommon before half the century was past. When, however, a chivalric reaction brought in a new type of duel, its introduction and popularity on the Borders were inevitable. The marchman's sword never knew

[1] Scots Acts, i. 561, 495, 508.

[2] Rot. Scot. ii. 35 b; Bain's Cal. iv. No. 303. The arms included an extra couple of pairs of gauntlets and greaves. [3] See ch. 68.

what rust was, and a state of chronic antagonism favoured such encounters.

Grant and Strother, 1380.

On 18th October 1380[1] a safe conduct was granted by Richard II. to Robert Grant, a Scotsman, to enable him to go to 'Liliattecrosse.' A duel was to be waged and fought there between him and Thomas de l'Strother, an Englishman, on Monday [12th November], the morrow of Martinmas. Liliat's Cross, synonymous with Lilliard's Edge, was a famous Border trysting-place on Ancrum Muir, between Melrose and Jedburgh.[2] The safe conduct, narrating that Grant had obliged himself in great sums of money to make his appearance duly, takes into the royal protection Grant himself and certain other Scots, his companions, whatever might be their rank, and whether armed or unarmed. It authorises them to go to the duel and to return without molestation, and endures until the morning after the duel, 'till sunrise of the morrow of the duel day.'

The issue of this duel is not expressly on record, but the author of a famous Peerage says he found in a manuscript history of the Grant family that the Robert Grant here concerned (who was of course 'a man of remarkable fortitude and resolution,' like most peerage heroes) 'fought and vanquished an

1 Rot. Scot. ii. 29ab. Rymer, vii. 275.

2 Roxburgh and Jedburgh were still in English hands at this time. Wyntoun, ix. ch. 5. Hence the necessity of a safe conduct for a Scot to travel on Scottish ground.

English champion of undoubted courage and great strength of body in the beginning of the reign of Robert III.'[1] This makes it possible that Grant was victorious on the morrow of Martinmas, and his victory may have been one of the services for which a few years later he was in receipt of a pension from the royal exchequer.[2] It is, however, equally probable that he did not slay his adversary, for Thomas del Strother seems to have lived to fight another day. Fifteen years later a champion of the same name—presumably the same man—again appears upon the scene to fight a Border duel.[3]

Peerage evidence.

On 12th November 1381 a safe conduct[4] was given for another duel to be fought at Liliat's Cross on [25th November] the feast of St. Katherine. The combat was waged by consent of King Robert of Scotland and of King Richard of England. John Chattowe of Scotland, esquire, is described as the party appellant. 'Chatto,' it may be said in passing, is the name of a height in the Cheviots, in Hounam parish, Roxburghshire, a rounded grassy eminence of over 1100 feet. John Chattowe, it may be inferred, was a borderer.

Chattowe and Badby, 1381.

1 Douglas Baronage, ed. 1798, 342. Had Sir Robert Douglas not seen the writ in Rymer, query, would posterity have heard of that interesting passage in the family history?

2 Pension 'for services in France and elsewhere' in 1392. Exch. Rolls, iii. 313.

3 Strother *versus* Inglis, *infra*.

4 Rot. Scot. ii. 39b.

William of Badby, liegeman of England, was the party defendant. By another document[1] Henry, earl of Northumberland, is represented as detained in Parliament by the king's command, and his son Henry—known to history as Harry Hotspur—is ordained along with three other Border magnates to attend at the duel and see all things done as the earl would do were he there in person. For this duel Sir William Faryndon was sent north to the Borders to make the preparations, receiving £20 for his expenses on his return.[2]

Richard II. and Border duels, 1383.

In March 1383 King Richard or his council appointed wardens of the marches,[3] but a special rider to the appointments commanded that on any case arising in which a duel should happen to be offered or waged, the acceptance, offer or wager should be reserved to the king or his lieutenant.[4] One of the duties of the wardens was the hearing of pleas based on breaches of truce between the realms—march treason as it was called. They had cognizance of treason at large within their wardenry.[5] To the latter class of appeals it is probable that the writ of 26th March 1383 refers, and it

1 Rot. Scot. ii. 40a.
2 Bain's Cal. iv. No. 309.
3 Commission dated 20th March 1382-3. Rot. Scot. ii. 49b.
4 Rot. Scot. ii. 50b. Mandamus quod si in aliquo casu emergente in hac parte duellum aliquod offerri seu vadiari contigerit quod acceptatio oblatio seu vadiatio hujusmodi duelli ad nos et personam nostram vel ad locum nostrum tenentem in hac parte reservetur. Date 26 March 1383.
5 Scots Acts, ii. 43, in 1455.

would have the effect of placing such an appeal on much the same footing when a challenge was given as had become common elsewhere in the kingdom. It referred the case to the king as virtual head of the court. In fact, it sent it to the court of chivalry.

After the great tilting at London in 1390, noticed at some length in a future chapter, the Earl of Moray went on pilgrimage to France. In his retinue was Walter of Strathern.[1] Two years later on his return Walter did homage to the English king, and by special favour received an annuity of £10 for his good service for life.[2] Whether due to this change of fealty or otherwise he was accused of treason in 1395. His accuser was another Scotsman, Thomas of Beverley, an esquire, to whom King Richard paid £45 to provide himself with horses, armour, and other necessaries for the duel, giving about the same time a sum of £20 to Strathern.[3] The appeal of treason[4] was made before Sir John Cheyne, constable of England, and a day was ordained for the battle which was to take place at Berwick. The sum for which Beverley had to find pledges was £1000 of English money. For this large sum Sir Robert Logan and Sir John

Strathern and Beverley, 1395.

[1] Rot. Scot. ii. 105a. Bain's Cal. iv. No. 412.

[2] Bain's Cal. iv. No. 434-5.

[3] Bain's Cal. iv. No. 468.

[4] Rot. Scot. ii. 129b. Bain's Cal. iv. No. 468. Beverley appears to have gone to Flanders in 1389. Rot. Scot. ii. 100a. He had safe conduct to enter England from Scotland in 1393. Rot. Scot. 122b. Bain's Cal. iv. No. 458.

Ramorgny[1] became security, and on 19th August they received a safe conduct to enable them to fulfil their pledge and present their man in the lists at Berwick.

Happily there is at least one Border duel of this period which is not left half told. Most of the preceding instances have been stories which began but did not end. That which completes the quartette of this chapter has an ending definite enough. Thomas de Strother (supposed to be the same as he of that name whom Robert Grant, on Peerage authority, is said to have defeated in 1380) fought again in 1395. This time there is no doubt about the issue, and the record is short and decisive. In the year of our Lord 1395, at Reulhauch,[2] says Bower,[3] there was a duel between Sir Thomas Strotheris, Englishman and challenger, and Sir William Inglis, Scot and defender, in which the Englishman was slain. The wardens of the marches were present as judges—viz., Archibald, earl of Douglas,[4] and Henry Percy, the elder, earl of Northumberland. Nor is Bower the sole authority. The

Strother and Inglis, 1395.

1 Most readers will recognise the villain of the Fair Maid of Perth. He was suspected of a hand in the betrayal and murder of the king's son, the young Duke of Rothesay, in 1402. Bower, xv. ch. 12. Extracta, 208-9. Scott's hanging of him is a novelist's license.

2 Rule Water is a tributary of the Teviot. It is famous for its 'hauchs.' My own eyes can confirm the evidence of the New Statistical Account, Roxburghshire, 208.

3 Bower, xv. ch. 3. Extracta, 203.

4 Archibald the Grim.

old index[1] of a missing roll of charters by Robert III. contains the following entry :—'Carta to Sir William Inglis of the barony of Maner,[2] blench, vice-com. Peebles, for the slaughter of Thomas Struther, Englishman, in single combat; reservand the lands possessed by William Gladstanes[3] knight in the said baronie and superiority thereof.' The charter itself,[4] dated in 1396, bears to have been granted to Sir William 'in reward for a noble deed—viz., the slaying of Thomas de Strother, an English knight, whom he slew on the Borders in a duel.'

An interesting charter.

CHAP. 65.—"*Vegetius*" *in Scotland.*

VEGETIUS *de re militari* is a well-known work which Fordun does not once name, but which his continuator Bower, who flourished early in the 15th century, was never weary of citing.[5] Vegetius *de bello*

[1] Robertson's Index, 137, 18.

[2] Manor is a highly interesting parish in Peeblesshire. That it wa the home of the Black Dwarf is a minor attraction.

[3] The Gladstones—'Gladstain, good at need'—were of note in Peeblesshire, certainly as far back as the time of David II. Reg. Mag. Sig. i. 41; also many charters in Robertson's Index. In 1358 this very William Gladstone, under the name of William de Gledestanes junior, had safe conduct to Oxford or Cambridge University, as he chose, for purposes of study. Rot. Scot. i. 829b.

[4] Cited in Nisbet's Heraldry, i. p. 84. Douglas Baronage, 198. . . . . in remunerationem facti nobilis—viz., interfectionis Thomæ de Struthers, Anglici militis, quem super martiis in duello interfecit.

[5] Bower, vol. ii. p. 306, 392, 453, 491.

campestri, on the other hand, the work referred to in the opening lines of the 'Maner of Battale' in the next chapter, is not so easily discovered. Search has been made in the British Museum. Almost every book bearing the name of Vegetius has been examined, and not only has the 'Maner of Battale' not been found there, but there has not been detected so much as the material for its composition. There is indeed 'L'Art de Chivalerie,' which is almost word for word with 'L'Arbre de Batailles,' but neither of these books of chivalry contains an original for the 'Maner of Battale.' Various manuscripts arousing a suspicion that they might be the originals have also been searched, but without result. The old treatise must go to the reader with its puzzle unsolved.

'The Maner of Battale.'

No doubt its publication now made for the first time will soon lead to its identity being detected. An opinion is entertained that it may be traced to a French origin. But its value depends only in a minor degree on its source. Nor is it material to the argument in this book, although it would have been distinctly desirable, to determine its date. It is enough to say that it must have been held in high esteem in Scotland, for it is found in not a few of the best law manuscripts, with annotations to shew that it was viewed in a practical, legal, and not in any dilettante light. For the version now given three manuscripts, two in Edinburgh and one

A problem.

in London, have been collated, disclosing scarce a single difference except in spellings.[1]

CHAP. 66.—'*The Maner of Battale.*'

THE Maner of Battale within listes scilicet Vigesius *de bello campestri, etc.*

Heir techis Us Vigeis[2] in his buk of chevalry how battale within listis salbe governit.

It is to wit that ane king or ane prince havand power of batall, or ane deput for ane of thame, sal sit Juge in scaffald above the entre of the listes.[3]

And gif the appelour or the defendour be under the regiment governance or jugement of sindry kingis or princis awand to thai kingis thair obedience and allegeance, thai kingis or princis being adversaris of were, within quhat lordship or kinrik thai twa sall appeir to fulfill that derenye, of that land the king, the prince or the deput, or ane of thame, salbe Juge, and to that lelely sworne. And thereattoure[4] with the juge salbe [the] king, or prince or deput of the tother parte quhilk salbe to the forsaid Juge in that causs

1 John Bannatyne, MS. No. A. 7, 25, Advocates' Library, is the basis with a word or two as in the Monynet MS. Adv. Lib. A. 1, 28, folios 375-8, the older of the two from which indeed the first was copied. The version has been collated generally with that of the Harleian MS. 4700, in British Museum. There is not a single material difference. The contractions are extended, and my version is given for ordinary mortals rather than philologists.

2 Vigece is a French mode of spelling Vegetius.

3 Compare 'Order of Combats,' cap. iii. *infra*.

4 Thereattour, besides.

consuler,[1] and that thai may se that the Juge halds the law and govern that jugement be law and counsale.

Item, in the first the marschall and the constable sall gar devoid all maner of man out of the listis. And thai sall have within the listis sexteine knychtis or squyaris wele enarmit, and twa and twa be paris salbe set at ilk corner, at ilk side, and ilk end of the listis, for to keip and for to hald the listis voyd and undistrubillit.

How the constabill and the marschell sall minister in thare officis in keeping of the listis.[2]

The appelour sall appere and enter first. And gif he or the defendour duell our lang[3] or wald absent him, the constable sall gar[4] ane of his serjandis, or ane herald stand on a bar of the listis, or on ane stage at the entre of the barres, and call be name the prevare[6] or the defendour the quhilk that hapins to be absent, 'Enter and appere to fulfill thine appele as thow art oblist;' or the defendour be name, 'Enter within listis for to mak the defenss as thow art oblist.' And gif ony of thir[7] appeire nocht, than sall the borrowis[8] be callit to appeir in upone the pane writtin in thare appele with the repruf that folowis to the party absent.

The maner to call the appelour and the defendour to enter in listis.[5]

The constabill or the marshall sall inform the

[1] Consuler, counsellor. [2] Compare 'Order of Combats,' cap. vii.
[3] Tarry too long. [4] Gar, cause.
[5] Compare 'Order of Combats,' cap. iv.
[6] Prevare, prover, appellant. [7] Thir, these, them.
[8] Borrowis, pledges.

constable serjand or ane herald for to mak the kingis crya at ilkane of the four corneris of the barras in thir termez that folowis, 'We bid and comande on our liege lord the kingis behalf till all thai that ar here in tyme of the derenye[2] of quhat degre, condicioun, or of quhat stat thatever he be that ilk man of thame keip and yeymen[3] tentabilly[4] all thare wappinis fra the handis of thir twa personis that ar entrit now in thir listis for battale. And that na man mak ony signe or takin,[5] or contenance with heid, with e,[6] with hand, or with ony part of his body, or ony worde to speke throw the quhilk the ta party or the tother may have comfort or discomfort, amendment or parement[7] quhill[8] that the causs and the quarrell at Goddis will be determyt betwix thir twa forsaid personis. And that thir fornamit poyntis thus cryit and commandit be diligently and specialy yemit and kepit upone the pane of tynsale[9] of liff and lym, land, and all that thai[10] may tyne againe our liege lord the king.' And gif thare be liegis of sindry kingis or princis as is before said, the crya salbe maid sindry and baith in ane forme.

The parteis enterit, the maner to mak cry within listis.[1]

The appele and the ansuer of it aw and suld be

1 Compare the 'oiez' in 'Order of Combats,' cap. vii.
2 Derenye, the combat. See p. 183, *supra*.
3 Yeymen, to keep or hold.
4 Tentabilly (from verb to tent, to take care of) carefully.
5 Takin, token. 6 E, eye.
7 Parement, loss. 8 Quhill, till. 9 Tynsale, loss.
10 'Thai' in Harleian MS. not in Monynet or Bannatyne.

inclosit in writ under the selis of baith the prevour and the defendour, the quhilk salbe in the yemesale[1] of the Juge. The crya maid, the Juge sall deliver the writ to the constabill, and than the constabill and the marschall sall first show it to the prover sittand in his chyar at the este end of the listis, sayand 'Schir, kenys[3] thow this is thi sele and thine appele hale and undammyst as quhen thow set thi sele therto?' And richtswa[4] it salbe showit to the defendour with thai ilk demandis sittand in his chyar[5] at the west end of the listis. And gif baith be grantit, the appele and the ansuer to that hale and under thare selis, Than the constabill and the marschall sall gang agane to the provour sayand 'Schir, sen this appele and the ansuer of it is knawn to yow baith hale and under your selis ye mon se it oppinit and here it be red in entent that ye suld knaw your awne wordis, and that we berand office suld bere witnes quhat ye said therto.' And this done richt, than sall thai turne againe to the defendour and suld say till hym, 'Schir, we have oppinit this appele and red it to your folowar,[6] and he has ansuerit that his quarrellis ar guide and lele, and that gif God will he sall pruf be his body.' And than the defenss salbe red, and than sall thai say, 'Now we have red yow your

The schawing of the appele.[2]

1 Yemesale, keeping.
2 Compare 'Order of Combats,' cap. v.
3 Kenys, knowest.
4 Richtswa, just so.
5 Chyar, chair.
6 Follower, pursuer, appellant.

defence ye will say for your part.' And gif he consentis him than sall thai swere.

The maner of the aith within listis.[1]

The provour in his chyar at the est end of the listis as is before said in thir termez sall swere, 'My quarrell is gude and lele, and with help of God that sall I prove be my body, havand nane stane of vertew upone me, na wichecraft or enchantment or ony uthir maner of sorcery. I sall nocht trow bot anerly[2] in God and in the richt of my quarrell.' To that the great aith[3] sall be made. Than thai sall gang to the defendour, and in thai ilk[4] termez and articulis gar him swere that he sall mak his defence. In all this tyme ilkane[5] of thame sall have certane counsale lymmit[6] to be with thame quhill[7] thai be set in ther sadillis, and thare speris gevin thame in thare handis. And than sall thare counsalours be removit out of the listis alswele as all uthir men. They sall hufe[8] with thare speris in ther handis to byde quhill the Juge gar be cryit 'Moveth.'[9] And with that worde thare twa gluffis[10] that thai laid in wage salbe cassin[11] betwix thame and than thai proceid to ther devor.[12]

1 Compare 'Order of Combats,' cap. vi. vii.

2 I shall trust only.

3 Aith, oath. The great oath is still in Scotland a well-known phrase, once greatly used in ratifications by married women.

4 Thai ilk, these same. 5 Ilkane, each.

6 Lymmit, specially assigned. 7 Quhill, till.

8 Hufe, . . . to byde quhill ; behove, . . . to stay till.

9 Good Anglo-Saxon and old English imperative plural.

10 Gluffis, gloves. 11 Cast. 12 Devor, devoir.

The constabill sall have all the armouris and the wappinis that ar custumyt to have or hald for batall that is to say ane spere, ane schelde, ane lang suerde, ane schort swerde, ane sterop,[2] ane knyfe.

Of feis falland to constable or mershall of him convict within listes.[1]

The marschall sall have the horss with the apparell of the horss armyng and uthir covering quhat sua it be or anornment,[3] bot[4] he be convict and vincust within lystis departis fra his horss and be sa hard stad be eventuyr[6] that he leif ony of his said wappinis with his horss. It is nocht cleirly declarit in this buke quhether constabill or mershall sall have thai wappinis.[7]

The marshallis fee in the said case.[5]

And forthy[8] quhen sic[9] caiss or causs sall fall gif[10] athir of thame half and nowther all of wappinis left with horss for best conclusion and evin departing[12] of wappinis.

Of departing of the harnes.[11]

The constabill than at the north este corner of

1 Compare 'Order of Combats,' cap. viii.

2 Sterop, stirrup?

3 Anornment, adornment. Jamieson's Dict. has anorn, to adorn.

4 Bot, except, unless.

5 Compare 'Order of Combats,' cap. ix.

6 Eventuyr, adventure, by chance.

7 Compare 'Order of Combats,' cap. ix. note first.

8 Forthy, therefore.

9 'Sic,' such.

10 Gif, give.

11 This in all three MSS. forms the last clause of the treatise. But its tenor proclaims its true place to be as here printed. The error proves that the oldest version extant is not the original.

12 Evin departing, equal dividing.

the lystis sal gar be borne out of the barres him discomfyt and recryand, be he on life or be he dede, armyt or dispolyeit[2] of his armouris, at the will of the constabill.

How the man convict sall be demanit.[1]

The auctor of this buke of chevalrye sais that within quhat kynrik[3] or provynce that lystis be in for batall, the kyng or the prynce of that land havand autorite to be Juge of swyk[4] batell, his officiaris of were,[5] that is to say constable or marshall, sall minister within lystes as is before writtin, notaganestanding[6] the Juge and his consale sittand in jugement.

Of the Ministeris.

Explicit modus duelli, &c.[7]

CHAP. 67.—*International Tilting.*

THE three years' truce between Scotland and England, negotiated towards the close of 1389, was the beginning of a long but not quite unbroken

[1] Compare 'Order of Combats,' cap. vii. Demanit, demeaned.
[2] Dispolyeit, despoiled. [3] Kynrik, kingdom.
[4] Swyk, such. [5] Were, war. [6] Notwithstanding.
[7] The Monynet MS. and the John Bannatyne MS. have this note at the end :—Adde ea quæ dicuntur in 4ta parte Regie Majestatis in titulo *de aliquo cui imponitur ars furti* et titulo 92 in De judicibus et in cap. 18 in statutis Roberti tertii. The reference is to Ass. Dav. ch. 20, Scots Acts, i. 321; Regiam, iv. c. 12; to the 'De Campionibus,' ch. 28, *supra*, and to Act of 1400 noted hereafter. It shews plainly the practical business light in which the writers of the MSS. regarded the Maner of Battale, the Regiam, and the Act of 1400.

period of peace. The relations between the two countries soon became cordial, and the safe-conducts issued to Scotsmen travelling south present a wonderful picture of friendly international intercourse. Traders with their wares, knights in quest of adventures in the tilting-ring, pilgrims to Canterbury and St. James and the shrines of the Apostles at Rome, mingled with scholars journeying to Oxford and Cambridge.[1] John Barbour the poet had similarly travelled from his home in the north towards these seats of learning five-and-twenty years before.[2] From the year 1386 the Rolls of Scotland abound in safe-conducts given to enable the holder to perform feats or points of arms.[3] Some of these encounters may deserve attention.

Safe conducts.

The most famous tournament of them all took place in 1390, when the chivalry of the two countries, after the long war, first met on a friendly footing in the English capital, and before the English king. Sir David de Lindsay had challenged Sir John de Wells to do certain feats of arms with him.[4] These feats of arms were sufficiently serious, for the 'taylyhe' or indenture[5] between them was for battle

[1] Rot. Scot. ii. 100a, 122a.
[2] Rot. Scot. i. 886b.
[3] For example in 1387, 1391, 1392, 1413, 1414. Rot. Scot. vol. ii. 87a, 90b, 111ab, 117ab, 205a, 207a, 212a. Bain's Cal. in 1391, 1393, and 1405, iv. No. 425, 452, 711. Cal. Rot. Pat. in 1404, 248.
[4] Rot. Scot. ii. 103a, ad perficienda quedam facta armorum.
[5] Wyntoun, ix. ch. 11.

to the death. In early summer Lindsay went to London, where many other Scottish knights and nobles were at the time. Amongst them was Sir William Dalzell, who had gone thither ostensibly to buy arms.[1] On 6th May the great encounter took place[2] before Richard II. and his Queen seated in 'summer castle,' the decorated coign of vantage from which royalty surveyed such scenes. The Scotch chroniclers, who liked right well such stirring stories, tell with lingering minuteness of detail how

Before Richard II. 1390.

> The Lyndyssay thare wyth manffull fors
> Strak qwyte the Wellis fra his hors,
> Flatlyngis downe apon the grene
> Thare all his saddille twme[3] was sene.

A spiteful English whisper rose that Lindsay was tied to the saddle—a charge which he promptly refuted by leaping from his horse, kneeling before the king, and then, heavily armed though he was, springing to saddle again with a single bound.

When the agreed-on number of tilts had been run, the combat was continued on foot. At last Lindsay, fastening his dagger in his adversary's armour, closed with him, lifted him up, and then dashed him headlong to the ground—

Sir David Lindsay and De Wells.

[1] Rot. Scot. ii. 103a.

[2] This is the date given by Wyntoun, ix. ch. 11. It was on 25th May that the prizes were bestowed, so that probably Wyntoun's date is right. The encounter is described at length by Wyntoun only, but it was a famous fight, and is noted in Bower, xv. ch. 4; Liber Pluscarden. i. 331-2; Extracta, 204. [3] Twme, toom, empty.

the fall leaving him defenceless and defeated. In perfect accord with the savage contract, as well as the rules regulating the duel to the death, the victor now had it in his power to kill the vanquished. But Lindsay, with a courtesy far worthier of chivalry than the victory itself, extended his hand to his adversary, and, with the words 'Rys, rys, schir knycht,' assisted Wells to his feet. Then, leading him towards the Queen's seat, he gracefully delivered him to her—a prisoner.

There was a series of tournaments at this time, in one of which Sir William Dalzell, who was, according to Stow, the King of Scotland's banner-bearer, played a prominent part.[1] Who, save Sydney Smith and misguided Englishmen who vainly quote him, has ever doubted the high degree and quality of Scottish humour? At the court of King Richard, Sir William Dalzell upheld the reputation of his country. A witty reply of his completely silenced an English knight, whom Bower describes as 'sufficiently grandiloquent and verbose,' and who had jested somewhat ponderously at the expense of the Scots.[2] In the field Dalzell's humour displayed itself no less. Sir Piers Courtenay, a handsome Englishman whom Stow calls the King of England's banner-bearer, and a famous tilter,[3] had

The two banner-bearers.

[1] Stow's Survey, iii. 239. Annals, 308.

[2] The joke is at once too good and too bad to mangle into a foot-note. See Bower, xv. ch. 5.

[3] Bower, xv. ch. 6, says that he was commonly called the champion of

donned a brand-new surcoat bearing the embroidered device of a falcon. From the beak of the bird there hung a scroll with the words[1]—

> I beer a falcon, fairest of flicht ;
> Quha so pinches at hir, his deth is dicht[2]
> In graith.[3]

As soon as possible the Scot furnished himself with a like surcoat but with a device in caricature. Where Sir Piers had a falcon, Sir William had a magpie with the motto—

Dalzell's magpie.

> I beer a py[4] pykkand at ane pes ;
> Quha so pykkis at her, I sal pyk at his nese
> In faith.

So obvious an insult could not pass, and a duel with sharp lances followed. Sir William had purposely left his helmet unstrapped, and in the first two courses of the tilt the helmet yielding before Sir Piers's spear, the full shock of the encounter was avoided. In the third course Sir William knocked out two of the handsome Englishman's front teeth. Sir Piers in great anger complained of the unfairness of the Scot in not having his helmet laced. On this Sir William offered to ride six courses anew, on con-

the King of England, and calls him the brother uterine of the primate of England. The whole account of this adventure of Dalzell's is from Bower, xv. ch. 6. There are many proofs of Courtenay's prowess as a tilter. See Knyghton, 2706.

1 Need one cite Marmion's motto? 'Who checks at me to death is dight.' Canto I. stanza 6, note H.

2 Dicht, ready, prepared.

3 Graith, armour : still used in Scotland for a horse's harness.

4 Tytler reads 'pyot,' Hist. of Scot. vol. ii. ch. 1. Nese, nose.

dition that in all respects on mounting their steeds he and his adversary should be alike, and that a forfeit of £200 should be incurred if either party broke the contract. To this offer Sir Piers, 'blazing with wrath over the loss of his teeth,'[1] at once assented. The wily Scot, whose conduct savours rather of chicane than chivalry, then pled before King Richard that as he had lost an eye at the battle of Otterburn, Sir Piers must consent to lose one of his likewise, to put him on the same footing in terms of the bargain. This Sir Piers naturally refused to do. Sir William therefore claimed the forfeit of £200. This demand provoked an altercation and some fighting between the knights of the two nationalities represented. But at length King Richard adjudged the money to Sir William, declaring that he surpassed the Englishmen both in deeds and wit.

Sharp practice in chivalry.

After all the jousts were over, rich presents or prizes[2] were given by the king's command to the knights who had earned laurels in the lists. Cloth of gold bought from 'Richard Whytyngdone' formed part of one Scotsman's prize. John, Earl of Moray, whom Pitscottie calls 'aue man of singular bewtie and vertew,'[3] who had gone to London expressly for a

1 Irâ incandescens ob amissionem dentium. But such teeth did not help to victory in the chivalric duel as in Bracton's duel of law.

2 These appear in the Easter Issue Roll of 13 Rich. II., under date 25th May 1390. Bain's Cal. iv. No. 411.

3 Pitscottie (1814) 65. Bain's Cal. iv. pref. xxi.

joust of war with the Earl of Nottingham,[1] received money and silver plate.[2] By the king's command Sir William Dalzell received a present of £40, while Sir David Lindsay received in money £100, besides a silver cup and gilt ewer as a tribute to his prowess. Sir David appears to have had further business of a kindred nature on hand, for on the very day on which he received his prizes a safe-conduct was granted to enable a ship to carry from Dundee 'a full suit of harness of war for the body of David Lyndesey of Scotland, knight.'[3] He appears at this time to have gone to France, carrying his armour with him, and returning in 1391.[4] Scotch historians say that in England no less than in Scotland fame long kept alive the memory of his knightly worth.[5] Nor on his part was he unmindful of the gratitude due to the saint of chivalry for his triumph. On his return to his own country he founded an altar in honour of St. George, in the parish church of Dundee, and endowed chaplains there to chant a daily mass, 'which,' says the faithful chronicler to whom we owe the fact, 'the writer of these presents once heard.'[6]

Saint George.

1 Safe-conduct 16th March 1389-90. Rot. Scot. ii. 103-4.
2 Bain's Cal. iv. No. 411.
3 Rot. Scot. ii. 104b.
4 Rot. Scot. ii. 110b.
5 Bower, xv. 4.
6 Extracta, 204.

CHAP. 68.—*A New Conclusion.*

SO, then, St. George had come to Scotland too. Let us brush aside 'The Maner of Battale' in the meantime, ignore mere tiltings and feats of arms however deadly, and confine attention to the evidences given for the duel proper. Whither do they lead? Do they not make it clear that the renascence of the duel under chivalry, which was so pronounced in England, was a potent fact in Scotland as well? The detail of previous chapters was not without a purpose. It was meant to herald a conclusion not yet advanced by any historian. Seen by the light of what is to follow, it points with unhesitating finger to a SCOTTISH COURT OF CHIVALRY.

CHAP. 69.—*Precedents for the Inch of Perth.*

THE conclusion hinted at in the last chapter, and which some future chapters will amply confirm, has important bearings. It sets in a truer light the great problem of the conflict on the North Inch of Perth in 1396, which the greatest of novelists and the most widely-gifted of antiquaries has made familiar wherever the English tongue is spoken. That strange combat between the Clan Chattan and the Clan Kay has long been a landmark in history—

a beacon which casts a fierce light athwart a dark time. Notwithstanding, its place in Scottish history is a yet unsettled problem.

A solution has been suggested by an eminent antiquary,[1] to whose editorial labours Scotland owes much. 'Trial by Combat,' says the Scottish Lyon King, 'had in a previous age been a widespread and established mode of deciding questions of civil right, and perhaps we have here a late instance of this form of judicial process surviving in the Highlands after it had become obsolete elsewhere.' In this view the combat would have to be classed as an isolated vestige of barbarism, with some relation to a previous age, but with none to its own; it would be a survival—not an expression of a contemporary phase. In direct opposition to this it must be urged that judicial combats were not characteristic only of a past age; they were not obsolete elsewhere; and they were at that very time in the zenith of popularity. The event therefore was no isolated survival of barbarity. Regarded as a judicial combat it was in perfect harmony with the spirit of the period, no less in its chivalric than its judicial aspects.

A suggestion considered.

Had there been but two men instead of sixty the duel would have been a very ordinary affair. More than two combatants are never heard of in the

[1] Dr. George Burnett, Lyon King of Arms, in his preface to Exch. Rolls, iii. p. lxxx. I may here tender my hearty homage to Mr. Burnett for many valuable clues and hints in his prefaces.

duel of law. It is not so in the duel of chivalry, although actual examples fought are rare, unless in those tiltings and combats à outrance in which so many knights and nobles slew each other in what they miscalled a gentle and joyous game. Encounters of equal numbers in tournaments were very common. Nor were they confined to tournaments. In 1340, as we have seen, Edward III. proposed a judicial combat with Philip VI., to be fought with one hundred knights on each side. Richard II. made a similar proposal for four-a-side. The idea was thus not new in theory. Neither was it new in practice, for a few years before there had actually taken place a combat of the kind in France. Precisely the same numbers had fought there as were to fight at Perth. The combatants were English and French, and it is a certainty that the story, which told against England, had vogue and popularity in Scotland at the time. The analogy is strikingly significant.

Duels of more than two.

Hume tells the story in an appendix to his history.[1] His version is from a French original. How far the version of Père Daniel is exact is not a question which can be discussed here; but that the encounter was a fact is quite clear, for the Scots historians tell the same story with much circumstance. With

[1] Hume's History, ed. 1823, vol. ii. note 1. I have to thank my friend and neighbour Mr. John Gibb for this reference. Hume quotes as his author Père Daniel, ii. 536-7.

Hume's version we need not concern ourselves. Let us follow the Scotch chronicles.[1]

In 1355 (the date is not to be rashly trusted) the lord of Beaumanoir, a well-known French soldier, whose deeds Froissart often noted down, had taken prisoner an English knight. The captive was very arrogant, and spoke slightingly of the French, roundly declaring *more Anglicano*,

> Ane Ingliss man worthe Franche twa.

One day he was heard to wish for a combat with equal numbers, and Beaumanoir promptly said he might go to his own countrymen and select nine-and-twenty companions. He himself would do the same amongst his own kinsmen, and the companies would meet in combat. The bargain was quickly closed, and a place of meeting and battle appointed:

An Anglo-French precedent.

> By Kayne in Normondy it was.

Soon the Englishman gathered round him his needed twenty-nine, and punctual to his hour back he went to Caen. Beaumanoir's band was ready too, and their leader had arranged that the sweetheart or the wife of each should be present on the eventful day. He deemed, says the historian, that the sight of fair ladies would take away every thought of cowardice and give courage and strength.

> The day come sone, and in the place
> A stalwart barres maide thaire was.

[1] Wyntoun, viii. ch. 43. Bower, xiv. ch. 11. Extracta, 183-4.

The Frenchmen had horses covered in iron and steel. The English horses were not covered, and their riders made ready to fight on foot. The Frenchmen dismounted also, and the battle began with spears. One Frenchman was killed, and after long, hard fighting the battle was as undecided as when it began. Then a French squire left the ranks and went towards his horse, his lord telling him he little weened that he would be first to flee. The squire answered,

'The ram oft gais a-bak
That he the maire debaite may mak,'

and then he proceeded to illustrate the proverb. Mounting his steed he suddenly charged the English flank, flinging their line[1] into confusion; his countrymen improved the occasion and the fight soon ended. Nine Englishmen were slain and twenty-one were prisoners. The French lost one man.

Bower after his fashion closes the episode with an epigrammatic leonine couplet. Wyntoun draws the moral that there is no wit in despising other nations.[2] Shall not we too draw a moral? Our moral is that there was current in Scotland an Anglo-French precedent for a duel of thirty with thirty. How it came

[1] A formation according to Bower in the shape of a harrow—cuneum ad modum hericii conglobatum. At Creçy the English bowmen were drawn up in the form of a 'harrow.' Green's Short History. Probably the same triangular formation is implied.

[2] I thank Mr. J. T. T. Brown for an interesting parallel reference in the 'Religio Medici' (Golden Treasury ed.) p. 99.

matters not, though its French origin appears on the surface. It may have stirred the roystering, fire-eating spirits[1] in the allied French and Scottish camp, in the Scotch campaign against England in 1385. It needs no proving that the story was there—a precedent in chivalry.

CHAP. 70.—*Preliminaries—Inch of Perth.*

Clan Chattan and Clan Kay.

THE Clan Chattan and the Clan Kay had long been at feud with each other. By their dissensions the whole Highlands were disturbed, for they were two great clans, numbering many septs, and inhabiting a wide tract of highland Scotland. For an examination into their identity and the causes of their discord, Skene's 'Celtic Scotland' must be consulted.[2] Suffice it here to say that the feud was deadly, and Celtic in its bitterness. At last it was arranged that thirty men from each clan should fight on the Inch of Perth before the king, so that the decision of battle might end the long dispute. The question is, How came that mode to be adopted?

Tytler represents the clans as of their own motive taking up the idea and broaching it to the govern-

[1] That these adjectives are not misplaced will appear, from Scots Acts, i. 555. One of the rules of the army was that if debate arose the disputants were not to take arms against each other.

[2] Celtic Scotland, iii. 310-18. I have preferred to adhere to Bower's names for the clans.

ment. He seems to ascribe to it no judicial character.[1] Hill Burton is scenic and unsatisfactory —not to say shallow. In his eyes it was a lively variation in the monotony of the tournament.[2] Some countenance has been shown to the notion that the Scottish king allowed it as a convenient way of getting rid of sixty unruly subjects by mutual slaughter. But this is a stupid supposition — as if the loss of three score warriors could cripple the Highlands! Skene alone of historians has given the matter the attention it merits, and his masterly examination puts every other out of court.[3] He sees in the facts the indication of a judicial wager of battle. His view these pages confirm; but even he scarcely gives the incident its full and true historical setting. As to the origin of the expedient of battle he has said nothing.

Modern historians.

Turning from the moderns to the ancients it falls to be noted that Wyntoun[4] contents himself with a record of the encounter, and does not vouchsafe any explanation of inducing circumstances. But Bower is express in the statement that Sir David Lindsay and Thomas, Earl of Moray, used great diligence in treating with the clans. The proposal these noblemen made was that each clan should send thirty clansmen to fight before the king, so that the combat might end the contro-

The ancients.

1 Tytler's Hist. ii. ch. 1.

2 History iii. 70 *et seq.*

3 Celtic Scotland, 310-318.

4 Wyntoun, ix. ch. 17.

versy, and the land have peace. This proposal, says the old chronicler, mightily pleased both sides.[1] The Book of Pluscarden does not mention the Earl of Moray by name, but attributes the negotiation to Lindsay and other nobles of the land.[2] Probabilities strongly confirm the statement of Bower, for the earl and Lindsay were both closely interested in the pacification of these 'pestiferous caterans.'[3]

Thomas, Earl of Moray, was directly concerned, not only because his own province lay in the circle of disturbance, but because he was under obligation, sealed and sworn, to maintain order. Before he succeeded to the earldom, whilst John his father, the earl, was yet alive, a council had been held on 28th October 1389, at Inverness, presided over by the Earl of Fife, brother of the king and governor of the realm. That council had heard certain pleas between the Bishop of Moray and John, the earl. The bishopric had suffered terribly from the clansmen's forays, to which the bishop suspected the earl was accessory. The council, therefore, enjoined the latter to purge himself of all complicity with the caterans, and to ordain fit officers to punish crime. The earl purged[4] himself accordingly, and the whole proceedings witnessed, amongst others, by Sir David

Thomas, Earl of Moray.

[1] Bower, xv. ch. 3. [2] Liber Pluscarden. i. 330-1.

[3] Bower's phrase 'pestiferos cateranos.'

[4] This seems to have been by compurgation or wager of law. For an instance of this in 1292, see Scots Acts, i. 447.

Lindsay,[1] were recorded in a sealed indenture.[2] A few months later Thomas, the earl's son, and at that time Sheriff of Inverness—destined soon to become Earl of Moray himself—attached his seal to a deed whereby he became the warden and protector of the bishopric, and all its goods and property, against all malefactors and caterans.[3] He was to receive a rising yearly fee[4] in return for this contract of protection, which in the Cathedral at Elgin on 22nd February 1390 he swore to perform. The results of the contract little satisfied the bishop.[5]

Brynt the kyrk wes off Elgyne
Be wyld wykkyd Heland-men.

So Wyntoun[6] tells us. Still there seems no doubt that Moray made an effort to fulfil his part of the bargain. On 25th September 1394 Thomas, now earl, entered into a contract[7] with Alexander of the Isles, lord of Lochaber.[8] This second contract had for its object the security of the lands and possessions of the regality of Moray and all its ecclesiastical lands. Alexander was to receive a large annual

1 John de Ramorgny, Esquire, was also a witness. Moray Chart. 197-200.

2 Moray Chart. 201. Date, feast of St. Peter in Cathedra, 22nd Feb. 1389-90.

3 Contra omnes malefactores viros kethranicos et alios quoscunque.

4 The fee was £10 for 1390, rising to 35 marks in 1394.

5 This fact is sufficiently evinced by the title the writ bears in the chartulary, which heads it *Inutilis et dampnosa provisio.*

6 Book ix. ch. 12.

7 Moray Chart. 354-5.

8 It was in Lochaber in 1429 that Alexander of the Isles was deserted by two clans, Clan Chattan and Clan Cameron, during the expedition of King James against him. Bower, xvi. 16.

payment[1] in consideration of the clause which bound him to hinder to the utmost 'his own men or other caterans of whatever rank they might be'[2] from over-running and eating up the lands of Moray. These contracts incidentally mention other engagements of a like kind, and are a sure sign of an honest attempt by the earl to keep order and band together the Highlands for peace. It is evident that with the Earl of Moray peace was an object of concern. With Lindsay it was no less so, for his lands of Glenesk lay within the highland line. 'The land of the Lindsays' was dangerously near the centre of disturbance. A few years previously he had

Sir David Lindsay.

himself been badly wounded by the dying blow of a highlandman whom he had transfixed with his spear in an engagement in the Stormont—the doleful day's work at Glasclune,[3] when the rebellious clansmen routed a party of horse led by the Sheriff of Angus.

A contemporary in the bishopric which it was Moray's duty to defend has left a gloomy sketch of the time. There was no law in the land; the whole realm was one larceny; homicide, robbery, arson, and other crimes remained unpunished; justice herself an outlaw was banished from the kingdom.[4]

1 The payment was 80 marks a year drawn from certain lands.

2 Homines suos nec alios kethranos cujuscunque status fuerint.

3 Wyntoun's phrase, ix. ch. 14, where, under date 1392, he describes fully this encounter, which is noticed by Bower in xv. ch. 3.

4 Chart. Moray, 382. The date of this is 1398, but doubtless it was applicable to earlier years as well.

Perhaps the scribe sacrificed something to his epigrams, yet withal his picture is only too faithful. The episode on the Inch of Perth was no bolt from the blue.

The clan battle: its character and origin.

The duel was a blending of ferocity, chivalry, and law. It was on a scale fitted to satiate the Celtic thirst of blood. It had been preceded by many single combats duly waged and fought in a court of chivalric function on appeals of treason or kindred charge, and it was to be followed by others—some of them on the self-same spot. Whether the clans had fallen out upon some point of dignity, some question of chieftainship, or the like, the combat was part of a contract for the stanching of the feud. To that, it cannot be doubted, the respective parties gave solemn oath and bond—a contract which was to be sealed in the blood of the bravest of the long contending clans, and which having been so sealed was honourably kept for many after years. It thus possessed every feature to make it typical of its age. Without the element of chivalry it would not have been completely typical, and the presence of that element must be self-evident. Most natural it was that such a method as this should present itself to its prime suggestors, steeped in the chivalrous tradition. For the Earl of Moray's father was that earl who had fought with the Marshal of England in the lists at London in 1390. And was it not Sir David Lindsay who had vanquished De Wells? The expedient of duel, its suggestion by Lindsay wreath-crowned in chivalry, its eager acceptance by the unruly but ever gallant highlandmen, its authorisation[1] and appointment by the king and his counsellors, to whom a judicial combat was no new thing, its coming before a court which took cognisance of points of honour and dignity[2] as well as of charges of treason—these circumstances combine to place it in absolute harmony with the fitness of things. Only in degree is the incident remarkable; it was a judicial combat on the grand scale—a gigantic appeal in the Scottish Court of Chivalry.

It is not out of the question that the story of the duel in France told in the preceding chapter may have had some influence in determining the number of men taking part in the battle. It is certain that the number fixed[3] was fitted to avoid internal jealousies amongst the many septs composing the two great clans, for it would enable each sept to send its quota of clansmen to maintain its honour on the field of death.

[1] 'Rex . . . fecit appunctuamentum'—the king ordained it. These are the words of the Book of Pluscarden.

[2] As evidenced by duels on points of heraldry in England.

[3] For the number 30 in compurgation see last note on p. 78, *supra*. In the great wager of battle at the close of the French Song of Roland Pinabel has 30 pledges, who are all hanged after his defeat.

CHAP. 71.—*The Inch of Perth*, A.D. *1396*.

ON the North Inch of Perth, a broad alluvial holm on the south bank of the Tay, a barras was made. The spot it occupied lay between the river and the Black Friars' monastery[1]—the river forming one side of the field. History often, heedless of great causes, is mindful of petty facts. Whilst we grope in darkness to ascertain the nature of the quarrel of the clans, we know to a penny the cost of the barras for their battle. 'And for the wood, iron, and labour of making the enclosure for sixty persons fighting on the Inch of Perth, £14 2s. 11d.' So runs the lurid item.[2]

Preparations for battle.

When the champions of Clan Chattan and Clan Kay reached the place of battle one of the former clan lost heart and fled. Things were at a standstill for a time, for neither side was willing to fight save on equal terms, and it was no easy matter to find a substitute to take the caitiff's place. 'And no wonder,' says John Major[3] in a phrase borrowed from Horace, 'for it was no idle question about the wool of a goat to fight in doublet to the death.' But a man, 'a bargaining loon of only middling stature but

1 Wyntoun, ix. ch. 17.

2 Exch. Rolls, iii. 418.

3 John Major's Hist. ed. 1740, 280. Quia non erat quæstio de lanâ caprinâ in diploide ad mortem pugnare. [Bower says they fought without doublets—sine diploidibus.] For the phrase de lanâ caprinâ, see Horace, Epistles, book 1, 18. Ad Lollium.

fierce,' as Bower[1] comprehensively calls him, volunteered for half a mark[2] to take the dangerous post.

A defaulter.

He bargained however that if he left the barras alive he was to have his sustenance assured him for the rest of his days—a request promptly granted. It is said that the man who thus lightly took his life in his hand to aid the Clan Chattan was himself of that clan,[3] and like a true clansman hated its enemies. Tradition knows him as Gow-chruim, the crooked smith.

In high royal seat above the lists sat King Robert III. Near at hand was his brother the Earl of Fife, and around sat or stood the nobility of the land. A countless crowd had flocked to Perth to witness the event. Amongst them were many famous Frenchmen and Englishmen.[4] Doubtless there was a gallant show of Scottish beauty and chivalry. There sure enough would be the flower of knightly worth and courtesy Sir David Lindsay, and many a brave

The onlookers.

knight besides, and many a lady fair, whilst Hay of Errol, the high constable, and Keith the earl marshal,[5] with heralds and men at arms and all the chivalric pomp of office, made fitting proclamations and ordinances for the coming scene.

[1] Bower, xv. ch. 3. Stipulosus vernaculus, staturâ modicus, sed efferus.

[2] This is Bower's figure. The Book of Pluscarden makes it 40s.

[3] De eorum parentela fuit et alteram partem non multum dilexit. Book of Pluscarden, i. 330-1.

[4] Bower. Also Extracta, 203. [5] A pure inference.

Old Wyntoun tells that he 'herd say' how, in the selfsame hour of the selfsame day, the hosts of Christian and Saracen were fighting a great battle in Hungary. Wyntoun had heard aright; that day at Nicopolis a hundred thousand Christians, boasting at morn that if the sky should fall they would uphold it on their spears, ere even fell were cut to pieces.[1] In fate's calendar the 28th September[2] 1396 was marked with blood.

The men who were to act in the arena at Perth were lightly clad and without defensive armour. Each had a sword, a battle-axe, a dirk, and a bow with three arrows.[3] Thus accoutred and stript to the waist like their descendants in the charge at Killiecrankie, they waited only the signal to begin. An arrow of the Gow-chruim's shooting opened the battle and the record of death. Sword and axe and bow and arrow were plied with direful effect. 'As butchers slay bullocks in the shambles they slew each other.'[4] There was a slaughter pitiless and great, and when the fight was

The fight.

1 Gibbon, ch. 64 (iv. 388).

2 Hill Burton erroneously says 23rd October 1396. History, iii. 71. The date is quite clear. Nicopolis was fought on 28th September. Moray Chartulary, 382, says 28th September was the date of the Perth duel. Bower says Monday next before the feast of St. Michael. He errs only in the day of the week. Michaelmas, 29th September, was on a Friday, so that the battle took place on Thursday.

3 Book of Pluscarden limits the arrows to three. A limit must have been very necessary. Till the last arrow was shot the spectators would be in danger.

4 Bower.

ended the autumn sun looked down on full fifty corpses[1] on the Inch of Perth. The Clan Chattan had gained a bloody victory. On that terrible field the arm of the crooked smith had done right stalwart service. Valiantly he fought, say the historians, and he issued from the battle without a wound. Perth remembers him until this day.

Near the end of the combat, when but two of Clan Kay remained alive, one of them plunged into the river and escaped by swimming.[2] The other was taken prisoner, and his fate is left in doubt, for, while some say that 'by the assent of the other side he had mercy,' others say that he was hanged.[3] If the latter version be true, it will be remembered that hanging was the usual doom of a traitor vanquished in the lists.[4]

So ended the great battle, the high but stern and sad spectacle, on the Inch of Perth. It is not for one moment credible that these brave highlanders butchered each other in vain—to make a royal holi-

1 Wyntoun: 'Fyfty or ma ware slane that day.' Moray Chart. 382, says eleven survived. The Book of Pluscarden says seven. Major says twelve. Bower is silent on the point.

2 Bower does not mention this, but he makes the deserter at the outset escape thus. 3 Book of Pluscarden.

4 Major in a confused passage suggests this legal aspect of the case. The king he says might make two men charged with capital crime—duobus reis mortis—fight in his presence, or if one or other was charged with capital crime and the one accused the other, and it was not clear which was innocent, and they asked single combat for proof. 'But' he concludes, 'I should advise against this mode.' Hist. 281. As to Major's views, see ch. 80, *infra*.

day. Fifty clansmen did not die in cold blood to vary the monotony of a tournament. The combat decided some great matter of dispute, the cause of much bloodshed and many a raid for years before. As the feud had been Celtic in its bitterness, the duel had been fought with Celtic courage and ferocity; and the contract of concord, which was to follow on this decision of the plea in chivalry, and of which the battle was a condition precedent, was held-to with Celtic tenacity and good faith. There is every reason to believe that the great feud was stanched. 'Thenceforward for a long time,' says Bower, 'the north was at peace, and the raids of the Caterans at an end.'

Its consequences.

CHAP. 72.—*Facts and Suppositions, 1398-1412.*

THE tragedy of trial by battle in Britain had its great commanding scene on the Inch of Perth in 1396. By the side of that combat all other duels pale: it becomes almost a bathos to speak of those which follow.[1] The next in date was fought in England between two Scotsmen. Richard II. in the summer of 1398, according to Stow,[2] 'caused a Theatre to be made at Bristow for a combate to be fought betweene

[1] It may be as well to state that mere feats of arms are seldom noticed in this book. As has been said before a passage at arms was not necessarily a trial by battle. Passages at arms were numberless.

[2] Stow, 319.

two Scots, to wit the one being an Esquire appellant and the other a knight defendant, and the appellant was overcome and hanged.' His fate clearly indicates that the combat was a treason-duel. Why the Scots fought in England is not so clear.

In Sir John Skene's version of the Acts of Parliament in the statutes of Robert III. appears the following[1]:—

A supposed Act of 1400.

'*In quhat Cases singular Combat hes Place.* It is statute that in singular battell foure things are required:—

'*First*—That the deed for the quhilk the defender in appealed is capitall and may be punissed be the death.

2. '*Secundlie*—That it is quietlie and treasonablie done and committed.

3. '*Thirdlie*—That he quha is appealed be haldin suspect be conjectures or probable suspitions and presumptions.

4. 'That the cause or controversie may not be proven otherwaise bot be battell and not be witnes nor be instruments letters or be wreit.'

This provision it seemed good to the 19th century editors of the Scots Acts to omit bodily, denying it so much as a place in the *fragmenta.* Perhaps they were justified in doing so, and perhaps the editorial discretion was not an editorial indiscretion. At the same time the supposed Act appears in manuscripts

1 Skene's 'Auld Laws,' Acts, Robert III. ch. 16.

of high authority assigned, as Skene assigned it, to the reign of Robert III.[1] The resemblance of these four conditions for the duel in Scotland in 1400 to those for the duel in France in 1306 demands attention. The language of the Act in minutest particulars is borrowed from a treatise, believed to be of French origin, found in the Black Book of the Admiralty of England—the 'De Materia Duelli'[2] a commentary upon Philip the Fair's edict. Such a consonance of phrase could not have come by chance. That it is a genuine statute of Robert III. need not be insisted on as the basis of argument,

1 In Monynet MS. (Advocates Library A, 1, 28) page 330, and in John Bannatyne MS. (Adv. Lib. A. 7. 25) near the middle, it appears as the 18th Act of Robert III. as follows :—

Conditiones pro quibus cadit duellum

Nota quod quatuor requiruntur ad hoc quod cadat duellum, Primo, quod factum de quo quis provocatur requirat in se penam mortis [Et quod aliter non probari quam per duellum]; Secundo, quod proditionaliter factum sit in occulto; Tertio, quod ille qui provocatur per coniecturas vel verisimiles suspiciones seu presumptiones habeatur suspectus; Quarto, quod causa in se non potest aliter probari nisi per duellum, viz., non per testes neque per instrumenta nec per literas sive scripta.' The passage I have bracketed is an obvious repetition. There is very little difference between the terms of this Act and part of a section of the De Materia Duelli, for which see Black Book, i. 331. There the four conditions read thus :—Nota quod quatuor requiruntur ad hoc . . . quod in facto preposito duellum sequatur. Primo quod casus prepositus contra aliquem ad finem duelli requirat penam mortis. Secundo quod prodicionaliter et in occulto factum fuisse proponatur, et taliter quod per testes vel alios sufficientes probari non posset quam per duellum. Tertio quod ille qui super dicto casu provocatur, de dicto casu proposito per judicia vel presumpciones verisimiles habeatur suspectus. Quarto quod evidenter appareat factum de quo talis provocatur contigisse.

2 See last note.

but that it is so is far from improbable. Cases already described show the appeal of battle in practice. Cases which follow present with more or less exactness the precedent conditions which this supposed Act requires. Even if not a statute it might state the law. One notable case so late as 1537 shows that on the very lines of the provision the duel was not admissible where the proof was plain. Where the matter was determinable in the ordinary courts in the ordinary way battle did not apply, and in 1474 we shall meet a case where that objection was stated and sustained when an accused had 'keist down his hat profferand him to fecht.' The supposed Act viewed as its worst is a very respectable fragment indeed.

Supposed Act considered.

Between May 1400 and June 1401 there appears to have been another duel on the Inch of Perth, as an item of the expenditure of the authorities in the burgh contains the costs of 'wood bought for the enclosure for two men fighting at Perth, in the year of this account, and for nails and the labour of making the enclosure.'[1] No historical notice of this duel seems to be extant. Nor is there any for a similar entry at Stirling, 'pro barreris factis pro duello,' for making the barras for a duel[2] three years later.

More Facts.

[1] Exch. Rolls, iii. 526.
[2] Exch. Rolls, iii. 596.

In a brief calendar of events noted in the Chartulary of Glasgow there appears the following:[1]—

Bellum inter Joannem Hardy et Thomam Smyth,
MCCCCXII.

Fuller particulars of this treason duel are given by Bower, who says that it was fought at Batelhalch, the judge being Archibald, second of that name, Earl of Douglas. Smyth had charged Hardy with the crime of treason—falsely, as it proved. The accused was victorious, and Smyth died in the duel.[2]

Hardy and Smyth, 1412.

CHAP. 73.—*On 'The Order of Combats.'*

JAMES I. returned in 1424 from his long captivity in England full of ideas of government as he had seen it in the south, and with a zeal for law and order which was to cost him his life. He was familiar with all the institutions of chivalry. We saw him in 1407 sitting with Henry IV. as a spectator at the duel of Bolomer and Usana. There need be little scepticism, therefore, concerning 'The Order of Combats' forming the next chapter. It is from a manuscript copied in the end of the 17th, or early in the 18th century, from an original which belonged to James the First himself. This copy, which unfortunately modernised the diction,

[1] Glasgow Chart. 316.
[2] Bower, xv. ch. 23; Extracta, 216.

was found in the Errol charter-chest, a natural receptacle, for the Hays of Errol were hereditary High Constables of Scotland[1] from the time of Robert the Bruce. It was transcribed in 1842 for the Spalding Club by Dr. John Stuart, an eminent antiquary. The text in the next chapter has therefore been taken from the Spalding Miscellany.[2] Dr. Stuart remarked that nothing was known about the tract beyond what its title sets forth. He had not detected its kinship to a famous English treatise.

Source of the treatise.

But it is too plain to call for proof that the man who drew up 'The Order of Combats' knew each article and clause of Thomas of Woodstock's ordinance, of which it is a slightly shortened version with scarce a difference from the original.[3]

An old writing slumbers in a northern charter-chest, it is edited by a learned society, and at last its genealogy is traced to Thomas of Woodstock—after something like five centuries of separation from the parent stock.

[1] See charter in Spald. Miscel. ii. 211.

[2] Spald. Miscel. ii.; see pref. cxxi.-ii. There were two copies.

[3] Every sentence, with two or at the most three exceptions, has its close counterpart in the English Ordinance, as in the Black Book, i. 301-29, or Dugd. Orig. 79-86. The exceptions and differences are indicated in the notes.

CHAP. 74.—'*The Order of Combats.*'

THE ORDER OF COMBATS FOR LIFE IN SCOTLAND.

As they are anciently recorded in ane old Manuscript of the Laws, Arms, and Offices of Scotland pertaining to James I., King of Scots.

With the Office and Priviledges the Constable and Marshaell hes in them.

CAP. I.

First the cartell or bill of quarrell als weill of the Challengers behalf as of the Defenders, was brought into the court, befor the Great Constable. And when the truth of the caus could not be proven by witness nor otherways, then was it permitted the same should receive tryall by fforce of arms: the one partie by assailing, and the other by defending. The Constable as vicar generall to the King, assignd the day of battell, which was to be performed within ffourty days[1] nixt following; whereto both the Challenger and Defender condescendit. Then wer the combatants commandit to bring in sufficient pledges for surety that they and every one of them should appear and perform the combat, betuixt thc sun ryseing and gooing doun of the day appoynted, for the acquytall of their pledges; and that they, or

¶ In what sort the day of Combat was appoynted.

[1] English Ordinance has '*not* within forty days.'

any of them, should not doe or cause to be done any molestation, dammage, assault, or subtilty, against the person of his enemie, either by himself, his ffriends, his followers, or any other person whatsomever.

CAP. II.

The Kings pleasur being signified to the Constable, he caused lists or railes to be made and sett up, in lenth sixty paces, and in breadth ffourty. The place wheron the lists wer appoynted were ever upon plain and dry ground, without riggs, hills, or other impediments. At either end of the lists was made a gate or entrie, with a strong barr to keep out the people. For guarding of either gate, the Constable appoynted ane serjeant at arms, comanding him not to let any man approach within ffour foot. The one gate opened towards the east, being strongly barrd with a raile of seven foot long, as noe horse could pass over or under the same.

¶ In what sort the King comanded the place of Combat be made.

CAP. III.

On the day of battell, the King used to sitt on ane high seat or scaffold, made for the purpose, at the ffoot wherof was ther ane other seat made for the Constable, who calld befor him the pledges, als weill of the Defendent as of the Challenger,

¶ In what sort the King did sitt to behold the Combat.

to be shouen and presented to the King; there to remaine within lists, as prisoners, untill such tym as the Challenger and Defender wer come, and had performed all ther ceremonies.

Cap. IV.

The Challenger used comonly to come to the east gate of the lists, and brought with him such armours as wer appoynted by the Constable and wherwith he determined to fight. Being at the gate, he stayd till such tym as the Constable arose from his seat, and went to him. He being come to the said gate of the lists, and beholding the Challenger ther, the Constable sayd: *For what caus art thou come hither, thus armed? And what is thy name?* Unto whom the Challenger ansuered thus: *My name is A. D., and am here come, armed and mounted, to perform my challenge against G. D. and acquit my pledges; wherfor I humbly entreat your Honour this gate may be opened, and I suffered to perform my intent and purpose.*[1] Then the Constable did open the visor of his headpiece, to see his fface, and therby to know that man to be he who makes the challenge.[2]

¶ In what sort the Challenger used to present himself to Combat.

These ceremonies ended, the Constable comanded the gate of the lists to be opened, wherat the armed

1 See p. 191.

2 Cranstoun would have been found out when he took stout William of Deloraine's place.—'Lay of Last Minstrel,' canto v.

man, with his necessaries and councill, entered. From thence he was brought befor the King, wher he remained untill such tym as the Deffender was come hither.

In lyk maner the Defender compearing did make requeist unto the Constable, desyreing that he would be pleased to delyver and discharge his pledges. Whereupon the Constable, aryseing from his seat, did humbly entreat the Kings Majestie to release them, becaus the Defender is already come, and presented befor his Majestie, ther to perform his duty.

But in cace the Defender did not come at tym convenient, in the day appoynted, then did the King delyver his pleasur to the Constable, and he reported the same unto the Marishall, who ffurth-with did give order unto the liuetenant that the Defender should presently be called to appear, by the Herauld Marischall, after this maner: *Oiez! G. D., Defendant in this combat! Appear now! ffor in this day thou hast taken upon thee to acquitt thy pledges in presence of the Lord Constable and Marishall; And also defend thy person against A. B., who challenged thee to mentaine this combat.* This proclamation was made thryce at the end of the lists. But if, at the second tym, the partie appeared not, then the Herauld did add these words:

The day passeth and therfore come without delay!

And if in cace the said Defendant appeared not befor noon, but stayed untill the third hour after, then did the Herauld, by comandment of the Constable, in the beginning of the proclamation, say: *A. B. appear in haist, and save thyn honour! ffor the day is weill near spent wherin thow did promise to perform thy enterpryse!*

I. It was also used, that the Constables clerk should in a book record the hour of the combatants appearing within lists, either on ffoot or horseback, in what sort they wer armed, of what collour their horses wer, and how they were furnished.

II. It was anciently used that the Constable moved the King in favor of the combatants, to know whither his Majesty were pleased to appoynt any of his nobility, or other officers of reputation, to assist them for councill in combat.

III. The Constable did survey the lances and other weapons, wherwith the combat should be performed making them equall, and of even measur.

IV. The Constable also appoynted tuo knights or esquyres unto the Challenger, to keep the place ffree from impediments. The lyk was also done for the Defender.

V. The Constable did also move the King to know whither his Majestie in person would take the oaths of the ffighters, or give him authority to do it out of his presence.

VI. The Constable also did send the Marishall

unto the Challenger and his councill, to make ready his oath, declaring that, after that ceremonie, all protestations should be voyd.

After these things the Great Constable caused his clerk to bring furth the Book, wherupon the combatants were solemnly sworn.

CAP. V.

The Constable having caused the clerk read the Challengers bill, and calling him by his name, sayd:

¶ The First Oath.

Doest thow conceive the effect of this bill? Here is also thy own glove[1] *of defyance. Thow shalt swear by the Holy Evangelists, that all things therin contained be true, and that thow shall mentaine it so to be upon the person of thy enemie; As God shall help yow, and the Holy Evangelists.*

The oath thus taken, he was led back unto his former place; and the Constable did cause the Marishall produce the Defender, who took the lyk oath.

The oath was ever taken, the parties kneeling, unless it pleased the Constable to pardon that duty.

CAP. VI.

The second oath was also indifferently proponed to ather of them. *That they had not brought into*

[1] In some copies it is read gauntelit. [Original note on the Erroll MS.]

the lists other armour or wapons than was allowed; neither any engine, charm, herb, or inchantment; And that neither of them should put trust in any thing other then in God, and ther oun valours; As God and the Holy Evangelists should help them.

¶ The Second Oath.

That done, they were both again sent to their places of entrie.

CAP. VII.

The combatants being again called, wer comanded by the Constable to take one the other by the hand, and lay their left hands upon the Book; which done, the Constable sayd: *I charge thee A. D., Challenger, upon thy faith, that thow doe thyn outermost endeavour and fforce to prove thyn affirmation, either by death or denyall of thyn adversarie, befor he departeth these lists, and befor the sun goeth doun this day; As God and the Holy Evangelists shall help thee.*

¶ The Third Oath.

The very same maner of oath, in lyke maner used, was offered unto the Defender, and that done, the combatants returned unto ther places with their ffriends and councellors.

These ceremonies ended, the Herauld, by commandment of the Constable, did make proclamation at the ffour corners of the lists, thus:

OIEZ! OIEZ!

Wee charge and command, in the name of the

King and his Constable, that no man of what estait title or degree whatsomever, shall approach the lists nearer than four foot in distance; none shall utter any speech, voice, or countenance wherby either the Challenger or Defender may take advantage; upon pain of loss of lyfe, living, and goods, to be taken at the Kings good pleasur.

Then the Constable assignd a place convenient within the lists wher the King of Arms, Heraulds, and other officers should sitt or stand, and be ready if they wer call'd; ffor afterwards all things wer committed to ther charge, als weill on the behalf of the Defender as Challenger; as if any thing were forgotten in ther confessions, either toutching ther lands or consciences, or that any of them desyred to eat or drink: All these wants were supplyed by the Heraulds and none other.

But here it is to be noted, That no meat or drink could be given to the Challenger, without leave ffirst asked of the Defender, who comonly did not deny the requeist: And, after, the Herauld went unto the Constable and made him privie therunto, desyreing the favour that the combatants might eat and drink or ease their bodies if need were.

After these orders taken, the Constable and Marishall did avoyd the lists of all sorts of persons, save only one knight, and two esquyres, armed, to attend the Great Constable; and tuo esquires only to wait on the Marishall; ather of them having in his hand a launce without a head, ready to part the combatants, if the King did command.

Of more ancient tym,[1] the Constable used to have tuo lieutenents and four servents and the Marishall one lieutenent and tuo servents, within lists: one part to keep order on one syd, and the rest on the other. And if the Queen hapned to behold the combat, then the Conestable and one lieutenent, and the Marishall with none but himself, waited upon the Kings syd; and ther lieutenents attended on the Queen.

Then did the Constable alone, sitting doun befor the King, send his lieutenent to the Challenger to come unto him; and the Marshall accompanied the Defender.

The Constable thus sett did pronounce this speech with a loud voyce,

Let them goe! Let them goe! Let them goe!
and do their best![2]

Upon which words pronounced in the Kings presence, the Challenger did march towards the Defender to assaile him furiously, and the other prepared himself for defence the best he could.

In the mean time the Constable Marishall and their lieutenents stood circumspectly to hear and see if any word sign or voyce of yeelding were

[1] This paragraph not in English Ordinance.

[2] One need hardly say that this is a translation of 'Laissez les aller,' &c. See pp. 163, 186, 198. Compare 'Moveth,' p. 230.

uttered by ather of the ffighters; and also to be ready if the King should command the launces to be lett fall to depart the ffight.

Item, it belonged of old to the Constable to take heed that none of them should privily speak to other of yeelding or otherways, ffor unto the Constable appertained the record and witnessing of all things.

And in cace the combat wer for question of treason, he that was vanquished should be furthwith disarmed, within lists, by commandment of the Constable; also, the weapons and armour of the vanquished was in one end of the lists defaced to his disgrace, and after the same drauen out togither with his horse; ffrom thence also the man vanquished was drauen out unto the place of execution to be there headed or hanged, according to the custom of the countrey.

The performance of the said punishment of treason on the bodies of the vanquished pertains to the Marishalls, who, at the Kings command, must see justice duely administrat.

If the combat wer only for tryall of vertew or honour, he that was overcome therein was only disarmed and put out of the lists without furder punishment.

If it should happen that the King should take the quarrell into his hand, and agrie the parties without longer ffight, then did the Constable lead the one, and the Marishall the other, out of the lists, at severall gates, armed, mounted as they wer, haveing especiall regaird that neither of them should go the one befor the other; ffor the quarrell, resting in the Kings hand, might not be renewed, or any violence offered without prejudice to the Kings honour.

And becaus it is a poynt very especiall in matters of arms, that he who leaveth the lists ffirst incurreth a note of dishonour; therefor to depairt the lists in dew tym was ever precisely observed, were the combat for treason, or whatsomever cause els.

CAP. VIII.

¶ The Constables Fees.

The Constable should have all the armours[1] or weapons that are accustomed to have or hold ffree battell; that is to say, a spear, a sheild, a long sword, a square sword, and a knyfe, with the haill jewells and rings the vanquisht had about him at his entring in quarrell.

CAP. IX.

¶ The Marishalls Fees.

The fees of the Marishall[2] were all horses, broken armour, or other ffurnitur that fell to the ground efter the combatants did enter the lists, als weill from the Challenger as from the Defender. But the more inward abulyie-

1 Black Book French version of the Ordinance gives this perquisite to the Constable, the English version to the Heralds, Dugdale's version to the Marshal. 2 Here again the last note applies.

ments[1] pertaind to him that was victorious, whither Defender or Persewar.

The barrs, posts, railes, and every other part of the lists, wer also the ffees of the Marishall.[2]

Cap. X.

It is also to be remembered, That without the principall lists were ever certain counter lists, betwixt which tuo the servants of the Constable and Marishall did stand. Ther stood, also, the Kings serjeants at arms to see and consider if any default or offence wer committed contrarie to the Constables proclamation, against the Kings royal Majestie or the law of arms. These men were ever armed at all pieces to keep the lists, and also to arreist and apprehend any the Constable or his lieutenant should command.

¶ The Counter Lists.

Chap. 75.—*The Scottish Court of Chivalry.*

It is now necessary to knit into one compact argument[3] the scattered proofs of the conclusion stated in chapter 68. It is drawn from the combined evidence of analogy, chronicle, and document.

England had the beginnings of a court of chivalry

[1] This is cleverly burlesqued in Hudibras, after the knight's defeat by Trulla.

[2] All the versions concur in this point, but see pp. 211, 231, and *infra*.

[3] Every statement in this chapter has its foundation set forth in this book either *supra* or *infra*.

under Edward III., and one of the most noted duels took place in 1350. In Scotland the same symptoms manifested themselves quite as early. The constable had chivalric functions in 1332. In 1362 there was an appeal of battle resulting in a banishment.

In England the duel, used sometimes to decide the right to armorial bearings, did not make itself prominent until the reign of Richard II. Then it came in like a flood, and it was feared 'lest appeals of that kind should become too many in the land.' The Court of Chivalry, inchoate before, became definite, with a jurisdiction limited by Act of Parliament, by which, however, its elastic character was not restrained, and its scope soon widened to include any treason. At this very time duels became frequent in Scotland, with treason as the prevailing ground of the appeal. As was for a time the case in England, the appeal might be made in Parliament. As in England, the duels were rarely fought except in the royal presence, and as in England, they were often stopped in mid-fight by the king. He did this in virtue of a royal *nobile officium* peculiar to chivalry. In both countries he was the head of this battle court, and in both countries the functions and perquisites of constable and marshal were the same. In both, the presence of heralds goes without saying. In both, the vanquished was subject to punishment

English analogies.

and disgrace. A king of Scotland witnessed at least one English treason-duel. In his time, if not earlier, Thomas of Woodstock's Ordinance was carried to Scotland and found a welcome there. The complete analogy of English and Scots practice justifies a strong inference of a completely analogous tribunal.

Last of all there are three documents. 'The Maner of Battale' was found in several of the most valuable law manuscripts, the writers of which were not collectors of legal curiosities. The questioned Act of Robert III. is in wonderful harmony with its time, and several of its provisions are illustrated in actual cases. 'The Order of Combats' came from the charter-chest of the hereditary constables. These writings themselves, embodying or professing to embody the law and practice of a court in Scotland, raise an overwhelming presumption, independent of facts already given and facts which are to follow. All that is known of actual practice tends to confirm their general accuracy as the 'laws of arms.' If these three documents be not the veritable pillars of the SCOTTISH COURT OF CHIVALRY, they lend strength and finish as buttresses to the argument. The whole facts, what are they but long buried fragments of the ruined structure? And marvellously they fit together when recovered and upreared after the oblivion of centuries.

True it is that such a name has never been used, or such functions assigned to such a court before.

It is true there is more than one hiatus in the proof. But what argument as to government and law in 14th and 15th century Scotland is without its gaps and flaws? Nay, without claiming the excuse of that inadequacy which perforce attends its present enunciation for the first time, where is the argument that has so few[1] as this?

Conclusion drawn.

CHAP. 76.—*Stray Duels*, A.D. *1426-56.*

'ANNO DOMINI 1426 a single combat or duel[2] between a gentleman, Henry Knokkis, esquire, defender, and a certain plebeian tailor. This tailor, laying his charge against Knokkis before the king that he had spoken treasonably about him, Knokkis was therefore summoned, and denying the charges made against him, the tailor appealing him of treason, they fought at Edinburgh under the castle,[3] for some time in

Knox and the tailor.

1 In any view it cannot be gainsaid that the king, constable, and marshal exercised in connection with treason-duels the very same offices in Scotland as in England. In England the trio formed the court of chivalry. What else could they be in Scotland? The title alone appears to be wanting to complete the case, and a name is a very unimportant deficiency. If this tribunal was not *nominatim* the court of chivalry, it certainly guided its procedure by a 'buke of chivalrye'—was in short the king's court sitting as a court of chivalry. Even in that view the name I have given is no misnomer.

2 Bower, xvi. ch. 15. Extracta, 231.

3 Beside the king's stables, under the precipitous south-side of the rock. Lands there were, at a later time, held 'with the office of

the king's presence, but by the king's command they were separated.'

Every point and circumstance in this sentence of Bower harmonises with the last chapter. In the exchequer rolls there is a payment of 20s. made by the king's command, *pro mensa scissoris ante duellum*,[1] 'for the "table" of the tailor before the duel,' an entry which possibly indicates that in accordance with ancient practice accuser or accused who could find no pledges was kept under guard between the accusation and the duel. 'Let the gaol be his pledge' was what the old English judges were wont to say. The tailor had been in honourable custody, and his sustenance was an item of royal expenditure.

A continuator of Bower[2] places in 1446 a duel between Alexander Cunningham and a person surnamed Dalrymple. It was at Stirling before James II., who stopped it. Another author[3] assigns the same duel, 'faucht in

Cunningham and Dalrymple, 1446.

watching the tournament'—cum officio observationis hastaludii. See Abbreviates of Retours, Inquis. Spec. Edinr. No. 398. Exch. Rolls, i.; pref. clxiv. For earlier charters see Reg. Mag. Sig. iii. 484, 2925, 2952.

1 Exch. Rolls, iv. 411; pref. xcvii.

2 Bower, vol. ii. p. 515 (an error for 519). Extracta, 238. This follows immediately upon the notice of a famous combat, à outrance, between three Flemish knights and three Scotsmen. This is assigned to 1446, but as it really took place at the marriage of James II. in 1449, the confusion of dates is obvious. It was stopped by the king flinging down his gauntlet. Tytler's Hist. *sub anno*, 1449. The next date in Bower is equally out of joint. The battle of Sark occurring in 1448 is given to 1445. Such tit-bits of chronology are only too common.

3 Asloan MS. 55.

the barras of Strivling,' to the year 1456. More is not hazarded concerning it than that the chances are heavily in favour of its being a treason-duel; but its date and its cause are alike uncertain. It is half suspected that Alexander Cunningham was the future Lord Kilmaurs.

The same doubt might envelop another duel, of date 1453, had there not been three tell-tale words in an exchequer roll of the period. Alexander Nairn, of Sandford, for nearly twenty years comptroller of the exchequer, fought with Sir James Logan[1] on the North Inch of Perth,[2] and was killed. This was a unique fate for a Lyon king of arms.[3] Chivalry did not spare its own officers. In the exchequer accounts of the following year the words, *cujus bona eschaetabantur*, 'whose goods were escheat,' occurring after his name,[4] make it practically a certainty that the duel arose on a charge of treason.[5] On the same day, and at the same place,[6] William Heriot[7] fought with David Galfurde,[8] and

Nairn and Logan, 1453.

1 Bower, vol. ii. p. 515 (519). Extracta, 243.

2 This fact appears in the Extracta only.

3 Nairn is said to have held that office. Seton's Scottish Heraldry, 477.

4 Exch. Rolls, v. 672.

5 There seems something odd about Nairn's safe-conduct into England in June 1452. Bain's Calendar, iv. p. 406. Rot. Scot. ii. 358a.

6 Bower, vol. ii. p. 515 (519). Extracta, 243.

7 So in Extracta. Bower calls him Walter.

8 So in Extracta. Bower calls him Glaffurd.

William Hakat fought with John Seton. In each case the battle was stopped by the king, and the parties were separated with honour to both.

CHAP. 77.—*In Parliament and Burgh Court.*

JAMES I. had perished in his prime a martyr to an ideal of law which Scotland did not fully share. Much of the reign of James II. was a struggle with the Douglases. Earl James had been defeated in open battle, with banner displayed against his sovereign in 1455,[1] and a sentence of forfeiture for high treason had been passed upon him.[2] But, in safety across the border, a convenient English tool, he was for many years a standing menace to the tranquillity of Scotland—a Scotland of treasons, and factions, and murders innumerable. The great Scotch political device—that of getting hold of the person of the king and then governing in his name—had been developed early in this reign. During the childhood of the third of the Jameses, rumour had laid to the charge of Alexander, Lord Kilmaurs—possibly that Alexander Cunningham who fought a duel in the last chapter—that he was an accomplice of the traitor-earl, the banished Douglas. To attest his innocence he procured letters under the great seal in 1463.[3] But rumours

[1] At Arkinholm in Eskdale. [2] Scots Acts, ii. 76.
[3] On 8th Feb. 1462 [1462-3.]

are not killed by writ under the great seal, and in 1464 he felt constrained to bring the calumny to a decisive issue. This he did in a meeting of Parliament. As a baron he was himself a lord of Parliament, and his proceedings, assisted by two fore-speakers,[1] make it plain that his course of action had been carefully planned, and was on the lines of a great precedent.

The vindication of Lord Kilmaurs, 1464.

On 13th January[2] 1464, in his place in Parliament he first, after duly craving permission, caused to be read the letters under the great seal which he had obtained. They narrated how he had been 'blasphemed' by a rumour,[3] fomented by some who were jealous of him, as well as by divers others, concerning assistance and favours shewn to James of Douglas the traitor, and his accomplices, and how of all imputation of crime he had been declared innocent.

After the reading of the writ in face of Parliament the aforesaid Alexander, Lord Kilmaurs, says the special Act made for his benefit, with bended knee, in presence of the said lords of Parliament, offered, for the sake of putting an end to the flying infamy of the said rumour, three kinds of purgation: First, to underly an assize of lords, his peers, not suspected, chosen

A triple option.

1 Advocates.

2 13th January 1463 [1463-64.] Scots Acts, xiii. 29.

3 Blasphematus extitit rumore invido.

by our lord the king; Second, to produce the purgation of one hundred knights and esquires; Third, to defend himself of the said crime, according to the laws of arms, against any appellant whomsoever.

No feature in this triple option is so singular as its resemblance to the three modes of trial known to Bisset and his accusers in 1242. These were duel, compurgation, and visnet. In the case of Kilmaurs they were assize, compurgation, and duel. The resemblance could scarcely be accidental, for Bower's Scotichronicon had been written about twenty years before. Compurgation was almost certainly obsolete. The visnet of Bisset's time had become that assize of peers claimed by Kilmaurs. The third alternative was the same as Bisset's—with a difference. There was no phrasing about 'the laws of arms' in Bisset's challenge to his accusers. The laws of arms were a part of chivalry, and judicially a later growth. The court of chivalry was their embodiment. Had there been an accuser of Kilmaurs it is likely that there would have been one more duel in the records of that court; but none came forward to change the flying calumny into an appeal of treason. So the lords held the letters under the great seal ample to purge his lordship 'of the said voice and Rumor.'[1]

That Parliament was a competent place to begin

[1] An ancestor of Kilmaurs was on the assize which condemned Murdoch, Duke of Albany, in 1425. Bower, xvi. ch. 10. He himself was on an assize in a treason trial in 1464. Reg. Mag. Sig. ii. No. 812.

such a plea seems clear. It was not so in a burgh court. On 13th January 1475 William of Seton was accused[1] 'for the wrangwise strublance of William Cadiou cumand apon him in forthocht felony and breking of law borrowis.' Seton denied that he was under lawburrows—that is, that he had been bound over to keep the peace—and he submitted to an assize. The assize having been sworn, Seton repeated his denial. On this Alexander Menzies, a dignitary of the burgh, with the honours of the provostship[2] awaiting him after five-and-twenty years of public service, answered that Seton had found lawburrows not only to the alderman and bailies of Aberdeen, but also before the king and the lords of council. 'And thairapon,' says the record of this strange case, 'the said William avisit, come before the court, and keist downe his hat profferand him to fecht in the said querel; apon the quhilk the said Alexander Menzes askit ane testimonial of the court how he manasit and provokit him, sayand that it nedit nocht, na that he wald nocht fecht in the said querel, sen that it mycht be determyt be the law and the assize.'

A challenge in burgh court, 1475.

This plea was sustained, the challenge of battle was passed over, and the assize, ripely advised, found 'that the said William of Setoune had strublit

1 Aberdeen Burgh Records, 1398-1570. (Spald.) 406.

2 He was provost from 1501 to 1503. There are many signs of his energy.

William of Cadiou apon forthocht felony under law borowis,' and fined him accordingly. Strutting swashbuckler chivalry, casting down its hat,[1] and claiming the laws of arms in the end of the 15th century, had no place in the burgh court, which dealt only with matters determinable by law and assize.[2] The challenge was preposterous, and William of Cadiou, who, if the town records tell true,[3] had not at all times been a man of peace himself, was declared quit 'of all strublance of the said William of Setoune.'

CHAP. 78.—*Note on the Passing of Chivalry.*

COUNTLESS chivalric combats are left unnoted in these pages because not pertinent to real trial by battle. Such contests were long of daily occurrence. But, as has been said already, with gunpowder came in the discipline of infantry, the knight was

1 'Throwing the hat' is still, I believe, a term and a custom in the pugilistic ring. Sir Walter Scott uses the figure. Once, not figuratively but in fact, he 'threw up his hat' as a challenge at a football match. See Life by Lockhart (royal octavo, 1844), ch. 36 and 69, pp. 327, 615, 616. In early times the love, although a usual, was not the invariable gage of battle. See p. 37, *supra*. Du Cange *voce* Duellum speaks of 'a glove or any other thing' as the gage. In the old romance of Sir Tristrem, the Irish knight Moraunt, as prelude to his battle with Tristrem, 'waged him a ring.' Fytte i. st. 92 of Scott's edition.

2 In harmony alike with the English statute of 13 Richard II. and the questioned Scots Act of 1400.

3 In 1440 William of Cadiou had to find lawburrows 'for the hurtyng of Robert Cullace.' Aberdeen Burgh Extracts, 1398-1570, 394-95. Of course that William was perhaps another William.

superseded, and chivalry was suffocated in civil war. It had by no means fulfilled the bright promise of its youth, when it started on its career in Europe to succour the weak,[1] to fight for God and the right, and to make knighthood the essence of Christianity in arms. But it had done much in giving an outlet to some of the finest instincts of humanity, and had relieved the dark background of feudalism with many a shining and generous deed. It improved the tone of public life, and heightened the standard of private honour and faith. When it died out in Britain it was drinking out the dregs of existence on the continent. There its record after the middle of the 15th century is a rapid story of decline.

Chivalry and tilting.

With the rise of chivalry tilting had risen; tilting and chivalry were in their prime both of usefulness and popularity together; and together the two declined and died. The world had grown too serious for tournaments, or preferred to take its frivolity in a form which made a less demand upon its manhood. In Scotland events ran their course as elsewhere. Perhaps owing to French nourishment, and the encouragement of James IV., who 'loved nothing so weill as able men and horsis,'[2] chivalry and tilting, not as a mere spectacle but as a robust fact, lived a little

[1] James's Hist. of Chivalry, 12, 23. Hallam's Middle Ages, part ii. ch. 9 (reprint, 811). Titles of Honor, part ii. ch. 3, § 24.

[2] Pitscottie (1814), i. 245-46. Compare Pitcairn, i. 118,* 123.*

longer than in England, but the difference was slight. The second half of the 14th century was full of knightly encounters of the sternest type. These prevailed throughout the 15th, but were ceasing at its close. Early in the 16th century, speaking generally, they had ceased.

A late example of this extreme species of combat is noted in the next chapter, not only for its inherent interest, but because of a curious document resulting from it, in which certain rights of the constable are defined.

CHAP. 79.—*Pitscottie's Dutchman*, A.D. 1500.

A combat à outrance.

EITHER in 1499 or 1500 there came to Scotland, for the purpose of jousting, a certain John de Coupance. The Scottish exchequer paid the hire of his ship,[1] and he was well entertained during his stay. He was an esquire of the French king. Pitscottie[2] calls him a Dutchman, and mangles his name into Clokehewis or Cockbewis.

None was 'so apt and readie to fight with him' as Sir Patrick Hamilton, a famous knight, then sheriff-depute of Lanarkshire.[3] They met 'on great horses under the castle wall of Edinburgh, in the barrace.'

[1] Exch. Rolls, xi. 231, 235, 239; pref. lxviii.
[2] Pitscottie (1814), i. 248—(1728) 104.
[3] Exch. Rolls, xi. 351.*

At the sound of trumpet they charged, shivering their spears. Supplied with new spears they prepared to charge again, but Sir Patrick's horse would not face the second encounter. Alighting, the knight called for a two-handed sword. 'A horse is but a weak weapon when men have most ado,' he said, crying to the Frenchman to dismount and end the fray on foot. This Coupance promptly did. They fought for an hour 'with right awful countenance,' says Pitscottie, 'and everyone strake maliciously;' but at last Sir Patrick brought his opponent to his knees. The king, who sat on the castle wall, cast down his hat, the combatants were sundered, and heralds and trumpeters proclaimed Sir Patrick the victor. And Pitscottie certifies that he was a right noble and valiant man all his days.[1] But he left a son nobler still, whose name stands first in the martyr-roll of the Scottish reformation.[2]

The office of constable.

After the 'Dutchman's' defeat the town council of Edinburgh[3] appear to have taken possession of the woodwork and fittings of the barras in which it had taken place. For this they were summoned before the king and

1 He was killed in 1520 in the fray known as 'Cleanse the Causey.'

2 His son, Patrick Hamilton, was the first Scottish Protestant martyr—burned in 1527. See Rev. Peter Lorimer's 'Patrick Hamilton.'

3 All the information as to these proceedings appears in a document titled 'Ane instrument that the Erll of Erroll hes the barras of men fechtin in singular battail,' dated 30th July 1501, printed amongst the Erroll papers. Spald. Miscel. ii. 212-13. See also Extracts from Edinburgh Records, 1403-1528—(Burgh Records Socy.) 91.

the lords of his council, at the instance of William, Earl of Erroll, Constable of Scotland.[1] Their case was not strongly urged, for the provost and bailies had, as they said, little wish to stand in plea with the earl, and they paid him a sum of money with which he owned himself content. And the provost and bailies further, in return for favours received from the earl, 'promised to their honourable utmost to aid and fortify the earl in his said office of Constable.' A few years later,[2] in 1509, another way out of the possibilities of friction between the burgh and the constable was found. The earl appointed the provost and bailies as his deputes in the constabulary for the space of three years. They bound themselves during that period to do no prejudice to the office, but, on the contrary, to advance its privilege, honour, and profit. And, notwithstanding that the grant of the office included 'the unlawis and escheits of courtis and barras,' the earl if present might modify the fines and payments as he chose.

It is remarkable how seldom in the records of duels and deeds of chivalry in Scotland mention is made of either the constable or the marshal. The documents just noted shew that 'The Order of

[1] The summons was 'pro injustis intromissione et detentione ab ipso certorum lignorum et meremiorum cum aliis munimentis quibus efficiebatur ambitus et circuitus dictus Le Barras in qua conpugnarunt et certarunt Johannes Coupante Gallicus et Dominus Patricius Hammilton miles.'

[2] 17th Feb. 1508 [1508-9]. This second document is also one of the Erroll papers. Spald. Miscel. ii. 213-14.

'Combats,' assigning the woodwork of the lists to the marshal, does not rightly state the law in Scotland. For, by the charter of David II., the right of the constable to that perquisite is made as clear in 1332 as the writ last narrated makes it in 1509. These deeds, therefore, are a very emphatic contradiction to the statement of Craig in his Jus Feudale,[1] that the marshal alone in all such cases took the oaths, and was the marshaller[2] of the field; and that to him alone pertained the arms, the horse, and all the accoutrements of the vanquished. Some there are, says very positively the learned knight, who conjoin the constable with the marshal in this office, but they are supported by no reason whatever. Craig's view seems to have been somewhat warped by his ingenious effort to derive the word 'marshal,' not from the stables of the early Germans, but from the duty of that officer to marshal, or regulate duels. In fact, notwithstanding a wide learning which has made his best-known treatise a great classic of Scots law, Craig's fatal *a priori* predilections led him into many a blunder. Here he attributes to the word, in its origin amongst the ancient Germanic peoples, a sense

Craig contradicted.

[1] Jus Feudale, lib. 1, dieg. 12, § 13.

[2] 'Quod *Marischaller* adhuc dicimus.' Here 'marischaller' is perhaps a French verb, but the rendering in the text conveys the idea. Craig would have been charmed with the etymology by Matthew Paris, Marescallus quasi Martis Senescallus. Chron. Maj. iv. 492. Doubtless he would easily have explained away Fleta ii. ch. 74, where the stable connection is manifest. He expressly sets aside the true derivation.

derived from a function which was not attache(to the office until the rise of chivalry. Craig gav(too much rein to theory,[1] but possibly he is neare the mark when he states it as his opinion that wher(a man subjected himself to single combat or due he incapacitated himself, on the ground of deathbed from disposing of his heritage from the moment h(entered the place of battle.[2] This application of th(law known as *ex capite lecti* is nevertheless as mucl pure theory as some other parts of the Jus Feudale.[3]

CHAP. 80.—*John Major's Homily.*

NOT very long after the adventure of Pitscottie' Dutchman, John Major was writing his history o Scotland. He for the first time in Scottish chronicl(sounds a note condemnatory of the duel. He ha(in his work reached the period of the duel renä scence, the heyday of chivalry, when Richard II. wa King of England. Unlike his predecessors, Majo disdained to describe these things, and delivere(himself of a homily somewhat as follows:—

'Our annals,' he says,[4] 'relate many single com

[1] It is worth remembering that Craig, who condemned the Regiam o grounds mainly exploded now, did precisely with the Book of the Feu what the writer of the Regiam did with Glanvill.

[2] Jus Feudale, i. dieg. 12, § 38.

[3] The words 'toutching their lands,' in cap. vii. of the 'Order c Combats,' p. 268, *supra*, may refer to the making of a will. See Stai iii. 4, 27-30. The law of deathbed is now abolished.

[4] Major's Hist. (1740), 279-80.

bats between Scots and Englishmen. Over these I tarry not. Laws and judges sin in allowing such encounters. The accuser sins, and so does the defender, if he can in any other way protect his life. Besides, it has often been found that the vanquished had the just cause, for God wills not to reveal innocence in this bad way. It ought to be sought out by legitimate means. If, in other ways, a settlement cannot be found concerning the matter in dispute they should leave it in the hands of God, for men cannot give judgment except according to what is pled and proved. I add also that the victor has little glory, and the vanquished much shame among the people. Therefore he acts imprudently and ill who hazards his life on such a cast. And what a mockery is the confession which is made before the duel, seeing that the shriven sinner persists in his sin. Seeking to take his opponent's life he risks his own, which it is his bounden duty to preserve. Wherefore the priest ought not to absolve him at all, and if he die unshriven he will be damned.'

Trial by battle condemned.

Well said, John Major! He refers, it will be observed, solely to the duel-judicial, and his censure visits first the law and the judge.[1] His remarks are on the theoretical side, but are significant of progress. Bower, writing a century before, revelled

[1] He expresses himself in very analogous terms in condemnation of tilting. Hist. 234.

in the description of a duel,[1] and was incapable of Major's conception that God willed not to declare his justice 'in that bad way.' Otherwise that universal homilist, whose chronicle touches upon most things under heaven, would have dealt with the theme, and his views, copiously interlarded with passages from Augustine and Seneca, would have been rounded off with a rythmic iniquity all his own.

CHAP. 81.—*Under James V.*

THE reign of James V. was troubled. There were many State trials for conspiracy, prosecuted with what was thought vindictive severity. At this period, when such charges were rife and had serious consequences, two Dumfries-shire lairds, Sir James Douglas of Drumlanrig and Robert Charteris of Amisfield, appear in connection with a charge of treason made by the former against the latter. The precise points of treason involved have not transpired,[2] but a challenge was given and accepted. They 'provockit each other,' says Pitscottie, 'to the barrace for certayne poyntis of treasoun quhilk the on alleadgit upoun

Drumlanrig and Amisfield. A sand-blind fight.

[1] Citations already made prove this. He found useful, as so many had done before him, a figure drawn from trial by battle, when he described Bishop Treyle of St. Andrews as a 'pugil ecclesiæ.' Bower, vi. ch. 46.

[2] The son of Charteris married the daughter of Douglas. Douglas Baronage (1798), 151. Matrimonial alliances are often a cause of discord.

the other.' On Monday, 17th June[1] 1532, before the king, not under the castle walls of Edinburgh, as some historians say, but in the close of Holyrood[2]—'within the inner clois of the Abbay'—the combat took place between them, armed at all points.[3] The pavement had been lifted and the close levelled for the great 'debait.' It was a remarkable duel, for Drumlanrig was not only not in a judicial temper, but was ill fitted for fighting, as he was short-sighted—'sumquhat sand-blind.'[4] He was 'in ane furie so meikle,' to quote Pitscottie's piquant words again, 'that he knew not

1 The Diurnal of Occurrents (Mait.) 16, says 17th May 1532. It names the parties as 'Johne Dowglas of Drumlanrick, and [the laird] of Hempisfeild, defendare.'

2 To Dr. Dickson I owe the following most valuable extract from the Accounts of the Master of Works preserved in the General Register House, Edinburgh:—

'The brekin of the calsay and rising of the samin within the inner clois of the Abbay aganis the debait betuix the lairdis of Drumlanerig and Hempisfeld quhilk wes xvij Junij [1532].

'Item, imprimis to four qnaryouris rysand the said calsay and stanis, to ilk ane of theim xvj d. ; summa v s. iiij d.

'Item, to vij werkmen berand the calsay stanis and sand and makin of the feld plane on Tyuisday eftir none and Weddynsday befoir none, to ilk ane of thame on the day xij d. ; summa vij s.

'Item, for v dosane and v ladis of deid sand to be laid in the feld quhair the debait wes ; price of ilk dosane of laidis of sand ij s. ; summa x s. x d.'

From Account of Mr Johne Scrymgeour, Master of the King's Works, 24 Sep. 1531—3 August 1532.

By way of glossary it may be said that 'calsay' means pavement, 'laidis' loads, 'dosane' dozen.

3 'Like ancient Palladines,' says Drummond of Hawthornden. Hist. (1655) 209. Two editions of Pitscottie say 'unarmed at all parts,' but this is a plain misreading for 'enarmed,' which means precisely the opposite.

4 Pitscottie (1814), ii. 352.

quhom he hat nor what he hatt.' But at last the blind fury of the battle was stayed, for 'Hempsfeildis sword brake,[1] and than the king cried ower the castle wall to the heraldis and men of armes to red[2] thame.' Here another version adds: 'And so they were stanched, and fought no more.'[3] In the words of another annalist,[4] they were 'sinderit without skaith.'

To the account of this duel Pitscottie appends a statement of which there are variants in different editions. 'At that tyme thair was monie southland men appailed utheris to the singular combat befoir the king, for ane singular combat durst not be bot in his presence or be his consent.'[5] The other version is that they so appealed each other 'for certain crimes of lesemajesty.'[6] Both readings are useful. The latter shows the continued competence of duel in cases of treason. The former is proof of the non-existence as yet of the private duel.

Trial by battle[7] came before the courts in 1537, in

1 Drummond says it was the short-sighted combatant's sword which broke. 'Hempsfield' is a common form of 'Amisfield.'

2 Red, separate. Of course 'castle wall' is a mistake.

3 Pitscottie (1728), 150.

4 Diurnal of Occurrents, p. 16.

5 Pitscottie (1814), ii. 352.

6 Pitscottie (1728), 150. Lesemajesty, high treason.

7 I am enabled, again by Dr. Dickson, to give a singular if not puzzling entry in the unpublished MS. Treasurer's Accounts of James V.:

'*Item* [the first day of Marche, 1526-7], to Johne Drummond, callit the king's kemp, be his precept, xv. lib.'

What this 'kemp' or champion had to do does not appear precisely, but that he had some chivalric duty is plain from another payment made a case of treason for an attempt upon the life of the king; and in another case about the same time a fierce duel was fought. The Master of Forbes was accused of having 'imagynit and conspirit his Hienes dede and slauchter be ane schot of ane small gwne or culvering.' He denied the accusation, 'offerit to defend the samyn with his body,' and flung down his glove. His accuser, the Earl of Huntly, undertook to prove the charge by evidence; but in case he should fail to do so, he accepted the challenge and lifted the glove, or as the report of the trial words it, 'failzeing thairof he hes tane up the pledge.'[1] This was in exact accordance with the supposed statute of Robert III. It was only when proof was lacking that battle was competent. There is some mystery concerning the facts of the case of the Master of Forbes, but there is none regarding his fate. He was tried by jury, found guilty, and executed.

Trial of Master of Forbes, 1537.

CHAP. 82.—*Rise of Private Duels.*

MEN in a passion do not wait for law; but the duel in its modern sense, or rather the sense it had a century ago, fought by no law save a punctilio of honour, without the sanction of any legal court—

to him on 14th April in the same year, 'to by tymmer to mak listis in the Abbay, xxx. lib.'

[1] Pitcairn, i. 185.*

the private duel—was unknown in Europe before the 16th century.[1] That it owed its origin to trial by combat, and was an offshoot of chivalry, is beyond question. It is said that the custom first came into vogue in Europe after a famous personal quarrel in 1528 between the two greatest monarchs of their time, Francis I. of France and Charles V. of Spain.[2] When Francis sent his herald to declare war on Charles, Charles told the herald that his master had broken his faith, and was a stranger to the honour of a gentleman. Francis, incensed by the insult, sent his herald a second time to Charles—this time with a cartel and challenge to single combat. The challenge was accepted, but the king and the emperor ultimately gave vent to their feelings in mutual scoldings and scurrility, and the project of combat fell through. But the incident of the cartel was well known, and the example of two such illustrious personages had a great influence in bringing into fashion duels on the point of honour. A historian of Crime has ingeniously worked out, sometimes

Results of quarrel of Francis I. and Charles V. 1528.

[1] Hallam's Middle Ages, ch. 9, part 1, note. (Murray's reprint, 734). It is true that so far back as the 13th century the voluntary duel is condemned in Fleta, and the victor declared a homicide and guilty of mortal sin; but that is a duel fought under sanction of a judge who is in the same passage condemned for his share in the proceedings. It is, therefore, against a judicial abuse of the duel that the passage was directed. Fleta, i. ch. 34, § 26. Probably such things as Pembroke's wish to fight Fawkes de Breawte are referred to. See p. 41.

[2] Robertson's Charles V., sub anno, 1528. Herbert's Life and Reign of Henry VIII. (Ward, Lock & Co.), 328, et seq.

convincingly, a connection between punishments and crimes. He has very fairly shown that defacement as a punishment led to defacement as a common form of crime.[1] A kindred principle is manifested in the lawful duel leading to the unlawful. Soon this vitiated outcome of the judicial battle[2] became popular all over Europe, fostered not a little by a habit which had only lately grown up of wearing swords as part of ordinary attire.[3]

Scotland was never far behind the age where fighting in any shape was concerned. The latter part of the 16th century is full of these private duels. But all the while the duel remained judicial, and not private, in cases of treason, and when duly sanctioned by the king. Under these conditions it was still trial by battle, and the law of the land, although Craig's Jus Feudale admits it not.[4] The 16th century duel-by-license was a swifter, far less formal thing than the old treason-duel of chivalry. The two-handed sword was giving place to the rapier. The cumbrous chivalric ceremonial was being dropped too.

The duel-by-license.

An odd and transitional example is tainted with a suspicion of military law. In the operations which

1 Pike, i. 211-13.

2 Charles V. had himself ordained and presided over a judicial combat in 1522. Robertson, proofs, note 22. The relation of chivalry to the private duel is considered in a note, with references such as none but Buckle gives, in Buckle's Hist. ii. 137.

3 Hallam, where last cited.

4 He always speaks of it as a thing of the past.

continued the war begun by the battle of Pinkie in 1547, Lord Grey of Wilton, lieutenant of the north under Protector Somerset, had taken the castles of Lauder, Haddington, and Yester. At the assault of one of these three castles, it is not clear which, in the early spring[1] of 1548, a Scot in the garrison supposed to have been a man named Newton, had spoken contemptuously of the young king of England, Edward VI. When the castle was surrendered the whole garrison was set free, except Newton, who, for his insulting words, 'was appointed to die for the same.' But he denied the words, and attributed them to one Hamilton. Hamilton, 'valorous enough and wrongfully touched,' denied the accusation, and challenged Newton to combat. In the market-place at Haddington, within lists 40 feet long and 30 wide, the duel took place. Each combatant on his knees first took an oath that his cause was just. Next, proclamation was made prohibiting, under pain of death, all persons from entering within the rails surrounding the place of battle. Then the signal was given, and 'with mutual fury' they began the fight. In the encounter, rather through his being taken at a disadvantage than for lack either of courage or strength, Hamilton was slain. So says one version, but another declares that the defeated man was forced to confess his treason, and was hanged on the

[1] The date appears from Thorpe's Cal. and from Diurnal of Occurrents, 46.

spot. Speed's chronicle tells that 'the victor was rewarded with a great chaine of gold and the gowne that the Lord Grey wore at the present, though many maligned and accused him still to be the utterer of those base words.'[1]

CHAP. 83.—*An Interlude*, A.D. *1549*.

JAMES V. died in 1542, his reason shaken by the ever-haunting shame of Solway-moss. Soon the hand of his widowed queen, Mary of Lorraine, was sought by the chief amongst the Scots nobility. Her most ardent wooers were Matthew, Earl of Lennox, and Patrick, Earl of Bothwell, who vied with each other in extravagant gallantry to gain her affections. The queen-regent, however, was too astute to fall in love. 'Since she had been a king's wife,' she told Sir Ralph Sadler,[2] 'her heart was too high to look any lower.' At anyrate, she 'did nothing bot gave thame fair wordis that they might serve hir.' So says Pitscottie,[3] who sketches in lifelike colours the lover-earls. Lennox, he says, 'went verrie strecht up in his

1 Speed's History (1627), 837. Compare with Borthwick on Judicial Combats in remarks on Brit. Antiquities, 1776, p. 9-10, where the event is erroneously assigned to the time of Edward IV. instead of Edward VI. In the summer of same year a quarrel at dice in Haddington resulted in a duel in which Lamberd, a man-at-arms, killed Captain Cholmely. See letter 3rd June 1548, Thorpe's Cal. 86.

2 Sadler's State Papers (1809), i. 84.

3 Pitscottie (1814), 422-23—(1728), 182. Compare Buchanan's Hist. xv. 12.

passage quhairfoir he appeired verrie pleasant in the sight of gentlwomen. As for the earle of Bothwell he was fair and quhitlie,[1] sumthing hinging-shouldered, and went sumthing fordward,[2] with ane gentle and humane countenance.' Bothwell himself declared that the queen had promised him her hand, and in 1549 he offered proof of that promise—proof by battle. His challenge, dated at Hermitage in Liddesdale on 1st April 1549, was accidentally discovered not long ago.[3] By it the earl offers to fight 'ane hundreth men for ane hundreth men, or man for man, as the King of France's majeste will pleis command him thairto,' with any person who dares gainsay certain articles. Of these the chief is the statement that the queen-regent 'promest faithfullie be hir handwrit at twa sindrie tymes to tak the said erle in mariage.' Heroic evidence like this is of little value. Nothing came of the challenge dated on All Fools' Day, and the royal breach of promise was never proved.[4] Neither Bothwell nor Lennox was successful in his suit, and Mary of Lorraine remained a widow. The comedy of the two earls and the wily queen deepens the tragedy of their children —Darnley, and Bothwell, and Mary Queen of Scots.

[1] Quhitlie, pale.

[2] Fordward, stooping.

[3] National MSS. of Scotland, iii. No. 24.

[4] Next year, on 23rd May 1550, Bothwell was summoned for treason—for 'greit and hie attemptattis . . . towart our Soverane Lady. P.C. Reg. i. 100.

CHAP. 84.—*Two Historic Cartels.*

THE annals of the judicial duel touch on many a name writ large in history. Two famous cartels, or letters of defiance and challenge, in cases which are on the doubtful verge of the judicial, form a connecting link to carry the chain of narrative through the reign of Queen Mary. Darnley, her worthless husband, was murdered on 9th February 1567. The rivalry of the son of Bothwell and the son of Lennox for the love of Mary of Lorraine's daughter had ended in this. James Hepburn, Earl of Bothwell, was loudly accused by the public voice of having done the deed. On 12th April, after a quasi-trial, he was acquitted.[1] But, in view of the mockery of the trial, rumour became the more emphatic of his guilt. On the same day he caused to be posted up in the market-place in Edinburgh a cartel bearing that, although he had been acquitted in a court of law, he was willing—to make his innocence the more manifest—to fight in a duel according to the laws of arms with any man of honourable birth and reputation who dared to say that he was guilty of the 'abominable crime' for which he had been tried.

Bothwell's cartel, 1567.

1 It is interesting to note that the Constable protested that he was the only judge competent, as it was a case of slaughter within four miles of the presence chamber. Spalding Miscel. ii. pref. xcvii. This was, of course, a claim in respect of the Constable's palace jurisdiction, and had nothing to do with the long extinct court of chivalry.

Next day, in the same place, a reply appeared. It contained an offer to accept the combat on certain terms: a place of battle was to be assigned where there would be no danger of foul play. It was from a lord of Parliament and a baron (Moray of Tulibardine, it is said) that this acceptance came, but the opportunity for his disclosing himself was not afforded. Bothwell did not seek to fight with the proffered antagonist.[1] After the startling events which followed—the feigned abduction of Mary, her marriage with the abductor, the rising of Scotland against the ill-starred match—Bothwell and the queen, with their followers, were on Carberry Hill facing the army of confederate lords. There Bothwell repeated his challenge.[2] It was accepted, not only by Moray of Tulibardine, who had answered his cartel before, but by Sir William Kirkaldy of Grange. Bothwell would fight with neither. A mere baron, he said, who was neither lord nor earl, could not be his peer. He wanted an earl, so Morton accepted the challenge. But Lord Lindsay of the Byres craved the honour, Morton consented, and Bothwell could not with any decency refuse. Accordingly, Lord

[1] P.C. Reg. 9th July 1567. Scots Acts, iii. 7. Birrel's Diarey, 12th April. Spottiswood's Hist. (Spottiswood Socy.) ii. 50, 51. Calderwood's Hist. ii. 350-51. Thorpe's Cal. p. 214, 246. Libels and 'tickittis of defamatioun,' shewing the popular feeling of Bothwell's guilt and the hollowness of the pretended trial, were appearing even before the meeting of the packed jury which acquitted him. Anderson's Collections, i. 126. Calderwood's Hist. ii. 349.

[2] Date, 15th June 1567.

Lindsay made ready for the battle, and girt on the great sword of Archibald Bell-the-cat,[1] to prove that Bothwell was the murderer of Darnley. Nevertheless the duel was not to be. Bothwell was not keen for the fight, 'his hart cauldit ay the langer the mair,' and the remnant of his desire to fight vanished when the queen forbade.[2]

Bothwell and Kirkaldy.

That Kirkaldy, with whom Bothwell would not fight, pursued him to the Orkneys, scattering there his little fleet, urging still further over the seas the flight of the fugitive, who was to end his days as a pirate in a Danish prison. But a still shorter, and in some respects a darker, future lay before Kirkaldy, who, like Bothwell, had his day of need to issue a bootless cartel.

So long as Regent Moray lived the attitudes of parties are intelligible and distinct, but after he was shot in 1570 the rapid changes of that tortuous time are hard to follow. Kirkaldy had been a king's man, but joining the faction for the queen he, with Maitland of Lethington, held the castle of Edinburgh against the regent and the reformers—the lords of the congregation. John Knox from the pulpit called him a cruel man-slayer, an open traitor, and a 'plane

1 Morton gave him the sword, Calderwood's Hist. ii. 363-64. Probably this was the weapon with which, at one blow, Angus cut through the thigh of Spens of Kilspindie.

2 The account of the Carberry Hill episode is from James Melville's Memoirs (Maitland Club), 183-84. Calderwood, ii. 363-64. See also Thorpe's Calendar, 248.

throt-cutter;'[1] and more than Knox made the charge. He expostulated with Knox in the end of 1570; for his other aspersors he held out a threat of a different treatment. On 13th April 1571 he caused his cartel[2] to be put up and proclaimed at the market-cross of Edinburgh. Warmly denying the charges made against him, he said that if any gentleman undefamed, of his own quality and degree, belonging to the regent's faction, 'will say the contrarie heerof but I am a true Scotish man, I will say he speeketh untruelie, and leeth falselie in his throat;' and he goes on to say, 'I sall be readie to fight with him on horse backe or on foote, at time and place to be appointed according to the lawes of armes.' On 11th June 1571 the cartel was repeated in a shortened form, and was sent this time to the enemy's camp at Dalkeith. Three days later Alexander Stewart of Garlies, whose pen it must be said had some bias towards scurrility, wrote to Kirkaldy accepting the challenge. 'I will offer myself to prove thy vyle and filthie treasoun with my persoun against thyne, and as the lawe and custome of armes requireth.' At the same time Garlies took occasion to hurl at Kirkaldy the taunt that he had little need to talk of quality and degree, seeing that he had his descent from 'progenitouris for the

Kirkaldy's cartel, 1571.

[1] Richard Bannatyne's Journal (1806), 75.

[2] The facts as to Kirkaldy's two cartels, and the negotiations which followed, are mainly from Calderwood, iii. 62, 90, 107-111. Thorpe's Cal. pp. 312, 317, 320. Diurnal of Occurrents (Mait.), 206-7.

most part saltmackeris.'[1] This genealogical fling is explained by the fact that salters were still in a state of villenage in those days, and for long after.[2] Much correspondence ensued about the place of battle and the conditions. Garlies offered to fight on horse or on foot, armed with jack, spear, steel bonnet, sword, and whinger, on the Gallowlee,[3] between Leith and Edinburgh. He wanted a site out of range of the castle guns.[4] Kirkaldy replied, proposing for the scene of combat 'the barresse beweste the West Porte of Edinburgh, the place accustomed and of old appointed for such matters.'[5] This lay close to the Grassmarket just underneath the castle, and in easy range of the castle guns. He wished a different selection of arms, too, from those suggested by Garlies. Steel bonnet, jack, plate sleeves, spears, sword, dagger, corslet, morion, pike, two-handed sword, gauntlets, and two sword stripes or plates for the thighs and legs—with all these it was that Kirkaldy sought to have the right of riding into action. The gallant Garlies made blunt answer that all this multiplying of conditions was but a sub-

Kirkaldy and Garlies.

1 Richard Bannatyne's Journal, 185. Saltworks were numerous on the Forth, and the Kirkaldies' lands lay along the shore.

2 See Act 15 George III. c. 28, 39; George III. c. 56.

3 Here the Regent's party hanged their prisoners—an uncomfortable place, one would say, for Kirkaldy. It lay at the foot of the Calton Hill, and had been granted to the burgh of Edinburgh by James II. in 1456 expressly for tournaments and jousts. Charters of Edinburgh (Burgh Records Socy.) 82. Exch. Rolls, i. pref. clxiv. Greenside is its modern name. 4 Thorpe's Cal. 317.

5 Kirkaldy was right. See p. 275, *supra*.

terfuge. Kirkaldy, whatever his reasons—and they were probably politic rather than personal, about which perhaps the laird of Lethington knew something—did not care to carry out the threat of his cartel. In the middle of July the matter dropped, Garlies and the reformers reading in his refusal 'a confession of his own treasonable turpitude.'[1]

Garlies did not long survive his virtual victory, as he was killed at the surprise of Stirling in the end of the same year Kirkaldy was destined to a less honourable fate than if he had met his doom in the lists according to the laws of arms. Knox is credited with the prediction that he would come down from his crag with shame and slander like a hunted fox.[2] Come down he did when forced to surrender the castle in 1573. He met with no pity, but was hanged for treason, and men still debate—as Garlies and he were on the point of doing with sword and spear—whether he was a traitor or a true Scot.

Their fate.

CHAP. 85.—*The last Trial by Combat.*

WHEN the civil war in Scotland had subsided, and something like order began to assert itself, the private duel is found to have made a startling advance. The

[1] See Calderwood, iii. 62, 90, 107-111. Thorpe's Cal. 312, 317, 320. Diurnal of Occurrents, 206-7.

[2] Skelton's Maitland of Lethington, ii. 425. See also Mr. James Melville's Diary (Wodrow Socy.) 33, 34.

privy council set to work to grapple with the evil, but with a distinct admission from the beginning that the duel had a lawful place in cases of treason, and with the royal consent—a qualification which received consistent effect, and which, it needs no proving, was a relic of the king's headship of the court of chivalry. Constable and marshal had dropped out of sight in that connection, but the necessity for the royal consent preserved the tradition unbroken.

Privy council and duels.

In November 1580 the council made an ordinance against all 'infamous libellis and writtis' leading to challenges. Singular combats, they said, were forbidden, 'except the samin be in materis of tressoun quhairanent na uther triall is to be had,' and they gave order for proclamation that, in terms of the law, imprisonment and confiscation of goods would be the punishment of those who directed such cartels, libels or letters of reproach, or who dared 'to appoint or keep trystis for the combat' without the king's license.[1] But the repression of duels was no easy task—it was little short of impossible. It does not seem to have been till 1592, when James VI. was making his peace principles appear in council, that the policy began to take effect. Whenever a cartel was heard of, the sender and recipient were summoned and bound over to keep the peace; but withal duelling throve. In an old style-book of the period a form was 'Discharge

[1] P.C. Reg. 26th Nov. 1580, iii. 333.

of a single Combat.'[1] It must have been in no little request.

Meanwhile all duels were not of the illegal type. Some at least there were which were purely judicial, and perfectly lawful. Thus in 1595 John Brown was accused or challenged, on what precise ground is not recorded, by George Hepburne. By the king's warrant a duel was fought, and the judges found the challenge proved 'be the said George, quho overcame the said Johnne, and spared his lyff at the desyre of the saidis judges.' Notwithstanding, Brown bore feud for many years and sought Hepburne's life, but on being brought before the council swore he would quarrel with him no more.[2]

Duel by license.

Two years after this duel one still more remarkable was fought. In a previous year the name of Stephen Bruntfeld had been before the privy council regarding challenges passing between him and Robert Hog of Gellane.[3] But in February 1597 his name was brought up in council in a different connection. He had been murdered, or at anyrate slain, in a duel in which treachery was suspected,[4] and the Master of Ogilvy became bail for £1,000 for John Ur, a piper suspected of some hand in the deed.[5] Stephen, who

1 In style-book, of which contents are sketched in Fountainhall folio MS. Stirling's Library, Glasgow. See Scot. Law Review, iv. 261.

2 P.C. Reg. 26th Nov. 1605, vii. 150.

3 P.C. Reg. 11th Sept. 1592, v. 567; 31st July 1593, v. 598.

4 Mackenzie's Hist. of Scotland (1869), 477.

5 P.C. Reg. 25th Feb. 1596-97, v. 675.

was captain of Tantallon Castle, had a brother Adam, who was, or had been, in the service of Sinclair of Roslin,[1] and Adam charged James Carmichael with having by unfair odds taken a murderous advantage of his brother, and so killed him in the duel. Within a very short space after the murder Birrel, in his 'Diarey' under date 15th March, records, in his gossipy Scotch, the dramatic story of the prosecution. 'Ane single combat foughten betwixt Adam Bruntfield and James Carmichael. The said Adam Bruntfield challenged James Carmichael for murthering of his umquhile brother, Steven Bruntfield, captain of Tantallon. The said Adam purchest[2] ane license of his majestie, and faucht the said James at Barnbogill Links before fyve thousand gentilmen; and the said Adam, being bot ane yong man and of mean stature, slew the said James Carmichael—he being as abill a like man as was leving.' Another version of this truly judicial duel represents it as having taken place 'in ane small inche be the sie, neir to Barnbugell, my Lord Duke and sindrie utheris being thair judges.[3]

Last judicial battle fought, 1597.

It is believed that this licensed duel, so distinctly judicial in its character, was the last trial by combat actually fought in Great Britain.

1 P.C. Reg. v. 636-645.

2 To purchase meant to obtain in those days—not necessarily to buy as now.

3 MS. Adv. Lib. A. 4-35, quoted in Pitcairn in Auchmowtie's case, ii. 112-124.

CHAP. 86.—*The Act of Parliament of 1600.*

MEANWHILE the fulminations of the privy council in 1580 against private duels had been of little effect, and on 1st April 1600, bent upon a firm policy, they fulminated again. They said that the non-execution of former acts and prohibitions had brought contempt and disregard upon them, so that persons were not at all afraid to appeal others to single combat upon every light occasion.[1] They therefore ordered proclamation to be made prohibiting the lieges from all challenges to single combat, under certification that offenders would be punished with all rigour and extremity 'in example of utheris.'

A stern prohibition.

Within a fortnight they sent to prison one of two gentlemen who had been 'doing thair utter endevoir to have had utheris lyveis' in the High Street of Edinburgh,[2] although the brawl-detesting James VI. was resident in Holyrood at the time. Within three weeks a still worse case emerged, the council examined the facts,[3] and the surviving participant in a duel was sent to the high court of justiciary on trial for murder.

Privy council's proclamation unheeded.

Between Robert Auchmowtie, an Edinburgh sur-

1 P.C. Reg. vi. 97-8.
2 P.C. Reg. vi. 103.
3 P.C. Reg. 29th April 1600, vi. 860.

geon, and James Wauchope, this duel[1] had arisen out of certain injurious words. Early in the morning of Sunday, 20th April 1600, the parties, 'bodin with sword and gantillet,' met on St. Leonard's Crags. The fight appears to have been in all respects fair, and the surgeon was the victor. He struck his antagonist, according to the indictment, 'on the face and head with four bloody wounds,' and so killed him. So aggravated a contempt of the privy council as this probably explains the keenness of the prosecution. The lords of justiciary found him guilty of murder, and he was sentenced to death—'his heid to be strykkin fra his bodie.'

A severe example.

Had the victory been gained by any guile this severity would have commanded popular sympathy; but where it had been fairly and honourably achieved, the death penalty on the sabbath-breaking duellist appears to have occasioned some public murmuring. This may at anyrate be inferred, seeing that in the end of the year it was deemed advisable to stamp the law as laid down in the case with the authority of Parliament. On the 15th November 1600 the Act 'Anent singular combattis' was passed.[2] By it the legislature 'Considering the great Libertie that sindre persones takis in provoking utheris to singular combattis upoun suddan and frivoll querrelis, quhilk hes engenderit great inconveniences within this Realme,

1 Pitcairn, ii. 112-114. 2 Scots Acts, iv. 230.

Thairfor statutis and ordinis that na persone in tyme cummyng without his hienes licence fecht ony singular combat, under the pane of dead and his moveable geir escheat to his hienes use, and the provocar to be punischit with ane mair Ignominious dead nor the defendar at the plesure of his majestie.'

Act of Parliament.

With private duels, which, said Sir George Mackenzie,[1] 'are but illustrious and honourable Murders,' this work has no direct concern, and the subject cannot be pursued. Suffice it to say that despite the Act of Parliament duelling went on.[2]

CHAP. 87.—*A Final Episode.*

ONE of the last investigations which James VI. conducted—before Sir Robert Carey, booted and spurred, brought him the tidings of succession to the English crown—concerned a plot alleged to have been laid for his assassination by Francis Mowbray of Barnbougle. Mowbray was in London in correspondence with, and in the pay of

Mowbray of Barnbougle.

[1] Works (1722), ii. p. 106.

[2] I need only refer to P.C. Reg. vii. 4, 26, 32, 187, 228, 424, 435; viii. 127-28. The 'process for directing cartels' was a well recognised technical term in 1604. Such a period would naturally produce the worthy clergyman Scott mentions, who wore a steel head-piece for the express purpose of separating brawlers and duellists. Scott's Tales of a Grandfather, ch. 40. The subject of duels in England under James I. is touched upon in that work in chap. 35.

Sir Robert Cecil,[1] minister of Queen Elizabeth. In the year 1602 Cecil was informed by an Italian fencing-master, named Daniel Archideaquila or Archdeacon, that Mowbray had revealed to him the plot against the king of Scotland. The matter was enquired into, and correspondence with Scotland ensued, with the result that Mowbray and the Italian were sent north. Examined in Edinburgh, both persisted in their statements—the Italian that the Scot had confided to him his treason, the Scot that the Italian lied. On this, as no proof could be obtained, a challenge was given and accepted, and in 'the great closse' of the Abbey of Holyrood itself, the 'barasse' was made for a duel on 5th January 1603. Before the day arrived news of further evidence came from London, and the combat was held over. But in the interval Mowbray attempted to escape from Edinburgh Castle by lowering himself down the side of the cliff by an improvised rope. Whether the rope was too weak, or because it was shaken by a warder at the top, the fugitive had a terrific fall, and was picked up a few minutes later bruised and dying at the foot of the rock. Before the morning dawned he died. Being a prisoner accused of treason, and guilty of breach of ward, he was solemnly condemned and suffered the *post mortem* penalty due by Scots law

[1] The particulars of this strange case are from Spottiswood's History, iii. 107; Calderwood's History, vi. 160, 194-5, 203-4; Pitcairn, ii. 406-409; Johnstone's Historia, 282; Birrel's Diarey, 30th January 1603; with special thanks to P.C. Reg. vi. 531, *note*.

to a dead traitor. He was not the first of the name of Mowbray who had been sentenced for treason after he was dead; but, whilst Robert the Bruce in 1320 gave honourable burial to Roger Mowbray,[1] the sentence of Francis Mowbray in 1603 was duly carried out, and the lifeless body was hanged and quartered. A rumour arose that the Italian master-of-fence was to be knighted,[2] but it was ill-founded. He received a pension of 900 marks Scots, and reappears, after James VI. had become James I., to claim implement of repeated promises made for his betterment by the king[3] who was always so hard bestead with arrears of that sort.

CHAP. 88.—*On the Borders.*

THE annals of trial by combat in Scotland are now ended, and the rest of the narrative will chiefly concern England; but in the journey south it will be natural to rest awhile on the marches, and review shortly the record of the institution there during the years preceding the Union.

The duel of law had prevailed in the 13th century on the Borders as in both the kingdoms; the treason-duel of chivalry had been familiar there late in the 14th century, but from that time until the 16th century it seems to drop out of the records.[4] In the

[1] Bower, xiii. ch. i. Extracta, 150. [2] Thorpe's Cal. 820.
[3] Thorpe's Cal. 821. Cal. Dom. 1623-25, addenda, 545.
[4] I have met with no examples.

16th century the private duel came greatly into vogue, and was almost judicial.

One well-known example in 1558 was that between a brother of Lord Evers and Kirkaldy of Grange, whose history and fate were noted in an earlier chapter. Kirkaldy had a cousin bearing the same surname, who was held prisoner in Berwick. On being ransomed he complained that he had been too strictly used whilst a captive. Sir William, therefore, challenged Lord Evers, but as 'their degrees were not equal,' Ralph, Lord Evers' brother, accepted the challenge. In presence of neutral persons and a body of troops the disputants met on the side of Halidon Hill on horseback with spears.[1] It is said that Kirkaldy came armed in coat of plate with a cuirass over it, and that Evers had no cuirass. Some objection was made to this disparity, but it was waived. When they were in readiness, says Pitscottie, 'the trumpetteris soundit and the heraldis cryed, and the judges leitt thame goe, and they ran togidder verrie furiouslie on both sydis, bot the laird of Grange ran his adversar the Inglisman throw the shoulder blaid,[2] and aff his hors, and [he] was woundit deadlie, and in perill of his lyff. Bot quhidder he died or leived I cannot tell, bot the laird of Grange wan the victorie that day.'

Kirkaldy and Ralph Evers.

[1] Pitscottie (1814), ii. 525. Holinshed, v. 585.
[2] 'Hurt in the flank,' says Holinshed.

At the same time it is evident that the consent of the monarch, or of some high official on their behalf, was necessary to a legal duel on the marches,[1] and no evidences of such consents have been met with in the 16th century; it is not thought therefore that on the marches the duels of that time can be reckoned as truly judicial.

Of their popularity there is proof enough, but perhaps none more interesting than in the experiences of Bernard Gilpin, a pious preacher, who had once to step down from his pulpit to stop a fight in the church itself. At another time he saw a glove hung up in a church, and was told by the sexton it was a challenge to any one who should take it down. The sexton, when Bernard ordered him to hand it to him, flatly refused, whereupon Bernard took it himself, and used it in his next sermon to point a moral for the reformation of his wild flock.[2] These, however, are not international examples, but there is proof that between representatives of opposite marches such combats were in high favour. They were in use to settle the pretensions of rival clans.

Border duels.

On 1st June 1586 the king and lords of the Scotch privy council came to learn that some persons 'of the surename of Burne,' living in the middle march on the Scotch side, and certain of the English

[1] See pp. 220, 221, *supra*; 315, *infra*.

[2] Life of Bernard Gilpin (1753), 178, cited in Sir Walter Scott's essay on Border Antiquities.

borderers, 'have of lait appointet to entir in ane combat at ane certane day now schortlie approcheing, apoun som lycht purpois unknawne to his Majestie and the saids lords, and without licence cravit of his Majestie, or of his dearest sister, or her officiaris, as aucht to be in sic caissis.' The policy of both countries at this time was guided by the prospect of union. Encounters such as this were almost certain to lead to petty hostilities, which retarded that policy. The projected combat was to have been between six of the Bournes and six of the Collingwoods. At least four thousand spectators were expected, and in a mixed crowd so combustible, a spark might have set the international animosity aflame. Both the Scotch council and the English ambassador set themselves to stop the meeting. Proclamations made at Border market-crosses forbade the lieges in general, and the Bournes in particular, 'to entir in combatt' with any Englishman, and commanded them to stay at home on pain of treason.[1] Some of the Bournes were put in prison to make the surer that they would keep the peace. On the English side likewise the Collingwoods were forbidden, by proclamation and otherwise, to attend

Bournes and Collingwoods.

[1] P.C. Reg. iv. 81. The name of the notorious Geordie Bourne will occur to most readers of Scott's Border Minstrelsy. See account of him in Carey's Memoirs. He was doubtless one of the clan of Bournes who were to have fought the Collingwoods. The last of the real wandering Border minstrels was of this clan, being named Burn. Lockhart's Scott under May 1819. The Collingwoods had a scion who was the successor of Nelson at Trafalgar.

the rendezvous.[1] Notwithstanding, the Englishmen put in an appearance on the field. They had not been so well watched as the Scots, and some bitter

[1] See undernoted extract from the English ambassador Thomas Randolph's letter to Sir F. Walsingham in Record Office.

State Papers—Scotland.

Randolph to Walsingham.

June 10th 1586.

I wrote unto y^{r} H: soomwhat briefly of a Combat to bee fought between the vj Collingwoods of England and vj Bournes theeves all of the borders of Scotland. The K. sent mee woord to stay the comming of the Collingwoods as hee would doe the Bournes. I promised to doe my endevour but it took no suche effect as I wished. ffor notwithstanding twoe letters written to Sr Cuthbert Collingwood to forbear his coming to the place himself & his frendes cam to the field above vij persons & by his owne report would have ben above iiij thowsand if Sr John ffoster had not made proclamacion to the contrary & divers gentellmen had not ben otherwise stayed.
The K. having great care hearof caused iij of the chiefest of the Bournes to bee for that time imprisoned & proclamation upon pain of death to bee made in all market Townes about that noe Scottish man for that day should com upon that ground, which by them beeing observed & broken by the Collingwoods the whole number of theeves ar greatly offended & divers others think their warden touched in honour that imprisoned the other & the Collingwoods at libertie. And so hathe the warden written unto me of whose l^{re} I send y^{r} L: a copie as allso the lyke complaint is gon against mee from the warden to the K. self. I leave it to y^{r} L: and other my good Lordes that shall hear of this matter to iudge as you please & how the K. will take it I know not. But this will I say for Sir Cuthbert that though he have in this fact failed, yet he deserveth better for his service in this countrey against theeves (in pursueing of whome this quarrell did arise) then doth any man within many miles of the borders. What fell out that day upon the fields between Sr John Selbyes soon and Sr Cuthbert for that hee took not his part it beelongeth to other to write rather then to me. But I hope to make them friends again. I write nothing of this disordered countrey, it passeth measure and must soon be refourmed or all will go to nought specially hir Maties poor Tenants in the middle marches. . . . . . .

At Barwick xth of June.

feeling arose, which doubtless the wardens of the marches made it their business to soothe. Truly the Border blood is 'fet from fathers of war proof.'

Border tradition has preserved the memory of some of these international encounters. They usually took place at points on the Border line where, by long usage, the march-wardens held their courts. Thus Kershopefoot in Liddesdale, one of these march meeting-places,[1] was the scene of the duel between the son of the Laird's Jock—an Armstrong of the Mangerton family—and an Englishman named Forster. The great two-handed sword, which was once wielded by the Laird's Jock, was bestowed upon his son for the great occasion. But it did not avail to give him the victory. His father though bed-ridden was carried in blankets to witness the combat, and the fierce old borderer died of rage and grief when he beheld his only child fall, treacherously slain.[2]

Kershopefoot and Gamelspath.

Gamelspath, a pass in the Cheviots beside the head waters of the Coquet, was a forum for Border

1 Rymer, viii. 17. Liddell was passed by a well-known ford there, on the Scotch side of which there is an extensive haugh which must have been eminently suited for the tournaments once held there. Scott's Border Minstrelsy, notes to Jamie Telfer and Hobbie Noble.

2 Border Minstrelsy, notes to Dick o' the Cow. The curious reader may compare Uffo's duel with two opponents in Saxo Grammaticus (1644), 645. His father, Wermund, armed him with his sword called 'Screp,' and sat on a bridge to witness the combat ready to drown himself had his son been defeated. But his son's victory made that rash act unnecessary.

trials in the 13th century.[1] Watling Street, overgrown with rush and moss, but still distinct, passes through it, and a great Roman camp stands in the midst, commanding a limited view of bent-clad and heathery fells—a spot by no means of easy access, as bleak as any to be found between the Solway and the North Sea. Till the Union Gamelspath continued to be a famous place of trysts,[2] and, if tradition do not err, the scene of some duels. The 'renowned' Robert Snowdon—the adjective is a quotation—a Northumbrian marchman, when only in his sixteenth year is said to have there defeated and slain John Grieve, a 'celebrated Scotch champion,' in a duel with small swords. The date of this event is indefinite. It was 'sometime before the Union.'[3] Traditions have a habit of forgetting dates.

CHAP. 89.—*Scottish Summary.*

THE general history of trial by battle in Scotland is summed up in four short paragraphs, each applicable to a special phase and period.

It came in with Norman feudalism. Under the

[1] See ch. 37 *supra*. Compaspath, Gamblepath, Kemmelspath, and Gemmilspeth are variants of the name.

[2] Rymer, xi. 788. Bain's Cal. iv. No. 1409. Tomlinson's Northumberland, 350. A visit to it in August 1889 gave me a magnificent walk of over 30 miles.

[3] Mackenzie's View of Northumberland 1825, ii. 76-7. Tomlinson's Northumberland, 342, 351. The 'renowned' Snowdon's fate was as follows:—His black horse was stolen; he traced it over the Border; it

influence of that initial impetus the duel of law prevailed all through the 12th, and persisted down the 13th century. But by the year 1300 most of the facts tend to the view that it had fallen out of use.

By the touch of chivalry in the 14th century, in consequence perhaps of French, and certainly of English example, the decadent duel arose again in a chivalric guise in cases of treason and the like. Scotland, like England, unless some argument has been expended in vain, had a court of chivalry, and the duel was practised there. But it was quite different from the old duel of law, although it succeeded to, and carried on, its tradition to a qualified extent. After flourishing for something like a hundred years the duel languished, lingering on, however, until chivalry was dead and the 16th century well advanced.

Four stages.

In that age private duels were coming into vogue, and trial by battle ran a third course. The duel of chivalry was succeeded by the duel-by-license.

The annals of the duel by royal license are short. They and the history of trial by combat in Scotland end with the making of the barras for the last time in the great close of Holyrood, in January 1603. There did indeed remain a power to license duels still, but it was never exercised again.

neighed back in answer to his voice, and he entered the building to take possession. Whilst unloosing the steed he was run through by a concealed assassin. Thus, like a typical borderer, he 'lived a life of sturt and strife, and died of treacherie.'

PART VII.—BRITAIN, 1603-1819.

CHAP. 90.—*Last words on Scotland.*

SO far as Scotland is concerned trial by combat had no history after the Union. The private duel remained an unmastered evil for many a day,[1] but the duel by royal license only once reappears in legal annals as so much as in contemplation. When Lord Ochiltrie was tried in the justiciary court in 1631 for slanderously imputing treason to the Marquis of Hamilton, the chief witness against him was Lord Reay—a Scotch nobleman who figures prominently in a future chapter.[2] Reay's evidence was denied by 'the pannel,' Lord Ochiltrie; and there was talk in the pleadings that, if the matter could not be otherwise unravelled, 'the

A remarkable challenge.

[1] This is sufficiently vouched by Act of General Assembly of 12th August 1648, in Peterkin's Records of the Kirk, i. 516-17. Scots Acts, vi. part 2, 601 in 1650, 824 in 1654, x. 77 in 1696. The Scot abroad continued his fighting. See case of one Highlandman *versus* two Dutchmen (when the head of the one Hollander was cut off, and the skull of the other cloven to the chin) in Evelyn's Diary, 22nd April 1694. Evelyn, under same date, records another duel in England fought by a Scot named Laws, who was hanged for his victory. For much information on the subject of duels see Hume's Law of Crimes (1819), i. 224-227, 438.

[2] Ch. 92. There is an obvious connection between the two cases.

pannel is ready to hazard his life in a duel to the glory of God and to the clearing of the truth.' Strange as such an exemplification of God's glory may seem, still stranger was Ochiltrie's other alternative. 'If his majesty is pleased to admit torture before a duel-trial, the pannel is ready with him [*i.e.*, Reay] to bear out the torture, and to be tried thereby with the said Lord Rea.' As things turned out, neither rack nor rapier was called into play; the verdict of a jury found the charge proven, and Ochiltrie spent his next twenty years as a prisoner in Blackness Castle.[1]

The judicial duel was in total desuetude in Scotland, and the constable[2] had long ceased to have any duties in relation to duels. But the marshal continued —not to regulate the lawful duel as formerly, but to forbid and hinder those which were not lawful. One of his last appearances in this connection was on 21st June 1663, when two offenders who had appealed each other to combat were called before his court, and were ordained to keep the peace, 'and to agree together and chope hands—which they particularly did.'[3]

1 State Trials, iii. 426-483.

2 No reference to duels appears in the report of the commissioners to Charles I. relative to the office of constable on 27th July 1631. A copy of this is in the Fountainhall Folio, a MS. in Stirling's Library, Glasgow, part iii. folio 109; also in Spald. Miscel. ii. 229-31.

3 Document in Nisbet's Heraldry, vol. ii. p. 74-75 (part 6, ch. 11). The parties were John Stewart of Coldingham, and Malcolm Crawford of Newton.

One remark only is needed to complete all there is to say on the Scotch judicial duel. The reserved right of the Crown to authorise it has never been expressly renounced or taken away. The last Scots Act regarding private duels, passed during the reign of William III. in 1696, was 'without prejudice to the Act already made against the fighting of duels.'[1] This appears to refer to the Act of 1600, which applied solely to duels without the royal license. Both the Act of 1600 and and the Act of 1696 were repealed by Statute of 59 George III.[2] But no positive enactment has imposed upon the Crown a disability to sanction a duel.

Crown's right to sanction duel.

CHAP. 91.—*England under James I.*

THERE cannot be a doubt that but for the temperament of King James, not only would the private duel have been infinitely commoner than it was,[3] but the probability is that the temporary revival of a braggart chivalry,[4] visible during his reign, would have brought back to legal practice the duel in the marshal's court. 'Civility

James I. and duelling.

[1] Scots Acts, x. p. 77. See also p. 57, and appx. p. 13.

[2] 59 George III. ch. 70.

[3] How common that was is indicated in Calendars State Papers, Dom. 1611-18, 1619-23, and 1623-25 indexes, *voce* Duel. 'Tales of a Grandfather,' ch. 35, shews that the duel was a frequent vent of international spleen continuing between Scot and Southron after the Union.

[4] Cal. Dom. 1619-23, and 1623-25, index *voce* Marshal.

by the sword,' as Bobadil called it, was the order of the day.[1] There was much stir and not a little enquiry concerning the office of marshal and constable,[2] and there was an evident difficulty in finding any means except a duel for the satisfaction of honour.[3] But James had a hatred of duelling a degree deeper than even his hatred of tobacco, and he set himself to repress to the utmost the madness of fighting, the 'vesania pugnandi'[4]—as a worthy historian of the time termed it—which possessed the land. His edict in 1613[5] against duelling (far more effective than the counterblast to tobacco) was the assertion of a consistent policy. His lack of the characteristic Stewart courage, the shudder which ran through him whenever he saw a sword, helped the cause of public peace. Had he been made of the same mettle as many of the gallants at his court, England at his death might have been one degree further from civilization.

The duel was not restored to practice in the court of chivalry, but in the ordinary law courts it was still a form,[6] though, as in Queen Elizabeth's time, a form only, for no fighting took place. But the bare possibility of battle on a point of law James

1 See for example Edward Lord Herbert of Cherbury's Autobiography. Duels or challenges occur on almost every page.

2 Cal. Dom. 1619-23, pp. 435-36. Cal. 1623-25, p. 118.

3 Cal. Dom. 1619-23, p. 436.

4 Robert Johnstone's Historia, 490.

5 Cal. Dom. 1611-18, p. 208.

6 8 James I. Bradley *v.* Banks. Crokes' Reports, 'James,' 283.

seems to have desired to remove, unless it be an ill-based inference from the journals of Parliament, that bills introduced in 1620 and 1623 'to abolish all trials by battail' had the royal approval. They did not pass.[1] The law was to linger on, a dead letter but still the law, for almost two centuries.

CHAP. 92.—*England under Charles I.*

Reay and Ramsay.

DONALD Lord Reay[2] in the year 1631 accused David Ramsay, esquire, of a share in a treasonable design to set up the Marquis of Hamilton as King of Scotland.[3] Investigations failed to elicit the precise state of the facts; but the conspiracy had, it was alleged, arisen on the continent in the low countries. The case was thus one of transmarine treason; and as there was no proof, and both parties persisted in their statements, it was fit enough according to old precedent for the court of chivalry.

On 24th November 1631 King Charles I., therefore, appointed a marshal court to try the case. Lord Reay, 'tall, swarthy, black but comely,' presented his appeal and challenge, saying that if Ramsay denied

[1] Bill read, Journals of House of Commons, 28th February 1620. Committed, 13th March 1620. Recommitted, 18th March 1620. Bill reported by Earl Marshal as fit to pass with approved amendments. Journals, House of Lords, 19th March 1623. Bill committed in Commons Journals of House of Commons, 22nd March 1623. Reported not fit to proceed, 29th May 1623. These references are taken from Kendall, pp. 135-36, who quotes the notes from the journals.

[2] See ch. 90. [3] State Trials, iii. 483-514.

the charges he was a false traitor and lied falsely, and proferring by the help of God to justify the appeal 'by my body upon thy body' according to the laws of arms. Reay then threw down his glove, which the minute reporter tells us 'was of a red or brown colour.' Ramsay, whose fair bushy hair gave him the nickname of Ramsay Redhead, answered that the appeal was false, and that Reay lied falsely, as he was ready to prove in duel, and thereupon he threw down his white glove. The constable folded the appeal in Reay's glove, and Ramsay's answer in the other; he then folded both together, and adjudged a duel at Tuthill, on 12th April 1632, 'between sun and sun,' beginning his award with an invocation of the Trinity as 'the only God and Judge of battels.'

There was much protesting and petitioning about sundry details, the precise dimensions of the long sword, short sword, pike and dagger, with which the matter was to be ended; the right to have a surgeon in the lists, to have pavilions to rest in, to have a preliminary view of the ground and so on.[1] In these one detects the antiquary's hand, and as John Selden[2] was of counsel for Lord Reay it is easy to guess whose hand it was.

Selden counsel.

But the elaborate foresight of the protests proved

[1] Barrington, 295, on 8 Rich. II., waxes merry about these details; the bread and wine, hammer, nails, needle and thread, &c. But the duels recorded *supra* show how prolonged the combat frequently was, and after say three hours by Shrewsbury clock, rest, refreshment and repairs would assuredly be needed! [2] State Trials, iii. 502.

needless. On 10th April the duel was postponed until 17th May, and on the 8th of May the king revoked his letters patent and disallowed it altogether. And so,' ends the reporter, 'there was nothing more done in it.'

On the day he forbade the duel King Charles wrote a letter to the marquis, who was so closely concerned in the affair. He said he was satisfied there was no such treason as had been charged, but that Ramsay had his own loose tongue and 'foolish presumptuous carriage' to blame. The marquis was to have no dishonour, and the letter closed with the assurance that the king was not ashamed to have shewn himself the faithful friend and loving cousin of the marquis of Hamilton. There cannot be a doubt that there was a serious intention on the part of the authorities to have this duel fought; it was only upon mature deliberation[1] that it was ultimately stopped.

On 6th August 1638 the duel was adjudged in another case[2] on the writ of right, and even at that late date a point of law regarding champions was discussed and decided. The defendant in the case of Ralph Claxton against Richard Lilburn was the father of the pamphleteer and republican, John Lilburn, destined to make some noise in the world of Cromwell—the 'freeborn John,' of whom it was wittily said that he could not live without a quarrel, and if he were left

A convenient blunder.

[1] The words are those of King Charles, State Trials, iii. p. 514.

[2] Reported in Rushworth, ii. 788. Kendall on Trial by Battle, 292. State Trials, iii. 518. Barrington, p. 295-6 on 8 Rich. II.

alone in the world would have to divide himself 'and set the John to fight with Lilburn, and the Lilburn with John.'[1] To return from this digression to the point of law, it is reported in this case that after the battle had been adjudged and waged, and was on the point of being fought, the judge enquired of the two champions if they were not hired for money? They confessed that they were, but the exception was held to have come too late to suspend the combat. On the day appointed the champions appeared in the lists, with batons and sand-bags, but the clerk had made a convenient mistake in the record, and the duel was quashed.[2]

Proposed abolition of wager of battle.

During the reign of King Charles various proposals were made in Parliament for the abrogation of trial by battle.[3] In 1641 'Richard Lilbourne, gentleman,' presented a petition to the House on the subject. Was he the defendant in Claxton *versus* Lilburn? But Parliament soon had other things to do than to carry out minor reforms in law, and trial by battle was not abrogated. Both in and after the reign of Charles other inchoate examples are to be found.[4]

1 Carlyle's Cromwell, i. 227.

2 Rushworth, ii. 788-90. Rushworth dignifies this case as an omen; because next year the king's army and the Scots met and parted also without battle. I understand the sand-bag was a degenerate shield.

3 Kendall, 136. In 1629 a bill brought in and read twice. Another bill, Journals of House of Commons, 25th February and 11th March 1640. Lilburn's Petition Journals, 23rd July 1641.

4 A list of some appears in N. & Q. 7 S. iv. 462, in an article by Mr. H. W. Monckton.

Litigation had ceased some centuries before, to depend for its success, in the smallest degree, on the champion. The great humorist of the Restoration alluded to the virtues of long purses, in representing that certain Presbyterian brethren whom he satirised

> Engaged with money bags as bold
> As men with sand bags did of old.[1]

The last line is one of many hundreds which recall the fact that the author of Hudibras was much employed by that living library of learning John Selden.[2]

CHAP. 93.—*Appeal of Murder Act, 1819.*

AFTER a very long interval Parliament again in 1770[3] discussed the subject of trial by battle. The attorney-general moved for leave to bring in a bill to abolish it, but after debate the motion was postponed. Again in 1774 the question was raised and came to nothing.[4] Forty years later a decisive hour came.

On 27th May 1817[5] Mary Ashford of Erdington, in Warwickshire, was drowned[6] under circumstances

[1] Hudibras, part iii. early in canto 2.

[2] Life of Butler, prefixed to Hudibras ed. of 1744. See also Lives of the Poets.

[3] Kendall, 235-6.

[4] Kendall, 236-8, 296-304.

[5] Barnewall & Alderson's Reports, i. 405-461. This very full report embodies a most interesting discussion on the early law.

[6] She is buried in Sutton-Coldfield churchyard under an epitaph of the woful-ballad order.

which raised suspicions of murder against Abraham Thornton. He was put on his trial, and the indictment, with a robust survival of faith in the powers of darkness, said that he had been moved and seduced to commit the crime 'by the instigation of the Devil.'[1] By the advice of the judge the jury returned a verdict of acquittal. But there were facts and presumptions strongly against the accused, and feeling ran so high that the brother of the dead girl, aided by a public subscription, instituted an appeal of murder to try the case again. This procedure, though quite unusual, was competent, and on 17th November the prisoner appeared before Lord Ellenborough and three other judges. When asked to plead, he replied 'Not guilty, and I am ready to defend the same by my body.' Then he threw down a gauntlet without either fingers or thumbs, made of white tanned skin, ornamented with sewn tracery and silk fringes, crossed by a narrow band of red leather, with leathern tags and thongs for fastening[2]—a gauntlet as strange as the occasion, its white leather perhaps a reminiscence of the sheepskin armour of early centuries. It was the last time that such a challenge was to

Ashford *versus* Thornton, 1817.

[1] This allusion to diabolical agency continued for long after 1819. A common form of the phrase was 'to the great displeasure of Almighty God and at the special instigation of the devil.'

[2] For these particulars and for a print of a sketch of the gauntlet I am indebted to Mr. John Rabone, Penderell House, Birmingham. See article by him in *Birmingham Weekly Mercury*, 14th February 1885. N. & Q. 6 S. xi. 462-63.

be given in a British court of justice. Averse though the judges were to granting the duel, they had no alternative. 'It is the law of the land,' said Lord Ellenborough.[1]

No battle followed. Indeed actual battle was never contemplated, but the return to the antique defence served its object. In April 1818 the appeal was withdrawn and Thornton was set free.

An Irish parallel.

The case did not stand alone. In Ireland in 1815[2] a murderer, named Clancy, had escaped similarly by an unexpected offer of battle, when he was put on trial at the assizes.

Immediate legislation was therefore necessary to prevent the thing from becoming a standing obstacle to justice. The appeal of murder of which wager of battle formed an inherent part had been defended in Parliament in 1774 as 'that great pillar of the constitution.' In 1819 this great pillar had become a dangerous nuisance, and a bill was brought in to take it away. After not a little parliamentary eloquence and several petitions, it was read a third time in the House of Commons on 22nd March by a majority of 64 against 2.[3] On 22nd June it received the royal sanction and became law.[4] From that date, it enacted, all 'appeals of

At last.

[1] Barn. & Ald. Rep. i. 460.

[2] N. & Q. 2 S. ii. 241.

[3] Cobbett's Parl. Debates, xxxix. 415, 428, 434, 734, 1097, 1116, 1120.

[4] 59 Geo. III. ch. 46.

treason, murder, felony, or other offences shall cease.' For the future there was to be no wager of battle, 'nor shall issue be joined nor trial be had by battel in any writ of right.' This provision made an end of trial by battle, and of the possibility of pleading it in every case in which it had ever been known in England, in prosecuting ordinary crimes, in prosecuting treasons transmarine or otherwise, and in civil process on the writ of right. It is a questionable tribute to the English fidelity to precedent, and to the caution of law reform, that the law which stood to be repealed in 1819 was the duel of law as it had been put into shape in Bracton's time, and the duel of chivalry as determined in the court of Richard II. When Saint Foix, a Frenchman, not less distinguished for his duels than his plays, died at the age of seventy-eight—which a biographer calls a reasonable age, to be sure, for a duellist—a wit put up in the theatre, by way of obituary, the sentence, 'Here we fight no more.'[1] From 1819 the words have had an application in English law, in theory, as they had had for several centuries before, in fact.

CHAP. 94.—*The End.*

YET even the Act of 1819 did not abolish the champion of England. He was a simulacrum. True, he had never been anything else, as the jest of Henry

[1] Ici l'on ne se bat plus. Beauvoir, Duels et Duellistes, 50.

IV. at his expense bore witness. Still, before 1819 he was a simulacrum following a form of law. After that date, when the appeal of treason had been abolished, his occupation was legally gone. Nevertheless his venerable function, which was an appeal of treason of a kind, survived the Act,[1] and the champion of England, cased in iron or tin, and lifted into his saddle with little assistance, pointed the edge of Carlylean satire at his 'bottomless Inanity.'[2] But Carlyle was historically wrong; at the last two coronations[3] there was no mail-clad simulacrum, and the pageant was shorn of its stateliest tradition.

The champion of England.

To trace the influence of trial by combat in English literature, and on the English language—in the romances which fed the soldier-spirit of the middle ages, in ballad minstrelsy,[4] in the loftier realm of classic verse, and in words and phrases still on the common tongue—this would be indeed a fascinating task. But it is

In literature.

[1] The champion's challenge was duly made in 1821 at the coronation of George IV. Annual Register, 1821, 385-86. Sir Walter Scott witnessed the ceremony which was not up to his expectations, although he says, 'the young Lord of Scrivelsbaye looked and behaved extremely well.' Lockhart's Life of Scott, ch. 52.

[2] Past and Present, book 3, ch. 1. An interesting discussion regarding the performance of the champion's function, and in which a mare's nest is beautifully exposed, appears in N. & Q. 7 S. vii. 482; viii. 254.

[3] Economy, not a pedantic construction of the Appeal of Murder Act, was the explanation. There was no coronation banquet.

[4] See specially 'Sir Hugh le Blond' in Scott's Border Minstrelsy, and 'Sir Aldingar' in Percy's Reliques.

far beyond the aim and compass of this book.[1] Historians and romancers have ever loved to tell how men bore themselves when they pled with poleaxe and point of sword. The poets have added many a goodly wreath of song. Thus, in literature, trial by combat has a great epitaph, like the funeral pyre of Beowulf—

> a mighty pile
> With shields and armour hung.[2]

Probably the subject was never touched to finer issues than in the scene where the Templar falls dead before the spear of Ivanhoe. Yet, eight centuries before Scott, long before English literature itself began, the theme had been attuned to still more artistic purpose in the Song of Roland. For, in that old epic, of which some strains were chanted at Hastings in 1066, it is through the medium of wager of battle that the French minstrel ends his tale with poetic justice, punishes the treason of Ganelon, and

1 A very interesting chapter might be written on the place-name lore of the subject. The barras, so frequently mentioned in earlier pages, is memorialised in many localities both English and Scots. A part of Lochmaben is known as The Barras, and has been so called for at least 400 years. 'Joustingleys' is another common name recalling the tilting ring of chivalric times. A place on the outskirts of Dalkeith is so denominated. Near Annan there is the farm of Justenlees. Distant from it a mile or more is Barrasgate. Some 'gait' or road, here branching off the highway and leading to the barras at Justenlees, furnishes an unexceptionable etymology. Compare Batelhalch (battle haugh) p. 259, *supra*, Barrasford on the Tyne, and Barras bridge at Newcastle. History records itself in our topography.

2 Beowulf—as translated by Professor Henry Morley in (Cassells') English Literature.'

avenges the fall of Roland in the Vale of Roncevaux. The whole procedure, from the appeal, wager, and giving of the glove, down to the close of the stern meeting in the 'place' at Aix, is described with an exactness such as our British romance-literature cannot approach. In simplicity, and truth, and force, the story of that duel, in which Pinabel was vanquished by Thierry in presence of Charles the Great, remains supreme.

INDEX.

NOTE.—See *Duel*, *King*, and *Trial by Combat*.

Acra, *aera*, 125.
Age, essoin of, 46, 81.
Annandale, 141, 143, 214, 333.
Approver, 42, 121, 138, 147; the last, 154.
Athole, Earl of, his murder, 136.

Barbour, John, 233; quoted, 181, 212.
Barnwell priory, 68.
Baron courts, 83, 140.
barras, *barrace*, *barrers*, *barres*, 86, 112, 119, 185, 199, 210, 216, 227, 258, 272, 285, 286, 290, 303, 311, 333.
Baton, 54, 119, 149, 155, 156, 159, 327.
Borders, the, 75, 78, 122, 126; chivalric duels there, 218, 313; projected clan-battle there in 1586, 315; traditions, 314, 317, 318.
Bracton, 36, 49, 86, 157, 237, 331.
Breach of promise cases, 8, 298.
Bruces, the, 140.

Camisfurd, 127.
campfight, 7.
Carlyle cited, 57, 62, 332.
carecte, 153, 154, 163, 174.
Cartels, 261, 298, 299, 302.
Cattle, fines paid in, 85, 86, 114.
Challenges—see Duel.
Champions, 14, 15, 21, 46, 49, 51, 53, 69, 90, 113, 114, 194, 212, 326, 328.

Champion of England, 194, 332.
Charters, evidence of, 13, 64, 72, 76, 77, 81, 97, 98, 133, 139, 210, 224, 276, 303.
Chaucer quoted, 180, 212.
Chivalry, 8; rise of, in England, 71, 145, 164, 167, 177; decline of, 202, 204, 205, 283; in Scotland, 145, 210, 213, 215, 226, 233, 239.
Chivalry, court of, in England, 177, 193, 196, 200, 204; argument for similar court in Scotland, 239, 273.
Church and duel, 12, 50, 53; on the borders, 124, 126, 127.
Clan-battle of 1396, 239, 253.
Clan Macduff, law of, 121.
Coldingham, swineherd of, 135.
colpyndauch, 114.
comhrac, 20.
Compurgation, 5, 64, 78, 79, 81, 85, 97, 98, 112, 140, 246.
Constable, the High, 146, 167, 173, 177, 178, 190, 191, 193, 210, 211, 227, 260, 261, 271, 274, 280, 321.
Coronation challenge, 194, 195.
Courcy, John, 63.
Craig, Sir Thomas, 75, 103, 287, 295.

Dead body produced, 128; dismembered, 201, 312.
deraign, 52, 183, 228.
Devil, the; his aid in duels not allowed, 92, 153, 154, 159, 163; his special instigation, 329.
Domesday book, 32.

DUEL—(see also Trial by Combat)
1. Duels fought.
2. Challenges or inchoate proceedings.
3. Chronological.
4. Classified.
5. Rules in fighting.

1. *Duels fought*—
David *v* Goliath, 2.
Corbis *v* Orsua, 3.
Dog of Montargis, 16.
Carouge *v* Le Gris, 17.
Jarnac (1547), 17.
Liot *v* Egill Scallagrimson, 21.
Surter *v* Thorgisel, 23.
Randid *v* Thorgisel, 23.

DUEL—*Duels fought—continued:*
Alfuin *v* Olaf, 24.
Arthur *v* Flollo, 25.
Cnut *v* Edmond Ironside (1016), 26.
Mimekin *v* Rodingar, 28.
Miscellaneous (Henry II. to Edward I.), 39, 42.
Walter *v* Hobbe (1220), 43.
Blowberme *v* Le Stare (temp. Henry III.), 55.
William of Eu (1096), 59.
Orgar *v* Godwin (temp. Wm. Rufus), 59.
Essex *v* Montford (1163), 61.
Henry Parles (1213), 65.
Nicholas *v* Geoffrey (1100-1140), 67.
Ketel (1182), 67.
Arthur, a Scots traitor (1155), 132.
John, swineherd of Coldingham (1240-60), 135.
Abbot of Jedburgh's man (1264), 139.
Hugh Bolare *v* William the Long (1292), 142.
Fisher *v* Whithorn (1456), 154.
Sitsilt *v* Faukenham (temp. Edward III.), 168.
Visconti *v* De la Marche (1350), 168.
Annesley *v* Katrington (1380), 171.
Vilenos *v* Walsh (1384), 177.
Palamon *v* Arcite, 183.
Usana *v* Bolomer (1407), 198.
Gloucester *v* Arthure (1409), 199.
Upton *v* Downe (1430), 199.
Catur *v* Davy (1446), 200.
Parker *v* Vaughan (1492), 203.
The O'Connors (1583), 205.
Harding *v* Seintlowe (1312), 207.
Turnbull *v* Venale (1333), 212.
Keith *v* Mar (1362), 215.
Strother *v* Grant (1380), 219.
Strother *v* Inglis (1395), 223.
Lindsay *v* Wells (1390), 233.
Dalzell *v* Courtenay (1390), 235.
30 Frenchmen *v* 30 Englishmen (1355), 242.
Clan Chattan *v* Clan Kay (1396), 239, 253.
Pinabel *v* Thierry 250, 333.
Two Scots before Richard II. (1398), 256.

DUEL—*Duels fought—continued:*
A Perth duel (1400), 258.
A Stirling duel (1403), 258.
Hardy *v* Smyth (1412), 259.
Cranstoun *v* Musgrave, 263.
Hudibras *v* Trulla, 272.
Knox *v* the tailor (1426), 275.
Cunningham *v* Dalrymple (1446), 276.
Nairn *v* Logan (1453), 277.
Heriot *v* Galfurd (1453), 277.
Hakat *v* Seton (1453), 278.
Tristram *v* Moraunt, 282.
Coupance *v* Hamilton (1501), 284.
Drumlanrig *v* Amisfield (1532), 290.
Newton *v* Hamilton (1548), 296.
Hepburn *v* Brown (before 1595), 306.
Bruntfield *v* Carmichael (1597), 307.
Auchmowtie *v* Wauchope (1600), 309.
Kirkaldy *v* Evers (1558), 313.
Armstrong *v* Forster, 317.
Uffo *v* two opponents, 317.
Snowdon *v* Grieve, 318.
Sundry 17th century private duels, 320.
Ivanhoe *v* the Templar, 333.

2. *Challenges and inchoate proceedings—*
William the Conqueror *v* Harold (1066), 29.
Marshal *v* Breawte (1220), 41.
John Courcy (1204), 63.
Fitz Thomas *v* Vescy (1294), 70.
Segrave *v* Cromwell (1305), 71.
King Malcolm III. (1057-93), 75.
King Edgar *v* King Kenneth (959-73), 76.
Hoddom *v* Fitz Troite (1199), 133.
Sir Walter Bisset (1242), 137.
Widdrington *v* Tasca (temp. Henry II.), 150.
Widdrington *v* Prior of Tynemouth (circa 1346), 151.
Sir Thomas Colville (1346), 151.
Paramour's case (1571), 158.
Gaston of Bearn *v* Edward I. (1274), 164.
Edward III. *v* Philip VI. (1340), 165, 178, 241.
Burnel *v* Morley (1346), 168.

DUEL—*Challenges and inchoate proceedings—continued:*
Henry of Lancaster *v* Otto of Brunswick (1352), 170.
Richard II. *v* Charles VI. (1383), 178, 241.
Sir Nicholas Brembre (1388), 179.
Hereford *v* Norfolk (1398), 191.
Coronation challenge (1327, 1377, 1399), 194; (1820), 332.
Fitzgerald *v* Ormond (1445), 199.
Arblaster (1445), 200.
Heroun *v* Walayse and Prudhome (1354), 214.
Douglas *v* Erskine (1367), 216.
Mercer *v* Gille (1381), 217.
Strother *v* Grant (1380), 219.
Chattowe *v* Badby (1381), 221.
Strathern *v* Beverley (1395), 222.
Lord Kilmaurs (1464), 279.
Seton *v* Menzies (1475), 281.
Master of Forbes (1537), 293.
Francis I. *v* Charles V. (1528), 294.
Patrick, Earl of Bothwell (1549), 298.
James, Earl of Bothwell (1567), 300.
Kirkaldy of Grange (1571), 302.
Mowbray *v* Archideaquila (1603), 311.
Bournes *v* Collingwoods (1586), 315.
Ochiltrie *v* Reay (1631), 321.
Stewart *v* Crawford, 321.
Reay *v* Ramsay (1631), 325.
Claxton *v* Lilburn (1638), 327.
Thornton *v* Ashford (1818), 329.
Clancy (1815), 330.

3. *Chronological—*
(a) Early and mythical, 2, 3, 16, 21, 23, 24, 25, 26, 28, 29, 75, 76, 183, 207, 250, 263, 272, 282, 333.
(b) From 1066 to 1300, 41, 43, 55, 59, 61, 132, 135, 137, 139, 142.
(c) From 1300 to 1400, 168, 170, 171, 177, 207, 212, 215, 219, 223. 233, 239, 256.
(d) From 1400 to 1500, 154, 198, 199, 200, 203, 258, 259, 275, 276, 277, 278.
(e) From 1500 to 1600, 205, 284, 290, 296, 306, 307, 313, 314, 317.
(f) After 1600, 320, 323.

DUEL—4. *Classified*—
(*a*) Duel of law, 43, 55, 59, 61, 132, 135, 137, 139, 142, 150, 151, 154, 158, 214.
(*b*) Duel of chivalry, 17, 70, 71, 147, 161, 164, 165, 168, 170, 171, 177, 179, 183, 191, 194, 198, 199, 200, 203, 205, 207, 212, 215, 216, 217, 219, 221, 222, 223, 233, 235, 239, 258, 261, 272, 277, 289, 291, 296.
(*c*) Duel by license in Scotland, 295, 305, 306, 307, 319, 322.
(*d*) Private duel, 18, 205, 292, 294, 304, 306, 309; forbidden by Act of Parliament, 310.
(*e*) Norse duels, 21, 23, 24, 317.
(*f*) English duels, 24, 25, 26, 39, 42, 43, 55, 59, 61, 65, 67, 142, 154, 168, 171, 177, 198, 199, 200, 203, 219, 223, 233, 235, 242, 256.
(*g*) Scotch duels, 23, 77, 132, 135, 139, 207, 212, 215, 219, 223, 233, 235, 239, 253, 256, 258, 259, 263, 275, 276, 277, 278, 284, 290, 296.
5. *Rules in fighting*, 7, 9, 23, 40, 41, 54, 55, 56, 60, 65, 86, 112, 118, 171, 173, 177, 184, 189, 227, 235, 269, 296, 325.
Dumfries, ordinance of, 84.

Edinburgh, duels at, 216, 275, 285, 291, 303, 311.
enach, 121.
Exchequer, duel in, 39, 42, 138.
Exemptions from duel, 33, 64, 66, 67, 97, 109, 147.

Five wounds of God, 149.
Frotho, King, 10.
Forgery, 209.
France, 8, 13, 14, 25, 32, 70, 151; duel-edict there, 161; influence of in England, 164, 165, 166, 169, 170, 171, 178; do. in Scotland, 211, 215, 225, 242, 244, 252, 257, 319.

Gadlings, 169.
Galloway, 84, 85.
Gamelspath, 127, 317.
gatharion, 85.
George, saint, 162; a symbol of continental influence, 166, 170, 205, 238, 239.
Germany, 4, 8, 28, 170.

Gilpin, Bernard, 314.
Gladstone, 224.
Glanvill, 35, 36, 37, 82; compared with Regiam, 105.
Glasgow, bishop of, 122.
Glassonby, court of Bruces at, 142.
Glove as gage of battle, 37, 60, 148, 149, 158, 159, 160, 161, 163, 180, 195, 230, 266, 282, 293, 314, 325, 329, 334.

Halidon Hill, battle of, 211; duel on, 313.
handwarcel, 128, 131.
Hardyng, the forger, 207; his forged duel, 208.
Hat, flinging the, 258, 282.
hazelstangs, 11.
Heralds, 186, 203, 218, 227, 240, 268, 277, 285, 313.
Heraldry, 152, 168, 203, 207, 211, 236.
holmgang, 11.
Holyrood, charter of, 81; duels at, 291, 311.
hoo, 169, 183, 187, 198.
Horn-tip of baton, 54, 149, 155, 159.
Hudibras, 272, 328.

Idiots, Act concerning, 101.
inch, 12, 251, 307.
Inch of Perth, combats on, 207, 251.
Innes, Cosmo, 77, 103.
Inverness, charter of, 97.
Ireland, 20, 62, 70, 205.
Islands, duels on, 11, 12, 25, 26, 61, 69, 75, 77.

Jury, trial by, 34.

Kemp, the king's, 292.
Kershopefoot, 317.
KINGS AND QUEENS—
England—
Arthur, 25.
Edmund Ironside, 26.
Cnut, 26.
William the Conqueror, 29, 31.
William Rufus, 60.
Henry I., 32, 64, 66.

KINGS AND QUEENS—
England—continued:
Stephen, 39.
Henry II., 33; *duelliana* of his reign, 39, 40, 46, 61, 82, 122, 133.
Richard I., 40, 56.
John, 40, 41, 62, 65.
Henry III., 40, 54, 66, 68; decline of duel in his time, 72.
Edward I., 52, 70; his relations with law and chivalry, 71, 73, 99, 101, 144, 147, 164, 204.
Edward II., 164.
Edward III., 150; his chivalric tendencies, 165, 167, 169, 212, 213, 216, 241.
Richard II., 167; court of chivalry in his reign, 178, 179, 190; his relations to the duel, 193, 195, 204, 218, 220, 221, 222, 234, 331.
Henry IV., 194, 195, 196, 197, 198.
Henry VI., 199.
Edward IV., 203.
Henry VII., 203.
Henry VIII., 204.
Edward VI., 296.
Elizabeth, 205.
Scotland—
Kenneth, 76.
Macbeth, 28, 30.
Malcolm III., 75.
Alexander I., 76.
David I., 78, 79, 81.
Malcolm IV., 77, 132.
William the Lion, 82, 97, 104.
Alexander II., 104, 113, 134.
Robert the Bruce, 207, 312.
David II., 210, 215.
Robert II., 217, 220.
Robert III., 224, 250, 252: a supposed statute of, 256, 274.
James I., 198, 259, 261.
James II., 276, 278.
James III., 278.
James IV., 283, 285.
James V., 290.
Mary of Lorraine (Queen-regent), 297, 299.

KINGS AND QUEENS—
Scotland—continued:
Mary, 298, 299.
James VI., 305, 308.
Britain—
James I., 312; dislike of duelling, 323.
Charles I., 324, 326, 327.
George IV., 332.
King's headship of court of chivalry, 169, 175, 188, 192, 208, 216, 221, 226, 250, 254, 262, 271, 273, 276, 277, 291, 298, 305.
Knox, John, and Kirkaldy of Grange, 301, 304.
Kyle, duel in, 139.

Laissez les aller, 163, 186, 198, 269.
Lanarkshire, a sheriff of, 284.
Langland quoted, 182.
Legal metaphor, 181.
Leicester, duel abolished at, 66. *Note.*—Add to references Hist. MSS. Com. 8th report, pp. xvi., 406.
Lindsay, Sir David, of Glenesk, 234, 238; arranges for clan battle, 245, 248, 250, 252.
Literature, 181, 332.
Lochmabenstane, 117, 127, 214.
London, charter of, 33, 64, 68.

Macbeth and the thieves, 28, 30.
Macduff, law of Clan, 121.
Magic, 22, 23, 91, 152, 153, 159, 163, 192, 230.
Major, John, his homily against duels, 288.
'Maner of Battale,' 225, 274.
March law, 75, 122, 126, 218.
Marshal, the, 145, 163, 167, 169, 177, 178, 227, 265, 271, 287, 321.
Marshal, Henry, the, 63.
mayhem, 46, 47, 111.
Melrose, monks of, 134, 139.
Moot-hills, 117.
Moray, John, Earl of, 237, 246, 249; Thomas, Earl of, 247, 249.

Norse duellists, 10, 21.
Northampton, foul play in duel at, 68.

Oaths, 5, 48, 60, 91, 94, 159, 162, 170, 174, 189, 229, 266.
Ordeal, 1, 79, 81, 82, 83, 111; abolition of, 113, 116, 140.
'Order of Combats,' 259, 274.
Origin of trial by battle in Britain, 18, 30, 32, 75.
ornest, 20, 37.

Parliament, appeal in, 61, 71, 171, 179; this appeal abolished, 196; case in Scotland, 273, 280.
Parliament, Acts of, &c., 77, 82, 83, 84, 98, 99, 101, 108, 113, 114, 147, 172, 179, 190, 196, 256, 274, 279, 293, 309, 322, 324, 327, 328, 330.
Perth, assize of, 84; Inch of, duels there, 207, 251, 258, 277.
Philip the Fair's edict, 160, 257.
pigun, 49, 52.
Piggun, Elias, loses his foot, 49; William, 52.
place, 159, 172, 185, 200, 334; *palatium*, 210; *palacia*, 86, 210; *palice*, 86; *platea*, 80, 121.
Place-names, 127, 333.
Plea-cairns, 117.
Pope and duel, 12, 15; on the borders, 122, 123.
Prerogativa Regis, 102.
Privy Council of Scotland represses private duels, 305, 306, 308.
pugil, 51, 57, 134, 152, 153.

Queen's presence at combat, 234; provided for, 269.

Ramorgny, Sir John, 223.
Recreancy, fine of, 38, 39, 45, 48, 92.
Reddenburn, 127, 129.
Regiam Majestatem, 82, 93, 96; examined, 99, 104, 110, 116.
Right, writ of, 35, 38, 47, 87, 106, 134, 148, 150, 151, 158.
Riston, charter of, 135.

St. George, 162, 166, 170, 205, 238, 239.
Samson, Abbot, 57, 62, 67.
saraad, 210.
Scone, duel of, 76.
Scotland and England, comparisons and contrasts, 73, 82, 97, 98, 104, 105, 141, 144, 145, 260, 273.
Seal, a curious, 54.
Selden, John, 19, 30, 55, 177, 178, 325, 328.
Service of heirs, 109.

Shakspeare cited, 51, 181, 192, 201.
Shaving of champions, 55, 56, 58, 148, 153.
Skene, Sir John, 77, 256.
Smithfield, duels at, 199, 201.
Solway, 117; its etymology, 127, 129, 130.
Song of Roland, 250, 333.
stengesdint, 11.
Stirling, assize of, 83, 140; duels there, 115, 258, 276.
Stow, John, his false servant, 201.

Tailor's duel, 275.
Teeth used in duels, 22, 47, 157, 237.
theam, 80, (49), 143.
Thebal Guth Guthani, 153.
Thomson, Thomas, 77, 103.
Tilting, 136, 178, 180, 211, 213, 232, 283.
Treason, appeal of, 20, 58, 59, 61, 70, 71, 196, 216, 221, 222, 280, 296, 311, 319.
Treason, *post-mortem* penalty of, 201, 311, 312.
Treason-duel, 60, 61, 70, 71, 167, 171, 179, 188, 190, 193, 196, 205, 254, 259, 270, 275, 277, 280, 292, 296, 320.

TRIAL BY COMBAT—

In Europe, 1; origin in Britain considered, 20; early British legends, 23, 24, 25, 27; conclusion as to its origin, 30.

England, 1066-1300—

Introduction by William the Conqueror, 31; legal outline in England (1066-1300), 31; charter of exemption to London, 33; sphere of trial restricted under Henry II., 33; trial by jury superseding it, 35; Glanvill and Bracton, 35; procedure sketched, 36; duel in finance, 39; approvers, 42; champions and their contracts, 46; duels, &c., in history (1096-1163), 58; story of John Courcy, 62; charters of exemption growing in number at close of 12th and beginning of 13th centuries, 64, 65, 66, 67; signs of a chivalric reaction, 70; Edward I. refuses to countenance duel of chivalry, 71; review of the law showing rapid decline of duel in 13th century, 72.

Scotland till 1300—

First authentic mention in 1124, 76; evidence of practice about 1180, 77; compurgation basis of early law, 78; wager of battle in King David's laws, 80; under William the Lion, 82; English

Trial by Combat—
Scotland till 1300—continued:
influence, 82; in Galloway law, 85; statement of law on writ of right, 86; argument as to its date, 93; charters of exemption by William the Lion, 97; Regiam Majestatem considered, 99; case for early 13th century as its date not yet closed, 102; present text not final, 103; conclusion, that its law is that of early 13th century, 104; parallel with Glanvill, 105; curious systematic omission of battle on writ of right in Regiam, 107; crime in Regiam, 110; statute of champions in 1230, 114; the Scotch duel described, 117; March law, 122; duel on borders condemned by Pope, 124; still prevalent in 1249, 126; scattered evidences of duel in practice till 1300, 131; review of the facts—duel believed almost extinct, 144; chivalry not yet infecting law, 145.

England, 1300-1603—
Continued decline of duel of law, 147; the last approver's duel, 154; duel on writ of right virtually a legal fiction, 158; rise of duel of chivalry—a French edict of 1306, 161; rise of chivalry traced, 164; St. George, 166; great chivalric duels, 168, 171; court of chivalry established, 177; its jurisdiction defined, 179; Chaucer's knowledge of the laws of arms, 180; duels of law and chivalry contrasted, 188; the coronation challenge, 194; its existence before the 14th century questioned, 194; some treason-duels, 196; the end of chivalry, 202; duel of chivalry at same time dies away, 203; summary, 204.

Scotland, 1300-1603—
A spurious writ, 207; *pervenire ad duellum* in 1312, 210; the 'law and custom' in 1354, 213; chivalric duels (1362-96), 215, 218; border duels, 218; an old treatise, Vegetius on the 'Maner of Battale,' 224; text, 226; international tilting, 233; renascence of duel under chivalry, 239; indications of a Scottish court of chivalry, 238; the combat of the clans in 1396 considered, 239; an Anglo-French precedent, 240; how the great Highland duel was arranged, 245; conclusion, that it was a gigantic appeal in the court of chivalry, 249; the combat on the Inch of Perth, 251; instances from 1398 to 1412, 255; a supposed chivalric statute, 256; its connection with a French original, 257; the 'Order of Combats' considered, 259; text of that ordinance, 261; argument for a Scottish court of chivalry, 272; duels from 1426 to 1456, 275;

TRIAL BY COMBAT—
Scotland, 1300-1603—continued:
duel-incidents in Parliament and Burgh Court, 278; chivalry passing away, 282; tilting and chivalry, 283; a late example of a combat à outrance, 284; perquisites of the Constable, 286; Craig's error on the point, 287; John Major's reprehension of trial by battle, 288; combat before James V., 290; rise of private duels, 294; judicial combat at Haddington in 1548, 296; curious challenge by Patrick, Earl of Bothwell, in 1549, 298; James, Earl of Bothwell's cartel in 1567, 299; Kirkaldy of Grange's cartel in 1571, 302; Scottish privy council tries to put down private duels, 305; instances of duel by licence, 306, 307; the last fought in Scotland, 307; a stern example made of the victor in a private duel, 309; confirmatory Act of 1600, 309; Mowbray of Barnbougle and the Italian, a final episode, 311; on the borders, 312, 314; duel of Evers and Kirkaldy, 313; projected combat of Bournes and Collingwoods stopped, 315; English ambassador's dispatch concerning it, 316; some border traditions of Kershopefoot and Gamelspath, 317; Scottish summary, 319.

Britain, 1603-1819—
Last words on Scotland: challenge by Lord Ochiltrie in 1631, 321; royal power to license duel never expressly abrogated, 322; policy of James I. in England, 323; his dislike of duelling, 323; proposals to abolish wager of battel, 324; case of Reay and Ramsay in 1631, 325; parliamentary proceedings in 1641, 327; renewed discussions in 1770 and 1774, 328; case of Ashford *v* Thornton, 329; Thornton's challenge, 329; Act of 1819, 330; champion of England survives the Act, 332; influence of trial by combat on literature, 333; song of Roland—a supreme literary monument, 333.

Tuthill, duels at, 65, 158, 325.
Tynedale, 139.
Tynemouth, Prior of, 52, 149.

Uniot (Vniot), William, his charter, 77.

Vegetius, 224.
Visnet, 78, 85, 116, 138, 139, 280.

Wad, 37, 79, 88, 128, 130.

wager of battel, 37.
Wager of law, 64, 246.
Welsh laws, 20, 210.
White leather armour, 152, 155, 159, 329.
Witchcraft—see Magic.
Woodstock, Thomas of, 173, 177; his ordinance cited, 173, 174, 175, 177, 184, 186, 187, 188, 190, 260, 274.
Wyntoun quoted, 75, 137, 191, 193, 234, 243, 247, 253.

William Hodge & Co., Printers, 26 Bothwell Street, Glasgow.

www.ingramcontent.com/pod-product-compliance
Lightning Source LLC
Chambersburg PA
CBHW061046270926
51784CB00018B/6
9781584770756